The Zeek Phe

Zero to $1 Billio

Robert Craddock
The Zeek Phenomenon™
Includes Index and Color illustrations
ISBN 978-0-915960-03-3

Publication Data
Craddock, Robert 2. Multilevel Marketing (MLM) 3.
Ponzi 4. SEC 5. Investigation 6. FBI 7. DOJ 8. Penny
Auction 9. Zeekler 10. Zeek 11. Entrepreneur 12.
Network Marketing 13. Penny Auction
14. Auction 15. Wealth 16. Business 17. How To 18.
Zeek Rewards

Published by Ebon Research Systems Publishing
P.O. Box 915115
Longwood, FL 32791
Telephone: 407-682-6744
Email: ZeekPhenomenon@gmail.com
Website: ZeekPhenomenon.com

Preface

Zeek Rewards was the path to financial freedom for millions of ordinary Americans and foreigners during a period of time when the global economy was suffering one of its worst downturns in history. *The Zeek Phenomenon*™ created the opportunity to participate in a Program where one could grow a small amount of money to more than one million dollars within a year. In many instances, fortunes were made by persons who had given up hope of ever living a debt-free life and/or reaching the goal of the "American Dream".

After the founders realized that the millions of dollars that were provided for membership fees and penny auction bids created a problem for their local bank, they devised many methods to accept and pay large sums of money using online merchants and a variety of other domestic and foreign banks. Since many of the deposits were in excess of hundreds of thousands of dollars, the *phenomenon* soon attracted the attention of state and Federal regulators. Additionally, the unexpected growth of the Company overwhelmed its management system and resulted in slow payouts causing complaints being filed with local and Federal Governmental agencies. Civil and criminal investigations soon followed the probes of several state and Federal authorities. Finding *"probable cause"* of wrongdoing, the Security and Exchange Commission (SEC) seized the assets of the Company annihilating the aspirations of more than two million Zeek Rewards participants in the United States and abroad. It's unfortunate that the payouts for bid purchases and membership referral fees allegedly did not meet the rules and regulations of the US Government since when SEC seized Zeek Rewards, the dreams of many persons who previously had no hope came crashing to the ground.

> *"On August 17, 2012, the U.S. Securities and Exchange Commission (SEC) filed a complaint against defendants Burks and Zeek Rewards, based in North Carolina. Burks ran Zeek Rewards, a membership fee opportunity that promised*

participants returns by sharing in the profits of Zeekler, a penny auction website. Money invested in Zeek Rewards earned returns of 1.5% per day. Participants were encouraged to let their gains compound and to recruit new members into a "forced Matrix" to increase their returns. The SEC contends that this forced Matrix payout scheme constitutes a pyramid scheme. New participants had to pay a monthly subscription fee of between US$10/month to $99/month and provide an initial membership fee of up to $10,000. The higher the initial membership fee, the higher the returns appeared. The SEC stated that the Zeekler website brought in only about 1% of the Zeek Rewards company's purported income and that the vast majority of disbursed funds were paid from new membership fees. The SEC alleges that Zeek Rewards is a $600 million Ponzi scheme affecting 1 million participants, which would be one of the largest Ponzi schemes in history by number of affected participants. A court-appointed Receiver estimated that the $600 million amount could be "on the low end" and that the number of participants could be as many as 2 million. Burks paid $4 million to the SEC and agreed to cooperate with its investigation.[1]

The Zeek Phenomenon™ is a chronology of these events as well as an examination of the motives that lead to the demise of one of the most innovative attempts in modern history to bring about the transfer of wealth to the ordinary person. This is a must read book for all who believe in the American Dream and believe in an opportunity for the common person to experience the riches of this great nation.

Todd Disner

---

[1] http://en.wikipedia.org/w/index.php?title=High-yield_investment_program&action=edit&section=3

Foreword

I gave a great deal of thought as to whether I should write a book about Zeek Rewards and some of the events of one of the fasting growing Multilevel Marketing (MLM) companies in the world. Having been a participant shortly after it started and having the experience of interacting with many of the *"net losers"* and *"net winners"*, I felt these associations gave me a unique vantage point where I could shed some light on the occurrences that caused the demise of this fascinating business venture that had promised to lift many common people from an ordinary life to one of wealth and fortune.

It is my belief that *The Zeek Phenomenon*™ can serve as a guideline for all who wish to pursue a MLM business and operate within the framework of the rules and regulations of our Federal Government. The *lessons learned* from this book could very well prevent serious mistakes during the MLM developmental and operational phases. *The Zeek Phenomenon*™ stresses the importance of anticipating rapid growth since once the business is expanding, it is mandatory that the growth be consistent with the abilities and resources available to avoid its spiraling out of control.

As a bonus for the reader, I included a *"How To"* section in the Appendix for those who wish to start their own MLM. It is important to apply the laws of the states and the Federal Government during the early stage of the business. Surround yourself with competent legal advisors who are familiar with the ever-changing rules and regulations governing network marketing and investment ventures. Use the experience of *The Zeek Phenomenon*™ to avoid the pitfalls of underestimated rapid growth and insufficient staff and resources.

I wish to convey very clearly that I am neutral with respect to whether or not Zeek Rewards should have met such a sudden and untimely death. Every citizen should strive to live by the laws of the country to which he or she holds allegiance. It is my opinion that when our Government evenly applies the law to the "net losers" and "net winners", everyone receives fair and just treatment.

The main purpose of this book is to bring to all who aspire to a better life through MLM business opportunities the *lessons learned* from *The Zeek Phenomenon*™.

Robert Craddock

4

Table of Contents

THE BEGINNING

In the 1980s and 1990s, the Shreveport, Louisiana native toured nursing homes in the South as a magician with country singer David Houston[2]. Paul Burks moved to Lexington, North Carolina in the early 1990s because his wife was from that area. Burks mostly kept to himself; and few locals knew very little of anything about the quiet, balding man with thick glasses.

Beginning at least as far back as 1997, Paul Burks operated a number of generally unsuccessful multi-level marketing businesses through Rex Venture Group, LLC (and related entities) with names such as Go-Go Hub, My Bid Shack, New Net Mail, Signed Numbered International and the Free Store Club. The Free Store Club was a shopping business that Burks had operated for several years.

In 2000, Burks ran for the North Carolina State House as a Libertarian, but he collected only 330 votes. It was then he became a local celebrity. Most afternoons, Burks frequented the same downtown restaurant with an entourage of followers.

Many people thought that Paul Burks was the architect of the Rev-Share Program[3] but really he was not. Andy Bowdoin, founder of the Ad Surf Daily MLM,

---

[2] http://www.charlotteobserver.com/2014/02/01/4657316/850-million-ponzi-scheme-player.html#.U_YHJ2fQPIU
[3] Rev-Share is a concept where you earn a percentage of the total money you make for the enterprise.

was actually the "*Father of Rev-Share*". Burks' business experience included nearly four decades in multilevel marketing programs — such as Amway and others — including failed attempts to launch similar businesses of his own. Burks apparently never made a comfortable living from his various business ventures, but his financial situation was to soon improve with the innovations brought to him by Dawn Olivares.

Dawn was working with Burks in his online business opportunity, Free Store Club, in Lexington, North Carolina when she conceived of the idea of a creative way to make more money. Dawn felt that adding a MLM component to Burks' shopping business would bring about a much-needed profit. Dawn had experienced the operations of Ad Surf Daily as she was one of the early participants in that Company with Todd Disner and other networkers. She used Ad Surf Daily, a MLM company that sold advertising, as a model for the new company.

Having experienced the early success of the Ad Surf Daily, Dawn felt that eliminating any problems of Ad Surf Daily and applying the features that worked well to Burks' shopping business was just the change that was needed to take his company to a new level. Once Dawn seized the opportunity to convince Burks that she could correct the problems that took the Ad Surf Daily[4] model down, she put her plan in action.

---

[4]Find the Bowdoin Case Study # 1 in the Appendix 1. It discusses the Ad Surf Daily Model that gives a percentage of the total advertising dollars that participants bring into the business. Ad Surf Daily was deemed a Ponzi.

Dawn knew most of the leaders who were involved in Ad Surf Daily and enlisted their assistance with her new idea. Working closing with former Ad Surf Daily participants, Dawn first introduced an essential element of Ad Surf Daily to the new venture — the **2 x 21 Forced Matrix.**

For anyone who does not know how a Forced Matrix works, a brief explanation will be provided now. The Matrix is built by each person bringing into the company two persons — resulting in 2,097,152, on the 21st level, but to get the total participants in the 2 x 21 Matrix, you need to add all levels together, and this total is 4,194,302. Participants enter the Matrix from left to right on vertical levels. The 2 in the Forced Matrix represents the number of persons each person is to recruit and the 21 represents the total number of recruitment levels. As more persons are recruited for the Matrix, the current rung is completed and a new level is

Level	
1	2
2	4
3	8
4	16
5	32
6	64
7	128
8	256
9	512
10	1,024
11	2,048
12	4,096
13	8,192
14	16,384
15	32,768
16	65,536
17	131,072
18	262,144
19	524,288
20	1,048,576
21	2,097,152

started for the next recruit; thereby *"forcing"* the specific placement of each participant. The Forced Matrix is generally shown using a triangle-shaped form but can also be shown in a 21-level vertical graph like above. In the triangle-shaped form, the participants are placed from left to right *"forcing"* the levels to be created in an orderly fashion with no vacant spaces in the team.

If you can earn one dollar from every person in your Matrix team each month, you can receive from that income a total of $4,194,302 dollars because you have the potential of 4,194,302 people in your Matrix when you are at the top. There will be a lot of persons in the company making a lot of money since money flows from the bottom up. Everyone earns a percentage of money spent by each person below him or her in the Matrix. The higher the person is on the Matrix rung, the more money the person makes. However, in the real MLM world, participants drop out, participants do not recruit their two persons and only about 20% earn most of the money.

Secondly, Dawn needed a product for the new business; and knowing that the Advertising Model used by Ad Surf Daily was problematic, she selected the Penny Auction Model. Below is an explanation of the Penny Auction Model.

> "A **bidding fee auction**, also called a **penny auction**, is a type of all-pay auction in which all participants must pay a non-refundable fee to place each small incremental bid. The auction ends after a period of time, typically ten to twenty seconds, without new bids; the last participant to have placed a bid wins the item and also pays the final bid price, which may be significantly lower than the retail price of the item. The auctioneer makes money in two ways: the fees for each bid and the payment for the winning bid, totaling typically significantly more than the value of the item.[11] Such auctions are typically held over the Internet, rather than in person.

> Participants pay a fee to purchase bids. Each of the bids increases the price of the item by a small amount, such as one penny (0.01 USD, 1¢,

*or 0.01 GBP, 1p; hence the name of the auction),
and extends the time of the auction by a few
seconds. Bid prices vary by site and quantity
purchased at a time, but generally cost 10–150
times the price of the bidding increment. The
auctioneer receives the money paid for each bid,
plus the final price of the item.*

*For example, if an item worth 1,000
currency units (dollars, euros, etc.) sells at a final
price of 60, and a bid costing 1 raising the price of
the item by 0.01, the auctioneer receives 6,000 for
the 6,000 bids and 60 as the final price, a total of
6,060, a profit of 5,060. If the winning bidder used
150 bids in the process, they would have paid 150
for the bids plus 60 for the final price, a total of
210 and a saving of 790. All the other, losing,
bidders collectively paid 5,850 and received
nothing.*[5]

In early 2010, with the encouragement of Dawn, Burks started an on-line business he called the Zeekler Penny Auction. In January 2011, Burks incorporated the 2 x 21 Forced Matrix into his penny auction business and launched Zeek Rewards.

In addition to being rewarded for recruiting team members, Zeek Rewards offered a daily profit share of the penny auction's profits for participants who purchased bids. The persons who joined Zeek Rewards were expected to promote Burks' Zeekler Penny Auction online business on their Zeek Rewards website. Also, using the 2 x 21 Forced Matrix model, Zeek Rewards

---

[5] http://en.wikipedia.org/wiki/Bidding_fee_auction.

participants recruited team members who were encouraged to purchase Zeekler Penny Auction bids.

Daniel Olivares, Dawn's stepson, was the Master Programmer and nearly singled handedly developed the computer programs for the new business. Under a complicated formula developed by Daniel, participants and their team members were issued "points" that grew everyday based on the number of bids purchased.

Membership fees were capped at $10,000[6], but people could purchase memberships on behalf of their spouses, children or other relatives. Some mortgaged homes to raise their membership fee. The membership fees were used to purchase bids for the penny auction where a proprietary computer program *"compounded"* the money at an advertised 1.5% daily. Also, a commission was earned for each referred participant who joined Zeek Rewards.

Ready To Officially Launch Or Was It?

Now with most of the pieces coming into place, Burks and Dawn needed one last key piece of the puzzle, **Startup Cash**. Dawn came up with a very creative idea — *Zeek Founding Members*. Each person would invest $1,000 dollars to secure an early position, ensuring a high placement in the Forced Matrix. In addition, this person would not have to pay the $100 monthly fee required by the Rex Venture Group (the financing arm of Zeek

[6]

http://www.usatoday.com/story/money/business/2013/03/30/authorities
-600m-scheme-incubated-nc-town/2037975/

Rewards) to continue to participate in the Program. This was pitched as: *"Pay Your First Ten Months and Pay No More!"*

In some cases there were people who secured several positions, and one such person was Durant Brockett. Durant knew Burks from the earlier Free Store Club days. Durant quickly handed over several thousand dollars to control the 11 top spots in the Matrix knowing that little work, if any, would be required. He also knew that he would benefit from the efforts of others in the large team that would expand under him. He and

How Durant was Placed in the Matrix

The 2 X 21 Forced Matrix will grow to over 2 million people quickly

other Founders were at the right place at the right time to make millions of dollars. The following illustrates Durant's position in the Zeek Rewards 2 X 21 Forced Matrix.

The way Durant structured his placement assured that he would earn money from everyone in the company except the 3 people above him, and with a program that had in excess of two million members, that was a great position to occupy.

It was not Durant's years of MLM skills that earned him millions, as he did not have much MLM experience, but rather the understanding of the power of a 2 X 21 Forced Matrix and starting at the top. Coming in as the fourth person, Durant knew he needed to control the next 11 positions as the flow went from left to right, allowing for himself to quickly earn money from everyone except the three positions superior to him as shown in the diagram. The red dots represent all the positions Durant held and the green dots were team members below him. Everyone from that point had to go under a green dot and that worked out perfectly for Durant.

The last thing needed was the *cherry on the top*, a website that would show the people the money they were earning each day (virtual money) and provided hour-by-hour updates of the earnings. Daniel Olivares, (remember Dawn's step son) was tapped as the 29-year-old web genius. With Daniel writing the code, Dawn would have a unique controlling position in the entire business without being the owner.

Loyal members of Zeek Rewards were required to login at least once a day, post an advertisement and give away bids to lucky recipients (Real People). If the people to whom they gave bids used the bids, it was expected that they would provide their credit card to buy more bids online. Once the bids were purchased and the profit for the Company was realized, the participants shared a portion of that profit each day.

The sites illustrated an ingenious innovation—*"show the activity each minute."* A participant could log in at 8am and see the activity from several hours earlier. When one logged in a few hours later, the website showed that more money had been earned if the person purchased more bids. This instantaneous reporting of money growing in the website was infectious. Zeek Rewards members would tell others that they couldn't stop logging in every hour, sometimes every minute; it became an addiction of sorts. Participants were making more money than ever before with a MLM business. They felt rich and wanted to show everyone who would listen how they were *making money 24/7*. It did not take long for people to ask, *"How can I get in"*? It was reported that some people would *"squeeze the last dime out of their home equity, savings, 401-k, and/or kids' piggy bank"* to get as much money working for them in Zeek Rewards.

The more money showing on the personalized website, the greater status the leaders had with other members. When the website earnings were displayed, it was very common for others to think that they were *"paper millionaires"*.

The developers realized that if they provided a website where people could log onto and show them that they were making money every minute, this was better than the *"proverbial money tree"*. The allure was so great; it captured the attention of almost everyone who saw the website. For example, if your regular income was $30,000 a year from a job, you quickly realized how you could triple your money or more. The same was true if your current income was $250,000 a year, you then had dreams of $2 to $3 million dollars from being a part of

Zeek Rewards. Depending on where you were financially, the dream grew proportionally.

Dawn directed that complex spreadsheets be built by her stepson to show *"what if projections"*. These spreadsheets were extremely useful because the simple calculators most people owned would crash because of the limitations to handle the large numbers and complicated formulas. One of the key factors for the success of Zeek was the excel spreadsheets that went from 0 to 365-day projections. Other spreadsheets went a step further and took the potential earnings projections to a 730-day level. The spreadsheets allowed participants to change the withdrawal amounts requested and the amount of bids repurchased. The spreadsheets could make adjustments based on earnings from the team members recruited to the Program. You also could see your earning increase when your referrals repurchased bids. Some enterprising people predicted earnings using the data from the last 90 to 120 days to project income for themselves and their team members three or six months in the future.

The spreadsheet tool was very powerful; it would hook the toughest prospect. But let's be honest, there were no tough prospects; in reality, people were begging you to *let them in*. Zeek Rewards was the *hottest ticket out there*. The spreadsheets were evolving daily and all it took was someone with a little more experience in excel to dress up the latest version and add some additional features. Sharing the latest and greatest spreadsheet version became an obsession, leaders could not wait to show it off, as this equated to more money in their pocket when their team members raved about the riches.

Zeek Rewards attracted the "Who's Who" of people around the globe. It was not uncommon to meet and work with attorneys, elected officials, police officers, banking managers, state and Federal judges, business owners, other pillars of the community as well as your next door neighbor. I remember one meeting that I attended that was being held at the Daytona Beach Airport, and in attendance were a couple of banking professionals, a retired Air Force General and a pilot who just landed. They all were there to tell their stories of huge financial success to the "*newbees*" in the room.

Zeek represented a promise of better things to come. Once it was off and going, the promise quickly turned into dollars landing in the hands of Zeek members willing to tell anyone of their newly found wealth.

Circulating the world were stories of people who were behind in child support payments who quickly paid the back money owed, people on the verge of losing their home who paid off their mortgage in a couple months and others who accumulated savings far beyond their wildest dreams. Stories were commonplace of people taking trips around the world and making new friends (to eventually recruit as team members) as money was flowing into their bank account at a *phenomenal* rate. The news of newly found Zeek wealth was talked about at meetings happening all across the country and abroad.

As the participant numbers continued to climb and people around the world could see that this was something that could *pay off big,* thousands more joined. This tremendous growth propelled an excitement that was contagious. The large payouts and increases in participants fueled the impetus that captured the attention of tens of thousands of people both domestically and internationally.

The ability to work with people in other countries was much simpler than in earlier years due of the Internet; but one of the challenges for Zeek Rewards was getting payments and receiving payments from foreigners. The normal merchant accounts tended to stray away from the MLM business as the risk was just too high. The usual response for a typical Network Marketer, who more than likely was unhappy with the earning results, was to dispute their credit card sales, cancel the product or service purchased and walk away. Not so with Zeek Rewards, the participants not only stayed and made more bid purchases, they recruited their friends, relatives and strangers to join in large numbers.

At first, Zeek Rewards responded immediately when participants sought to cash out-- that became the best advertisement of all: *happy participants with their large checks, posing for photos on Facebook.* Facebook postings and other social media activity started a frenzy of people anxious to join Zeek Rewards. People who didn't trust the mail traveled long distances to drop off checks at the cramped office building where security guards allowed only seven people inside at a time. Overworked employees collected money and provided receipts at the office cluttered with dozens of plastic US Postal mail bins on the floor stuffed with cashier check-filled envelopes.

Because of the sheer volume, when the participants wanted to withdraw money, they went online to their website, sent an online request — or called — and then had to wait for a check in the mail, sometimes 5 to 6 weeks. The office in Lexington was grossly unstaffed and the management struggled to keep up with the daily onslaught of new participants.

By the end of 2011, it seemed like everybody in Lexington was talking about Zeek Rewards and the large sums of money earned. Many saw it as a way to make extra cash, pay bills or help family members. The word-of-mouth advertisement permeated all socio-economic levels and was very successful in bringing novices into the business with little expense to the Company for advertisement.

As Zeek Rewards grew, Burks made conference calls with participants and posted information about the Company on *YouTube.* He produced glossy brochures touting the Company. As a result of his marketing, Burks brought in hundreds of new participants. Brochures featured the mass sums of money one could make: "*In addition to the mind-blowing savings, you can create more wealth than you have ever thought possible with Zeek Rewards' geometrically progressive matric compensation plan*". The brochure gave fancy words for the simple 2 x 21 Forced Matrix shown below:

The 2 X 21 Forced Matrix will grow to over 2 million people quickly

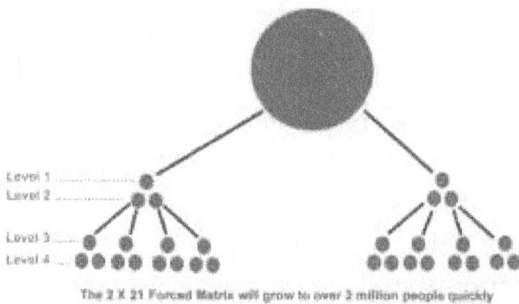

Burks also hired some of the industry's top attorneys and analysts to promote his Company. The publicity paid off. When the Association of Network Marketing Professionals held its annual convention in March 2012, it called Zeek Rewards *"The Model of Legal Compliance"*.

The most bizarre part of this story was the volume of money sent in the form of cashier's checks to a little town in North Carolina. If you were lucky to visit the 3,000 sq. ft. office[7], (a converted laundry mat), you waited in line for two hours to *give them your money.*

After giving Zeek your money, you could see an online report showing your daily earnings in your personalized website. Strangely enough, none of this seemed unusual to anyone as the excitement was uncontainable. The greed for most of the people was *"off the charts"*. Anyone at the scene would see the parade of people lining up each day. Around 8:00 am each day, people would form a long line waiting for the 9:00 am opening. Once the door opened, the people rushed in

---

[7] http://myfox8.com/2012/08/17/zeek-closes-headquarters-in-lexington/

and handed over their own money, or money from their team members (referred to as their downline). Everyone wanted to make "*1.5% compounded daily*". When they saw the dollars growing in their website, they would not want to waste one minute putting in more money. The average person standing in line was holding between $40 to $200 thousand dollars in cashier's checks.

The people, all arriving at this unique time and place created what is called the *PERFECT STORM,* in network marketing (the point when all factors align). The *PERFECT STORM* ignited a **"phenomenon"** that no one could have ever anticipated. The simple and unexpected factors that led to the success, and later the downfall of Zeek Rewards will most likely never be duplicated.

To fully comprehend the conditions leading to the uncontrollable growth, you first need to understand the leaders, their backgrounds and most of all, their motivation. One must examine what led them to a position that would forever change so many lives and perceptions regarding revenue sharing programs (Rev-Share), passive income and Forced Matrix pay plans.

In the past, MLM recruits would go into a room, sometimes a hotel, a restaurant or a living room and listen to the latest and greatest home business opportunity. They would hear promises of riches and then buy into a program to create a team of workers under them (their downline) to purchase "*lotions, potions and pills*". They would do this with the hope of becoming financially independent mostly through the efforts of others. The ever-elusive goal being sought was the dream millions of people worldwide wished and prayed for each and every day — *financial freedom*.

The people hosting these meetings knew the odds that if they had 100 people in the room, the statistics would show:

> *5 most likely will be financially self-sufficient, 20 will have some money, but most likely sit on the sidelines, 50 will cross their arms feeling suckered into wasting their time, and the last 25 people will listen and visualize themselves making enough money to change their lives forever; they will opt to join the program.*

Until Zeek, the MLM recruiting efforts mostly comprised of drawing circles that depicted persons on your team at various levels and making the recruiting of your workers seem so simple that anyone could do it with only a 20% success at best. **So how did Zeek capture almost 80 to 90% of the people in the room?** Some say, *"Greed"* and others say a chance to pay bills and live a better life.

"No one was in it to get rich," said Mary Bell, a 75-year-old seamstress from Lexington who scraped together money to join Zeek. Sarah Chavez wanted extra money for her daughter's frequent hospital visits for leukemia[8]. Her husband worked in a factory, and they

[8] http://www.aliefpost.com/2013/03/zeekrewards-scam-leaves-nc-town-millions-poorer/

paid $7,000. *"It's hard to believe in something like that. But everyone told us it was a sure thing"*, she said.

In most MLMs, the owner has several homes, buys expensive cars, travels on private jets and lives a lifestyle that most would dream of, not Burks. Burks did not change his residence in the home where he had lived for years, did not buy fancy new cars, and did not expand his lifestyle like most people who owned MLMs. Now that is not to say that the people working the Program did not expand their lifestyle, because many transformed their life completely and lived in a *grand style*.

Let's look at the numbers: relatively small amounts of money for startup, two million people joining in less than 18 months, payouts totaling $400 million dollars, ewallets and cashier's checks waiting to be deposited in amounts in excess of $600 million dollars, and a website with over three million visitors daily. The website was developed by one person, David Olivares, with a limited $50,000 budget; this was unheard in the MLM industry prior to Zeek. The Health Care.Gov website could have taken a lesson from the Zeek web developer.

How the Zeek Rewards Strategy Worked

If you want to comprehend the most viral and rewarding marketing machine *"On the Planet"*, take a look at Zeek Rewards. Just how the Zeekler Penny

Auction and the Zeek Rewards Programs worked was a mystery to the MLM world.[9]

Let me say that this probably is the most fun you're likely to ever have while creating wealth on the Internet. First let me give you the terminology used by the developers: *"Zeek Rewards is the 'Collective Advertising Division' of Zeekler Auctions, a popular Entertainment Penny Auction Shopping Site."* I am sure your first impression is *"What does that mean?"*

To enable Zeekler to play competitively with the *"big boys"* in the online penny auction marketplace, it would normally call for a huge advertising campaign which would cost the Company hundreds of thousands of dollars. Instead of going the traditional advertisement route, Zeekler's sales team made a decision to compensate its subscribers instead of Google or another firm to place ads and drive traffic to the Zeekler Penny Auction site.

Zeek Rewards invited members to discover what it's like to share in the business's financial success just by placing one FREE AD on a daily basis! ZeekRewards was the only website available showcasing the exclusive *"24-hour Compounder Incentive System"*!

The costs associated with each monthly subscription were:

Free = $0.00 per month

Silver membership = $10 per month

---

[9] http://zeekrewards16.tumblr.com/post/7705096173/zeek-rewards-exactly-how-does-it-work

Gold Membership = $50 per month

Diamond Membership = $99 per Month

It is important to note that even a free member could earn money once he or she joined Zeek Rewards without any out-of-pocket expense.

Little Work Was Needed to Play the Game

Every night after the close of the business day, the Company added up its sales for the day and shared a part of the revenue with all qualified members*. (*Members who paid their monthly fees became a qualified participant able to generate income as soon as the money is recognized by the system, and that usually was the same day the money was received, barring technical difficulties.) A qualified member holds an activated Silver, Gold or Diamond Membership and has added his or her advertisement for that day. Below is a scenario where one could be getting $2,000 to $3,000 per calendar month PASSIVELY.

Usually the typical daily cash-back percentage was around 1%; therefore, I will use a 1% daily cash-back figure in this particular case in point. (You should NOTE: This is just an example and the exact amount varied from day to day). Let's say you've achieved 10,000 bid credits inside your account, then you would commence doing an 80/20 cash-out plan (Be aware: this was NOT a requirement, some participants used a 100% cash-out plan — allowing

them to withdrawn all monies earned without having
any reserve for future bid purchases.)

Pay close attention...When you hit 10,000 bid
credits in your profile, if the daily cash-back
percentage is 1%, which is about the average, Zeek
Rewards will be furnishing you with $100.00 per
day! First of all, did you catch that, you are making
$100 per day...it's YOUR MONEY! So now, here's
the way the 80/20 plan operates: You will take 80% of
that $100 (or $80) and put it back into your own
future growth simply by doing exactly what you've
been doing on a daily basis, which is mostly just
bidding at your auction site and inserting your one
advertisement every day. Then, take out 20% of the
$100 (or $20) and put it to use however you want!
Now I know $20 does not seem to be a lot, BUT,
wouldn't getting paid out $20.00 Every Single Day,
be of SOME help to you? That's an extra $140.00 per
week, or about $560 per month, in YOUR pocket, in
PASSIVE INCOME!   Keep in mind...these amounts
can continue to grow every single day and month
after month. Where else can you achieve this profit
without working a job or running your own
company?

BUT WAIT - There is MORE!

Zeek Rewards has an incredible 2x21 Forced Matrix
for its paid members that will completely *"blow your mind."*
You can generate about $3.50 per Diamond, $1.50 per Gold
and $.40 per Silver on every single paid subscriber within
your Matrix...month after month, after month! Even free
Zeek Rewards members were able to earn money when

they referred persons or bought bids for the Zeekler Auction!

Alright now, this is a quick schedule of one's 10 minute work day.

1.) Login to ZeekRewards. Place your free advertisement for your credit for the day with the Zeekler Penny Auction Program. This Is Very Important! If you do not post the advertisement, you do not quality to get any earning for the day.

2.) Post your advertisement using your ZeekRewards' back-office with the Zeekler Penny Auction Program.

3.) Keep *compounding* through the Zeekler Penny Auction Program (sharing in the day-to-day profits) and receive your daily payout until you are where you desire to be moneywise!

There it is, your 10 minutes with Zeek Rewards! Now go play sports, or visit the work out center. Inform your Facebook, Twitter, family and associates about it or whatever you actually want to do! After these 10 minutes with Zeek Rewards playing with the Zeekler Penny Auction Program, the rest of the day is yours to do whatever you desire.

The Zeekler Penny Auction Program combined with Zeek Rewards produced a ground-breaking, trend-setting, new business model. The main feature was an exciting, on-line, *"entertainment shopping"* experience using the website called Zeekler.com or ZeeklerAuctions.com. The Zeekler Penny Auction Program offered new, brand-named products at 90%, 95% or even up to 99% off the retail price. Products included iPads, laptops, jewelry, housewares, money, gift cards, and much, much more. There were items that could be purchased for pennies on the dollar! From the amazing penny auctions to the wholesale stores, the Zeekler Penny Auction helped saved the winning shoppers millions of dollars!

To further comprehend how the Zeekler Penny Auction Program operated within Zeek Rewards, the following example is provided:

Zeek Rewards Penny Auction Model

Let's assume there is a penny auction going on right now and you want to enter it for the chance of winning an item at a great price. If someone enters this auction now and won by placing only one bid, and the winning bid was $1.80, you would only pay $2.80 to win the 50 bid voucher, that would break down to a net cost of 5.6 cents per bid. Hey that's not *too shabby* is it? But the thing is that will never happen. Let's say you had won a previous bid pack for $.10 cents per bid and it took 20 bids to win the bid pack, now if they win the bid pack they will be out of pocket $4.80 and will have paid 9.6 cents per bid for each bid in the bid pack. Now that doesn't seem all that bad either does it, except there's a catch, the likelihood of winning after only 20 bids was extremely rare.

Let's assume there are 16 other bidders in this auction, and more people will enter it as they think the item will come to an end. You could be competing with over 20 people for the bid pack in the end, and who knows when anyone is going to *throw in the towel*. There have already been, in the example above, 280 bids on that one bid pack and this thing is just getting started. Let's say the people bidding have won their bids at a value of $.25 cents per bid, these people together have spent $70 bidding on this thing, no one has won, and only one person will win after battling everyone else for hours. Yes, it is true that you could be the last one standing after only spending a few dollars' worth of bids… But out of all the other people also in the auction, do you really think that is very likely?

Penny Auction style websites will tell you that you need to have a system in place that gives you an advantage, a theory that will allow you to be the last bidder… but everyone else you are bidding against is thinking the same thing. So at this point, we can agree that $.25 cents per bid is a good number to stick to. Ten cents per bid is very hard to come by, $.60 cents per bid is what you pay when you join; $.25 cents per bid seems at least feasible. So we will use that number for the rest of this example and in others to base everything from in terms of costs on these penny auction websites.

So now let's see where that 50 Bid voucher auction ended, $5.80 or 580 bids. Spending no money per bid, that works out to $.11.6 or $.12 cents per bid. If someone bid 20 times at $.25 cents a bid the total cost for the bid voucher would be $10.80. That works out to $21.6 or $.22cents per bid. If someone had to bid 40 times to win that voucher, they would have spent about $.31 cents per bid for each bid in the bid voucher. All in all, collectively people spent $145 bidding on the bid pack. And you wonder how they can sell items so cheap?

If an initial 80 bids turn into 1000 bids by continuously winning bid vouchers using only the original bids, the result is amazing? These is very possible if the player is extremely lucky, but remember, there is fierce competition out there, people may be willing to pay higher than the cost of an item just so that they will not have wasted all their money on the penny auction with nothing to show for it. Some people are even trying to make a name for themselves by being fearless and never losing an auction so that they can intimidate other users from trying to compete in future auctions (sounds crazy doesn't it? But it REALLY happens!).

Now that was fun, but what is the true cost of bidding on actual penny auction items, like those MacBook's and iPads people win for less than $50.00? Well, let's take a penny auction for an iPad as an example so see how it works. Retail, this iPad costs $499.00 (Funny they tell you this model's value is $699 but it is really $499)… That is how much you could waltz into an Apple Store and pick one up right now if you wanted to… Let's break down an auction and see how much people are really spending (this will reveal exactly why penny auction websites are capable of selling items so cheaply.

Penny Auction Example of an IPad Auction

Let's assume one enters the auction to get an iPad, and this auction received 11,570 bids!!! At a cost of $.25 cents per bid, people have already spent $2892.50 just bidding on the one IPad! Even at a super duper value of $.10 cents per bid, people would still have spent $1157. On information for a knowledgeable person, this is the profit model Dawn saw and combining it with a Forced Matrix Rev-Share Model, this was going to push everyone's **"greed button"** really hard and Dawn counted on it.

The person bidding at an auction should be prepared to shell out as much as full retail value. Penny Auction websites do a great job of making a person forget how much bidding really costs. All of the testimonials about how people won items for one penny, a dollar or some absurdly low price, do not tell the story of their total loss. But how many auctions did they lose before winning that one auction? How much money have they spent bidding in total before winning that one item? Sure, the final auction cost was $1.00 but they may have spent $500 losing other auctions before finally winning one.

Now the pricing on Zeekler.com, the Zeekler Penny Auction site was a dollar for every bid, so the math is simple. To generate the money to support the Zeek Rewards Program, Dawn needed a reason to have people pre-purchase bids and that was in part what was learned from Ad Surf Daily. She needed the people to invite others to the penny auction site and use the bids given to them to try and hopefully get hooked and spend more money--kind of like fueling an addiction. This method is a well-known marketing technique called the *"Puppy Dog Approach"*. In the *"Puppy Dog Approach,"* you let someone try it for a short time, and soon they find out they can't live without it and they will pay whatever it takes to keep the *Puppy dog.* In this case the continual bidding on items at a perceived low cost is the *"carrot"* to pursue the *"Puppy Dog Approach"*.

Several months after the launch, speculations began to surface that Zeek Rewards was an investment opportunity. The more sophisticated called Zeek Rewards a *security* and referred to the participants as *investors* and the business as an *investment.* With increasing membership, written instructions were sent to all participants in an attempt to avoid the appearance of an investment. Controlling the hype and information transmitted across cities, states and countries proved to be a formidable challenge for the rapidly- growing business.

In response to the chatter, Dawn reached out to some well-known MLM compliance attorneys and tasked them to prepare a compliance course for Zeek Rewards participants. Considerable effort was made for all participants to take the course and receive a certificate upon completion.

In order to dispel the notion that Zeek Rewards was an unregistered security, every participant had to read a Disclaimer at the beginning of a recruitment meeting. Prior to bringing a new person into the

business, the new recruit had to acknowledge and accept the following Disclaimer:

"If you make a purchase from ZeekRewards you are purchasing a SUBSCRIPTION to the penny auction site or you are purchasing BIDS OR ADVERTISING. You are NOT purchasing stock or any other form of "investment" or equity. You MUST actually use the bids or advertising units that you purchase. Affiliates who present the products to others in a misleading manner or in a way that leads the buyer to believe he or she is making an investment or purchasing equities will be terminated and all commissions will be forfeited. Buyers MUST read the entire How It Works and Get Paid pages on the ZeekRewards website and the Legal Disclaimers".[10]

To sustain the growth momentum, Dawn sought professional marketing tools and hastily approached a group of talented people who were skilled in building a marketing system with videos that would capture the attention of the average person. She struck a deal with Robert Mecham and OH Brown; this talented team was the creative talent behind the videos, presentations and website called *One Penny Billionaire*. Participants were encouraged to purchase the marketing tools to build their team membership.

The online MLM bloggers were posting every hour it appeared and the sole reason was *impression and*

---

[10] Created by Zeek officials to be passed out at every recruiting meeting. The Disclaimer was also sent to all participants by email.

click revenue — a way to make money just by driving people to a website and clicking on the ads. Zeek Rewards was a hot topic on the web and with millions of people trying to get any information they could, all anyone had to do was mention the word Zeek, and they would attract thousands if not hundreds of thousands of people to their web site, and this translated into ad revenue for them. Postings good or bad, it made no difference; just that you were giving timely Zeek Rewards updates was all it took to drive people the website.

At the same time, there were other companies that tried to replicate *The Zeek Phenomenon* ™; namely: **Bids that Gives, Bids for Kids, WCA (World Consumer Alliance), Go Fun Places, TelexFree** and about 30 more.

These new companies allowed the current people in Zeek to join them with the same type of money-making excitement, only one problem, the companies did not operate like Zeek. There were a lot of people in those new companies who were disappointed. Later they ceased to operate, in fact most closed up so quickly that there just was no time for any regulatory action to get up to speed. So very little came of their operations, with the exception of TelexFree[11]. The main point is that these new upstarts most likely created some of the regulatory focus on the operations of Zeek Rewards.

---

[11] See more information about TelexFree in the Appendix Exhibit 2.

Burks Hires a Manager to Cope with the Spiraling Growth

In early 2012, Burks recognized he was in for challenging times, as signups were picking up rapidly causing serious administrative and management problems in the inadequately-staffed office. Burks reached out to Gregory J Caldwell (Greg) to assist him in running the Company and to help manage the tremendous growth. Greg was a private investigator; and it is not known why Burks felt he was the person to help operate the Company, but Greg was his choice. Others have said that Greg had no idea that he was being asked to manage one of the fastest, perhaps the fastest, growing network marketing companies in the country.

To understand a little about Greg, he owned and operated private investigation agencies in Florida, Tennessee and Ohio. Initially, Greg used the company name, White Hat Solutions, and later in life he adopted a new role and marketed his brand as an expert of MLM compliance. When the State of North Carolina came knocking during the first quarter of 2012, one would assume that Greg would have dropped everything and provided whatever documentation requested; obviously that did not happen. We are not sure why Greg did not deliver the requested documents but, the facts are, requests from the state went unanswered. Perhaps other problems were distracting Greg from the state's requests and in particular, the ever-present threat of the websites going down.

In March, 2012, the Zeek website, that was built and managed by Dawn's stepson, was experiencing serious operational issues. The daily calculations would sometimes take 20 or more hours to complete. Other problems involved site outages, both on the auction side and in the member's back office. Burke addressed the computer problems in his newsletter on March 26, 2012:

> *"But what does all that traffic mean in terms of the servers? Well, it means that the number of computers around the world trying to connect to ZR was outstripping the servers' ability to respond to those connection requests. Over the past two weeks we have been in "upgrade" modality to meet the increased demand. We have added several new servers and drive arrays including the superfast SSD San drives. The engineers, Alberto, Guido and Javier have worked with total dedication with The Master programmer, Dan Olivares, to*

expand the capacity with as little interruption as possible to the flow of your business. I compare it to trying to change a car's sparkplugs with the engine running! It's not an easy task and they have done a remarkable job.

When you are already dealing with server issues and you throw in a few other challenges it can be a little frustrating. For example, we also just changed credit card processors, we are in the middle of implementing a new eWallet payment system, we are nearing the launch of the new Compliance Training system, we are transitioning away from the 5cc system and we've made huge expansions in the support staff".

It was not because the images were so large or the Internet connection was not function correctly, but it was reported that the server publishing the sites was getting hammered by the mountain of increased traffic. Greg recognized this problem and attempted to solve it.

Greg had to put on his best diplomatic hat, and tried to develop a plan to bring up a duplicate site and do this without the current site being interrupted until the new site was ready to be installed. This was the start of Greg's *three-month nightmare*.[12] Right about that time the rumors were circulating that accounts were getting hacked, money was being transferred out of accounts

---

[12] Conversations with Author and Greg Caldwell

unknowingly with participants losing thousands of dollars. The panic was alive and well.

Another problem, and perhaps more serious, was that Zeek was being viewed as a passive income opportunity, in a sense an investment, with a great return. The people signing up these people would say, *"Give me $10,000 and I will manage it for you"*. Some people managed accounts for 50 to 100 people. The passwords would be something simple and easy for the person managing the account to easily remember. Allowing a person to manage Zeek accounts and login with privileged passwords each day to perform the required advertisement task created a huge privacy problem.

When these accounts started growing, it was common place for people to get on webinars using a service like *"Go to Meeting"* and type in the account password to display information contained in the back office for everyone to view. Because there were hundreds of meetings going on each day, when someone saw account information that would allow them to ramp up their recruitment efforts, they would copy down the login information and enter the account at their meetings to show their audience the power of Zeek. It all seemed very innocent, but abuses were reported.

Perhaps the people managing accounts were not aware of the potential problems they were creating due to the unauthorized access to sensitive, privileged information. There would be people who would turn off repurchase conditions or place repurchase conditions on the account to show how simple it was to send money to the website accounts. Also, once the money was in the back office, unauthorized repurchase bids could take place. This may have accounted for some of the statements that accounts were being hacked, when in fact; it may have been bad judgment on the part of the account holder. It probably was the case that some illegal transfer of money occurred, but probably less often than initially suspected.

Around June 2012, there was an idea advanced to introduce a secure device where no one would be able to log into anyone's back office unless the participant was plugged into his or her personal computer. With the secure device in place, people with other participants' passwords would no longer be able to access the back office of the sites they managed. Use of this device would have been important because it removed the liability from Rex Venture Group and Zeek Rewards. It must be noted at the time that effective policies governing privacy infringement were not present. Despite his efforts to improve the situation with the new device and other techniques, Greg did not provide the participants with a workable solution to their website problems.

REGULATORS TRACE THE MONEY

Now, with Zeek Rewards and its predecessor Ad Surf Daily, what made the initial success was simply that the people who joined did not leave; they actually made money and lots of it. In most instances, network marketing companies do not pay well, or at least only a few at the top make money; but Zeek Rewards and Ad Surf Daily members shared a different experience. When people joined the two companies, they were shown how to make money each and every day. The new recruits would naturally tell others and the cycle would continue. So in this global economy and with instant communication, the word would spread quickly, and spread it did! Both companies experienced rapid initial growth. It was understandable why Dawn patterned Zeek Rewards after the initially successful Ad Surf Daily when she looked for a MLM company as a model.

It was not hard to find someone who was withdrawing money and *"living like a king"*. People, who a few months earlier were in fear of losing their home, had not only made their home loan current but, paid it off. Kids were going to college and no student loans were needed. Retired couples were taking trips they never thought possible. Miraculous things were happening and everyone was buzzing with the possibilities of riches beyond their wildest dreams.

Each night there were hundreds of conference calls, some in Spanish, some in Portuguese and others in different languages. The team leaders would use the calls to discuss the power of the website in motivating them and others to embrace Zeek as their primary business: *"You could look at your Matrix displayed in your backend web portal and see it filling up with money each day, sometimes every minute"*.

Life was good. Little did we know it was like a scene from the Titanic where the day before they were to hit the iceberg everything was *"Great"*. No one knew what was to come and how the next day, August 15, 2012, would change their lives forever.

Everyone was in this euphoria state; and many agreed on one thing, they were going to need a bigger safe as banks started questioning the large amount of cash everyone was walking around with. You see, the Government in its wisdom keeps placing increasing restrictions on banks, and that impacts the general public on how they manage their finances. This is not a Zeek thing, but the world we live in.

After 9/11, the Patriot Act demanded that all financial institutions be more diligent in processing transactions and collect identifying information on their customers[13]. These requirements were interpreted in a variety of ways; but in general, banks would not cash checks for people if they did not have an account with the bank and/or banks would not cash large checks from anyone. This unique challenge hurt Zeek participants and caused a serious problem for the banks. Because of the reluctance of banks to cash large Zeek checks, many participants rushed to their banks and withdrew their

---

[13] http://en.wikipedia.org/wiki/Know_your_customer

money and closed their accounts. Participants sought other avenues to deposit the large checks creating a potential shortfall in the reserves that all banks are required to have. The banks' reporting to the Feds the many closed bank accounts and the attempts of depositors to cash large checks were among the triggering events that captured the attention of state and Federal regulators including the **IRS, SEC, FTC, NC DOJ** and let's not forget the **FBI** and **Secret Service**.

Once Zeek Rewards was in full swing, crazy amounts of cash were going around. To better comprehend the challenges everyone was having receiving and paying money, you have to understand a few more important facts. The banks were having issues with the volume of money being deposited and/or paid out to the Rex Venture Group. To respond to this unforeseen problem, Burks used up to 15 bank accounts [14] to spread the deposits around as the banks felt there was no way any legitimate business could go from zero to that much money in such a short period of time. Burks was not trying to hide anything, but just trying to do business in this complex world we all live in.

The administrative staff at Rex Venture Group could not keep pace with the large amount of cashier's checks for bid purchases. The practice of using ewallets became a part of the business model in order to process the flow of money. Anyone who wanted to quickly post bids and receive commissions needed to have an ewallet account. Rex Venture Group enlisted the support of the following ewallet businesses: Payza, Solid Trust and NX

---

[14] http://www.sec.gov/litigation/complaints/2012/comp-pr2012-160.pdf

Pay Systems. NX Pay Systems was the only ewallet company that was in the United States. Arrangements were made for the money to be deposited or withdrawn from the ewallets by accessing the personalized Zeek Rewards back office.

Although the use of ewallets was not contemplated in the beginning, it evolved into a crazy plan where you could have money placed on your ewallet account and; additionally, you could accept cash from anyone. Also, someone with your ewallet account could post the bid purchases and pocket the payout cash if they knew your password. It was not long before illegal withdrawals were made by persons who crashed into the ewallet accounts or who used passwords given to them to process bids and advertisements for accounts others managed. This was not felt to be the norm, but the exception.

Network Marketing Companies Are In a Panic

Have you ever heard a large volume of water going down a drain? Just watching as the items in the water start to move faster as they get close to the whirlpool being created, the closer they get, the faster they move towards the drain. Now if you listen closely you start to hear a suction sound as the water is flowing faster and faster and the draining sound is now creating a hissing sound. That is the best way I can describe the flow of people leaving other MLM programs and going to Zeek Rewards.

Let me expand on the panic that was gripping other MLM owners at this point. Companies, like ACN, Fortune Hi-Tech Marketing, Mary Kay, and yes, even Amway, saw long-term leaders start *dipping their toes* in *The Zeek Phenomen*on™ because they saw a way to earn the same money, or more, in months with less effort. It would take some other leaders ten years to accomplish what was being accomplished in Zeek Rewards in 12 months or less. This was intoxicating and the excitement was overpowering.

From fear that the vast amounts of money would not last, most of the key leaders used aliases and got their team members to do so as well. Pretty soon terms like *"witness protection"* was being used to protect identities of leaders from other MLMs. If any member in another MLM was at a Zeek Rewards meeting or on a Zeek webinar, they used various methods to hide their names. You see, in the back of their minds if Zeek did not last, they wanted to preserve their position at the old company. As Zeek picked up steam, the traditional MLM companies saw a lot of their team members leaving. The drain of members created a crisis situation for the traditional MLM companies.

Once this happened, the MLM companies started recognizing the loss in money volume, cancelations of monthly auto ships (the life blood of the industry) and/or downgrading of monthly packages. These changes started a panic among traditional MLM companies. When the established MLMs started seeing their numbers drop drastically on weekly update calls, they knew there was a serious problem. It did not take long for the word to get out that everyone was heading to Zeek; in fact, there were some MLM owners signing up in Zeek as well. I guess they did not want to be left out on the flow of money. It was most definitely a *huge tidal wave*.

Based on the information from knowledgeable people, some companies had their legal departments call and do what they could to get the NC DOJ involved as they needed Zeek Rewards *"taken down"*. Owners realized that everyday ZeekRewards operated was a day their company was closer to going out of business. Someone should have mentioned that when a call is made to the authorities to complain, it also places the spotlight on the complaining company. This lesson was learned by Fortune Hi-Tech Marketing February 2013.[15] Consequently, Fortune Hi-Tech Marketing's call to the authorities complaining about Zeek Rewards resulted in an investigation of their own Company and eventually the problems that closed them.

State Regulators Request Documents

Behind the scenes in Zeek, there were troubling signs according to corporate documents, company emails and consumer complaints sent to various local and Federal authorities. The concerns of participants were not being addressed, the wait for money was taking longer and the banks were getting nervous. Dark clouds began to appear on the horizon for this fast-growing Company.

---

[15]http://www.usatoday.com/story/money/personalfinance/2013/01/28/fhtm-shut-down-pyramid-scheme/1870527/

The grievance calls to the authorities from other MLM companies, the complaints from Zeek participants who were upset due to the slow processing of payouts and the complaints from banks regarding suspected illegal activity all contributed to the Federal investigations that eventually lead to the closing of Zeek Rewards and Rex Venture Group. Once the state and Federal investigations were underway, it was a matter of time before the end was inevitable.

In the hardware store on South Main Street, Lexington, North Carolina, the owner pulled Carol Myers [16]aside to tell her about the best thing to happen in years to this declining furniture and textile town. *"Did she hear about the online Company, Zeek Rewards?"* He told her that for a small membership fee, she could make a fortune. Also, there were more and more people in Lexington, including doctors, lawyers, police and accountants who had given money to Zeek. Skeptical at first, Myers drove a few blocks to the Company's one-story, red-brick office and spotted a line of people circling the building. Observing the frenzy, she was sold and plunked down several thousand dollars; but months later, Myers, like hundreds of thousands of others, discovered that Zeek Rewards was reported to be a scam. *"I was duped,"* Meyer said. *"We trusted this man. The community is still in shock"*.

On Nov. 23, 2011 a complaint was filed with the North Carolina Attorney General's office, Wayne

---

16

http://www.usatoday.com/story/money/business/2013/03/30/authorities-600m-scheme-incubated-nc-town/2037975/

Tidderington of Florida called Zeek Rewards an "*illegal*"
Ponzi scheme. He said a relative invested $8,000 and the
Company guaranteed a return of 125 percent every 90
days. Although the Attorney General's Office could have
asked a judge to shut down the business because of
deceptive trade practices; instead it forwarded
Tidderington's complaint to the Secretary of State's Office
because "*it looked like it might involve securities*". The
Secretary of State's Office; however, declined to take
action because it didn't believe it had the jurisdiction,
spokeswoman Liz Proctor said. "*I put it all together,*"
Tidderington stated. "*I gave them the roadmap. I said,
'Here's a snake, Here's the gun, Here's the bullets, Shoot the
snake.' But they ignored me*". Over the next seven months,
the Attorney General's Office received nearly a dozen
more complaints.

In early June of 2012, the state of Montana gave
Zeek Rewards the boot. Montana requires multilevel
marketing companies to register. "*Zeek Rewards didn't
submit any paperwork — even after warnings*", said Luke
Hamilton, a spokesman for the Montana Attorney
General's Office. "*We started getting a lot of complaints,*"
Hamilton said. (In fact, it is doubtful that Zeek Rewards
registered initially in North Carolina, a requirement of
the state.)

But it wasn't until July 6, 2012, that the North
Carolina Department of Justice issued an order giving
Burks until the end of the month to turn over all Zeek-
related documents. He missed that deadline. You would
think with the money available in Zeek Rewards, he
would have simply hired a top legal team to meet with

the regulators and find a solution. Kevin Anderson, Senior Deputy Attorney General for the North Carolina Consumer Protection Department insisted his Agency handled the case correctly, saying the Office received thousands of complaints a year. *"We have to have more concrete evidence than a couple of consumer complaints before we go to court,"* he said.

In August, 2012, a North Carolina Employees Credit Union warned customers, not to invest in Zeek Rewards because it was a *"fraudulent company"*. The Credit Union refused to issue cashier's checks to the customers of the Bank if they were being made out to Rex Venture Group—the financial arm of Zeek Rewards. However, regulators had received complaints long before then and had not acted. The reason for the earlier inactivity is not known.

The SEC received similar complaints during the same period, but the Agency didn't begin its investigation until the summer of 2012. SEC spokeswoman, Christine D'Amico, declined to comment on the investigation except to say the Agency took action *"as soon as we believed we had sufficient evidence to obtain an emergency court order to halt the fraud"*. Or could it have been the fear of losing control of the funds?

Authorities say owner Burks was the mastermind of a $600 million [17] or now, reported $900 million Ponzi

---

[17]

http://www.sec.gov/News/PressRelease/Detail/PressRelease/1365171483920#.U_TbRWfQPIU.

[18]scheme — one of the biggest in U.S. history that attracted one million plus participants, including nearly 50,000 in North Carolina. Many were recruited by friends and family in Lexington, a quintessential small town where neighbors looked out for each other. It was reported that more than one quarter of the participants were foreigners.

At the time when they paid their membership fees, many participants did not know that state regulators had received nearly a dozen complaints about Zeek Rewards and the associated penny auction site, Zeekler.com. The North Carolina authorities failed to take action for months, leaving the Company free to recruit tens of thousands of new people without any interruption.

Inconsistent Management Creates a Problem

Most people did not know that Greg Caldwell did not live in Lexington, North Carolina; in fact, he did not live in the state of North Carolina at all. Each week Greg was the great commuter. When Burks hired Greg to help manage the fast-growing Company, he needed Greg in the office Monday through Friday; but after some negotiations, Burks agreed to Monday through Thursday. Burks leased an apartment for Greg. Greg would fly from Ohio on Sunday night and return to work Monday morning. On Thursday, Greg would leave by mid-day

---

[18] http://hamptonroads.com/2014/02/key-player-850m-nc-ponzi-scheme-pleads-guilty

and fly back to Ohio arriving in Ohio Thursday night.[19] This left Friday, Saturday and Sunday uncovered with the newly-hired middle manager who was tasked with the awesome responsibility of correcting the serious management problems.

From all accounts, Greg's part-time activity in the Lexington office continued until the morning of August 15, 2012 — the day that will live in the minds of all Zeek Rewards participants. On that day, the NC DOJ came to the end of their patience and demanded quite loudly the documents they had requested several weeks before. Let's not forget the banks that were suffering as they felt exposed under the Patriot Act and fear of a rush on the bank by their depositors.

On that day Greg was looking forward to heading home and catching his flight out of Charlotte, North Carolina. He was unaware that Zeek was in its worst predicament since the beginning. Burks was unprepared for what was to happen and the magnitude of the problem that was soon to come. You need several factors to come together culminating in a "*PERFECT STORM*" that turned into a *TSUNAMI* of epidemic proportions. Well on that day it did, like a well-planned explosion.

---

[19] Conversations with Author and Greg Caldwell

STATE REGULATORS MOVE AGAINST ZEEK

On August 15, 2012, Burks was dealing with some medical issues involving his wife, Greg was heading out of town and the NC DOJ was ramping up their requests. Burks asked his longtime friend and attorney, Noel Tin, to meet with the NC DOJ Civil Division and do what he could to resolve the issue regarding the requested documents. It is unclear if Noel was well versed in SEC litigation, but the information the NC DOJ was looking for involved security law, including areas that would fall within the jurisdiction of the FTC (Federal Trade Commission).

From the report of knowledgeable sources, it was learned that during the meeting, the following subjects came up *"Was Burks going to be arrested?"* and *"How could Burks escape jail"*? The NC DOJ, did their best *"Hail Mary Pass"* or *"Bluff"*, and said Burks could voluntary hand over all operations including the assets and, they would not go after him *"criminally"*. [20]

Now there are some key points to think about, firstly, the NC DOJ Civil Division would not be coming after Burks on a criminal complaint and secondly, how can Noel after an hour or two advise his client to do anything without consulting other attorneys that may have more experience in this type of law? Nonetheless, it was reported that a deal was struck at that one meeting. Also, it was reported that Noel made the deal for Burks to surrender the Company to NC DOJ without consulting

---

[20] Conversations with Author and persons close to Burks.

anyone in Zeek Rewards or Rex Venture Group, including Burks, Dawn or Greg. The validity of this unilateral action is unknown.

It is inconceivable what happened next. Noel had to go break the news to his longtime friend that Burks needs to give all his Company's money ($600 million) to the Government, close his business or better yet give it away to the Government and let two million people know the business they have been working for is now gone – not a great day for Burks.

Well it did not take long for Greg to get the news and with the attorney Kevin Grimes who did the compliance videos, Greg quickly did a three- way call to Burks and advised Burks not to sign anything until he had a chance to discuss the issue with him. Greg was driving to the airport, when the news of the proposed closure came, and quickly turned around and return to the office to deal with this most serious situation.

It was reported that around 4:30pm EST August 15, 2012, Greg arrived to learn that Burks has entered into an agreement to turn over Zeek Rewards and Rex Venture Group to the NC DOJ, (not the SEC). The document allowed them to take total control of the bank accounts with a reported $400 million dollars on deposit. By all appearances, Rex Venture Group had been sending out all auction items, paying all commissions, paying all vendors and payroll and was poised to continue to grow at a phenomenal rate. The seizure of the Company stopped all current activity and any future plans.

The NC DOJ asked Greg if he would stay on and help them sort through the items. Once he agreed, NC DOJ continued to pay him his consulting fee. Greg's first task was to obtain locks to secure the office and data files. Greg had the website taken down immediately. The absence of the website was the first sign to the participants that something very serious had happened.

The concern by regulators was the *"point system"* that they considered an unregistered security. The NC DOJ failed to understand that the *points* had **NO VALUE** and only a 90-day life. In fact, if Burks had declared that Zeek was not making any money, he was not obligated to make payouts based on the way the *point system* worked. Unfortunately, Burks never elected to do this and continued to show on the websites the 1.5% compounded amounts irrespective of the money earned from the auctions. Once the amounts were posted on the websites, it was alleged that payouts were made from other sources not related to the auction fees—hence, the situation may have prompted a Ponzi investigation.

The activities of other MLM companies that mimicked Zeek could have brought more regulatory attention to the activities of Zeek Rewards. The most visible companies that tried to replicate *The Zeek Phenomenon* ™ were; namely: **Bids that Gives, Bids for Kids, WCA (World Consumer Alliance), Go Fun Places and TelexFree**. Several of the new companies allowed excited Zeek participants join them. They were anticipating the same type of money they experienced in Zeek. Only one problem, it was reported that these companies did not operate like Zeek and there were a lot of people who were disappointed in their earnings. Many of these *copycat* companies closed so quickly that there was no time for any regulatory action to *get up to speed.*

Zeek received a great deal of attention from outsiders who made a living from blogging. The online MLM bloggers were posting about Zeek Rewards every hour it appeared and the sole reason was *"impression and click revenue"* — a way to make money just by driving people to your website and clicking on the ads. Zeek Rewards was a hot topic on the web and with millions of people trying to get any information they could, all anyone had to do was mention the word Zeek, and they would attract thousands if not hundreds of thousands of people to their web site, and this translated into ad revenue for them. Posting good or bad, it made no difference; just that you were giving timely updates is all it took to drive people to the MLM blogger sites and eventually to Zeek Rewards.

It is thought that the (1) attention on Zeek Rewards brought by the participants complaints, (2) the reports from banks regarding the closed accounts, (3) the complaints from the competitor MLMs, (4) the MLM bloggers' negative information on the Internet and (5)the *"copycat"* MLMers all contributed in part, to the interest by the state regulators.

North Carolina Department of Justice Seizes Zeek Rewards

Finally, on August 15, 2012, the North Carolina Department of Justice (NC DOJ) accepted a *voluntary surrender* of Zeek Rewards following a civil complaint lodged against the Company.   In addition to closing the Company, NC DOJ takes control of the assets of Zeek Rewards and Rex Venture Group.

Behind the scenes, the Security and Exchange Commission (SEC) was preparing documents to take control of Zeek Rewards for "selling securities without a license."

THE SEC TAKES CONTROL

The next day on August 16, 2012, the Securities Exchange Commission filed an ex parte motion[21]. The motion was for the Federal Government to take control of Rex Venture Group d/b/a Zeek Rewards and its assets. Why did the Federal Government tell the judge they had to act so quickly? That answer is simple, the Federal Government wanted to take control of the money to protect the interest of the participants!

The following describes how the Federal Government received the custody of millions of Zeek Rewards participants and their accounts:

> *"United States District Judge Graham Mullen appointed Kenneth Bell as the temporary Receiver, empowering him to take control of Zeek's assets and begin an investigation. Mr. Bell is a <u>Partner</u> at the <u>Charlotte</u> office of McGuire Woods, where his practice includes white collar crime. It is likely that Bell took control of Zeek's offices yesterday immediately after the Order was signed. In the Order, Judge Graham also ordered Burks to provide a list of all assets, employees, and creditors of Zeek to the Receiver within 10 days, and a full*

---

[21] http://en.wikipedia.org/wiki/Ex_parte. *Ex parte* / ɛks ˈpɑrtiː/ is a <u>Latin</u> <u>legal</u> term meaning "from (by or for) [the/a] party". An *ex parte* decision is one decided by a <u>judge</u> without requiring all of the parties to the controversy to be present. In <u>Australian</u>, <u>Canadian</u>, <u>U.K.</u>, <u>South African</u>, <u>Indian</u> and <u>U.S.legal doctrines</u>, *ex parte* means a legal proceeding brought by one person in the absence of and without representation or notification of other parties.
The entire text of the motion is found in Exhibit 3.

accounting of assets, bank accounts, and other property within 30 days".[22]

The Securities and Exchange Commission, in a press release, stated they closed the $600 million Ponzi, operated by Rex Venture Group on Aug. 17, 2014, and stated, Burks was selling securities without a license. It was alleged that the Ponzi scheme was using money from new participants to pay the earlier ones. During the month of August, 2014, Burks agreed to pay a $4 million civil penalty to the North Carolina Government; the SEC was not involved in this settlement. He also agreed to cooperate with a Federal court-appointed Receiver who was charged with recovering hundreds of millions of dollars from "victims".[23]

Remember Burks had handed over bank accounts totaling several hundred million dollars, so this was not the typical Ponzi, where there was no money to recover. In most Ponzi schemes, the authorities had to liquidate cars, boats and planes, but with Zeek, hundreds of millions of dollars was sitting in the bank or in ewallet accounts.

Investigators say Burks, a former nursing home magician, siphoned millions for his personal use. In his first public comments, Burks told The Associated Press he couldn't discuss details because of lawsuits by victims

---

[22] SEC information on the web and in other documents.

[23] http://www.usatoday.com/story/money/business/2013/03/30/authorities-600m-scheme-incubated-nc-town/2037975/

trying to recoup money. [24] It is important to mention, the lawsuits to recover money did not happen until the Government seized the money.

One of the main questions many asked after the shutdown of Zeek Rewards in August 2012 was *"when criminal charges would be filed?"* That question was at least partially answered December 20, 2013 when the U.S. Attorney's Office announced that two people, Dawn Wright-Olivares, the former Chief Operating Officer (COO) for Zeek, and her stepson, master programmer Daniel Olivares, plead guilty to investment fraud and other charges. Both also agreed to forfeit proceeds from the venture that totaled more than $11.4 million. The money reportedly was to go to those who lost money in Zeek Rewards.[25]

Still avoiding indictment at the time of this printing was Burks, Zeek's top executive. Documents showing Dawn Wright-Olivares[26]' and Daniel Olivares' pleas contained references to "P.B". The documents stated he was enriched $10.1 million, but failed to mention that over $7.0 million of the money was paid to the IRS for taxes owed. [27] People were wondering why investigators didn't act more quickly and why Burks was not charged at the inception of the shutdown.

24

http://www.usatoday.com/story/money/business/2013/03/30/authorities-600m-scheme-incubated-nc-town/2037975/
25

http://www.zeekrewardsReceivership.com/pdf/US_Net_Winner_Class_Action_Complaint.pdf

[26] http://www.arkansasbusiness.com/article/96427/two-arkansans-to-plead-guilty-in-900m-ponzi-scheme

[27] Zeek Rewards Receivership.com

Some of those who lost money with Zeek might want to see Burks punished criminally, but more importantly, at this point they probably want additional proceeds placed in the pool of money for *"net losers"*. So when would these checks start to be disbursed? *"Everything will come out in time,"* said Burks, standing in the doorway of his home. Asked if he had anything to say to victims, he shook his head. *"I never told anyone to invest more money than they could afford,"* Burks snapped. *"I didn't tell them to do that, ever"*. He said if they lost money, *"It's their fault. Not mine. Don't blame me"*.

Cal Cunningham, a former prosecutor [28]representing some participants in a lawsuit, slammed Burks — and regulators for taking so long to act. *"It's why we need a full hearing on what happened in a court of law — whether that is the civil case or a criminal proceeding. A lot of people were hurt,"* he said.

Civil Forfeiture Laws Used to Take Immediate Control of Assets

Recently enacted Federal Civil Forfeiture Laws were used in the demise of Zeek Rewards. The participants who had the ewallet accounts in the US would soon learn a civil forfeiture lesson and in some cases a million dollar lesson, as did Durant due to the freeing of his account. All Zeek Rewards US ewallet accounts were seized by the Federal Government after the shutdown of the Company.

---

[28] http://www.ibtimes.com/zeekrewards-class-action-plaintiffs-hire-prominent-nc-politician-lawyer-758437

In order to understand the far reaching effects of Civil Forfeiture Laws, details of two examples will be placed in the Appendix — See **Bowdoin Case # 1** [29]and **Dehko Case # 3**[30]. You may remember that Dawn used some of the techniques from her Ad Surf Daily experience to make Burks' shopping business more profitable. Andy Bowdoin was the founder of Ad Surf Daily, the company that is further detailed in Bowdoin Case #1.

Briefly, the Bowdoin Case involved the Ad Surf Daily business where the US Government seized $53.0 million dollars. In the Dehko Case, the US Government closed the bank accounts of the *"mom and pop"* supermarket and put the company out of business on a mistaken notion. It was suspected that the Dehkos were laundering money when, in fact, they made frequent bank deposits of $10,000 because their insurance company would not insure deposits larger than $10,000. These were perfectly legitimate deposits from their business' daily receipts, but the pattern of deposits gave the appearance of smurfing, an illegal act.[31]

The two cases had distinctly different outcomes. Criminal charges were filed in the Bowdoin case and Andy Bowdoin was found guilty of operating a Ponzi

---

[29] Dowdoin Case Summary is found in Exhibit 1.

[30] Dehko Case Summary is found in Exhibit 4.

[31] http://en.wikipedia.org/wiki/StructuringStructuring, also known as smurfing in banking industry jargon, is the practice of executing financial transactions (such as the making of bank deposits) in a specific pattern calculated to avoid the creation of certain records and reports required by law, such as the United States' Bank Secrecy Act (BSA) and Internal Revenue Code section 6050I (relating to the requirement to file Form 8300).

scheme, the same charge against Zeek Rewards. In the Dehkos case, the family finally got their money back, but their fight continues today with a lawsuit against the Federal Government that seeks to rein in some unintentional problems associated with civil forfeiture.

The Federal Agencies will continue to trace the money where it is perceived that laws have been broken — this is their responsibility in protecting the citizenry. MLM companies should be alert to the activities of their participants that run afoul of the law and put in place policies that prevent such infractions. *The Zeek Phenomenon*™ could have had a much different fate had the founders been cognizant of the state and Federal rules and developed policies that conformed to the dictates of the law.

A RECEIVER IS APPOINTED TO CONTROL THE ASSETS

On August 16, 2012, the Security and Exchange Commission (SEC) requested Senior Judge Graham C. Mullen in the Western District of North Carolina to sign a temporary order giving the SEC control of the assets of Rex Venture Group and appointing Kenneth Bell [32]as the Receiver. The Judge signed the order and shortly thereafter SEC issued the following press release:

FOR IMMEDIATE RELEASE

Washington, D.C., Aug. 17, 2012

The Securities and Exchange Commission today announced fraud charges and an emergency asset freeze to halt a $600 million Ponzi scheme on the verge of collapse. The emergency action assures that victims can recoup more of their money and potentially avoid devastating losses.

The SEC alleges that online marketer Burks of Lexington, N.C. and his company Rex Venture Group have raised money from more than one million Internet customers nationwide and overseas through the website Zeek Rewards.com, which they began in January 2011.

---

[32] http://www.mcguirewoods.com/People/B/Kenneth-D-Bell.aspx

According to the SEC's complaint filed in federal court in Charlotte, N.C., customers were offered several ways to earn money through the Zeek Rewards program, two of which involved purchasing securities in the form of membership fee contracts. These securities offerings were not registered with the SEC as required under the federal securities laws.

The SEC alleges that participants were collectively promised up to 50 percent of the company's daily net profits through a profit sharing system in which they accumulate rewards points that they can use for cash payouts. However, the website fraudulently conveyed the false impression that the company was extremely profitable when, in fact, the payouts to participants bore no relation to the company's net profits. Most of Zeek Rewards' total revenues and the "net profits" paid to participants have been comprised of funds received from new participants in classic Ponzi scheme fashion.

"The obligations to participants drastically exceed the company's cash on hand, which is why we need to step in quickly, salvage whatever funds remain and ensure an orderly and fair payout to participants," said Stephen Cohen, an Associate Director in the SEC's Division of Enforcement. "Zeek Rewards misused the

power of the Internet and lured participants by making them believe they were getting an opportunity to cash in on the next big thing. In reality, their cash was just going to the earlier investor".

The SEC's complaint alleges that the scheme is teetering on collapse with investor funds at risk of dissipation without its emergency enforcement action. Last month, Zeek Rewards brought in approximately $162 million while total investor cash payouts were approximately $160 million. If customers continue to increasingly elect to receive cash payouts rather than reinvesting their money to reach higher levels of rewards points, Zeek Rewards' cash outflows would eventually exceed its total revenue.

Burks has agreed to settle the SEC's charges against him without admitting or denying the allegations, and agreed to cooperate with a court-appointed Receiver.

According to the SEC's complaint, Zeek Rewards has paid out nearly $375 million to participants to date and holds approximately $225 million in investor funds in 15 foreign and domestic financial institutions. Those funds will be frozen under the emergency asset freeze granted by the court at the SEC's request. Meanwhile, Burks has personally siphoned several million dollars of participants' funds while *operating Rex Venture and Zeek Rewards, and he distributed at least $1 million to family members. Burks has agreed to relinquish his interest in the company and its assets plus pay a $4 million penalty. Additionally, the court has appointed a Receiver to collect, marshal, manage and distribute remaining assets for return to harmed participants.*

The SEC's investigation was conducted by Brian M. Privor and Alfred C. Tierney in the SEC's Enforcement Division in Washington D.C. The SEC acknowledges the assistance of the Quebec Autorite des Marches Financiers and the Ontario Securities Commission.

HUNDREDS OF PARTICIPANTS BAN TOGETHER

As the shock wave of what happened on the sixteenth of August was felt around the world, it was safe to say that confusion and rumor were flowing at a high rate. Leaders were making calls trying to retain the teams they had built and move them to different opportunities. There was widespread panic as many people were expecting money to be available in their e-wallet, but discovered none was there. There were so many people wanting to do something, but they simply did not know where to go or what to do.

The most amazing thing happened; people of different interests began to come together in an effort to keep Zeek alive. Former participants banned together under the Zteambiz.net site and registered to send money for retaining qualified legal counsel to represent the interest of the group. This was a formidable task at best since the effort was to get a law firm to represent one million plus people, many of who were out of the country.

It soon became evident that in this crazy world of network marketing, people develop long lasting friendships, and with the Internet, Skype and social networking, it is easy to see how this group comprised mostly of strangers coalesced. In the beginning everyone came together as one big family. This is consistent with the mentality of networkers, most will come to your rescue and *"give you the shirt off their back"* if you are in desperate need. The main goal of the participants was to keep Zeek Rewards alive. It seemed everyone focused on the continuation of the Company without considering the different interests, that is, the divergent interest of *net winners* and *net losers*. About ten days after the crash of Zeek, the goal was reached for securing sufficient funds to hire legal counsel to investigate the events of August 15, and 16 and determine if Zeek Rewards could continue to operate.

Soon the group began to see cracks in their comradery; it became evident that the goals of the *net winners* and *net losers* were not the same. *Net winners* were mostly concerned about any possible claw backs if the Ponzi charge was upheld by the courts. The *net losers* began to focus more on how they could recover the money they lost because the payouts were less than the money they paid into Zeek Rewards. In fact, many *net losers* had never received any payouts due to the waiting period *three months) established for them to become eligible to make withdrawals.

The Biggest Net Winners are Targeted

The *net winners* fear became a reality when the Receiver published a motion asking the court to approve a claw back action against the 9,000 people who received a profit of $1,000 or more. In this list he named the top ten *net winners* and published their names on the Receivership website. Among the most affected persons with respect to claw backs were the *net winners* who made in excess of $1.0 million:

Todd Disner "net winner" of more than $1,875,000

Trudy Gilmond "net winner" of more than $1,750,000
Jerry Napier "net winner" of more than $1,745,000
Durant Brockett "net winner" of more than $1,720,000
Darren Miller "net winner" of more than $1,635,000
Rhonda Gates "net winner" of more than $1,425,000
Michael Van Leeuwen "net winner" of more than $1,400,000
David Sorrells "net winner" of more than $1,000,000
T. Le Mont Silver Sr. "net winner" of more than $773,000 and $943,000
Karen Silver, T. Le Mont Silver's wife "net winner" of more than $600,000
Aaron and Shara Andrews "net winners" of more than $1,000,000
David and Mary Kettner "net winners" of more than $930,000
Lori Jean Weber "net winner" of more than $1,940,000

All total, this group earned $18,736,000 (Eighteen Million Seven Hundred thirty Six Thousand dollars)

Todd Disner occupied the top position in the *Net Winners* List, and in my opinion, he is one of those unique people who would *give his last dime to help someone.* He is not different from any other person with the exception that he possesses a unique talent; and that is, his ability to locate business opportunities that have a high probability of immense success. Accordingly, one of his most famous achievements was the development of a national sandwich chain, Quiznos. The Quiznos Corporation is the third largest chain of submarine sandwich shops, with more than 1,150 restaurants in the United States, Canada, Puerto Rico, United Kingdom, Australia, and Japan. Quiznos Italian-style deli offers

Italian submarines and other sandwiches, soups, salads, and pastas. The classic Italian submarine made with ingredients of a proprietary recipe housed in a fresh-baked soft baguette is the cornerstone of the Quiznos concept.

Todd Disner and his partner, Boyd Bartlett, formulated the brand concept and menu for Quiznos America while operating a popular Italian restaurant, Footer's, in the Capital Hill neighborhood of Denver, Colorado. Using their knowledge of Italian foods, they developed an Italian-style deli, serving submarine sandwiches, soups, salads, and a few pasta dishes. In Footer's kitchen, Disner and Bartlett created recipes for red wine vinegar dressing and a proprietary soft baguette and other essential ingredients in the classic Italian submarine that made the famous Quiznos a household word.

Trudy Gilmond, Jerry Napier, Durant Brockett, Darren Miller, Rhonda Gates, Michael Van Leeuwen, David Sorrells, T. Le Mont Silver Sr, Aaron and Shara, David and Mary Kettner and Lori Jean Weber round out the list of people that Kenneth Bell identified as the recipients of $18 plus million dollars jointly. From all accounts, this group of people shares a common bond, and that is simply the desire to help others.

Now that may sound strange, but here in what I think. The position these people were in was great, but they did not need to be part of Zeek Rewards. They joined Zeek because they had a desire to help many other people. Most of them paid for several people to get started, to my knowledge, none of them every asked for a dime back. They spent countless hours and thousands of dollars to travel and help others. Yes, their growth in Zeek depended on the efforts of their team members; but it was reported that the membership fees paid for others were far greater than the original money spent with Rex Venture Group and Zeek Rewards, in the form of travel, and business-related expenses to promote the business opportunity.

Despite the attempts to persuade the SEC that Zeek Rewards was not a *"security"* or *"Ponzi scheme,"* the Receiver filed a motion to claw back the "illegal gains" of the *net winners*.[33] In an effort to prevent the claw backs, *net winners* formed various groups to challenge the Receiver in Court. Some of the larger *net winners* sought their own legal counsel.

The First Legal Dream Team

The decision was made by a large group of *net winners* to retain the law firm of SNR Denton and now through mergers and such, it is now called, Denton's. The lead attorney was Glenn Colton [34]and assisting him was Gene Besen [35]and Dan Gibb[36]. These were highly qualified attorneys that practice SEC litigation.

To locate attorneys with this much experience and respect in the legal community was a stroke of luck, but that luck quickly turned to disappointment. The overwhelming talent of MLM bloggers that have a talent of pinning stories to fit their goal of painting everyone in

---

[33] See the entire text of the motion in Appendix Exhibit 5

[34] http://www.dentons.com/en/glenn-colton

[35] http://www.dentons.com/en/gene-besen

[36] http://www.dentons.com/en/dan-gibb

the MLM community as crooks, liars and thieves was alive and well. The bios of these attorneys with contact numbers were posted on the web.

Can you envision one million telephone calls in a day; well that is about what happened. Due to the harassment, it did not take long for the talents of Gene, Dan and Glenn to quickly disappear. One of the reasons may be the simple fact that the online MLM bloggers did a great job of spreading fear and misinformation. It is normal for people to want to verify the facts and ask to hear the information first hand, but when you have a group this large if a small percentage of the people just make one call you end up with hundreds of thousands of calls being made. That will *blow the doors off* of any company and that is just what happened.

The attorneys did not understand the power of network marketing, and were the beneficiaries of a crash course in group communication. The game plan in hindsight should have been a conference call where the legal team would be introduced and answered twenty prepared questions. Of course, this is hindsight and the leaders of the group did not anticipate the problem. Unfortunately, in the end, the Zeek *net winners* and others lost the team as the Internet bloggers just *blew them out of the water*!

The Second Legal Dream Team

Quilling, Selander, Lownds, Winslett & Moser, P.C. was the second firm approached. This firm's qualifications were very impressive and, best of all; they were willing to take on this monumental task. To explain what got the group so excited about this new firm, the group looked into the prior cases handled and discovered that Mr. Michael Quilling functioned as a Receiver in cases throughout the United States and Canada. He handled prior Receivership cases like Ann Nosratieh, as Executrix on behalf of the Estate of Robert Laird Lindsay, as Representative Plaintiff- and- Strategic Metals Corp. and Capital Alternatives Inc., Defendants; (Court of the Queen's Bench of Alberta, Judicial District of Calgary). Other Quilling cases reviewed by the group were:

Quilling v. Cristell, No. 3:04-CV-252, 2006 WL 316981 (W.D.N.C. Feb. 9, 2006)
Quilling v. Grand Street Trust, No. 3:04-CV-251, 2005 WL 1983879 (W.D.N.C. Aug. 12, 2005)
Quilling v. Compass Bank, No. No. 3:03-CV-2180, 2004 WL 2093117 (N.D. Tex. Sep. 17, 2004)
Quilling v. Gilliland, No. 3:01-CV-1617, 2002 WL 373560 (N.D. Tex. Mar. 6, 2002)
In re Pro-Snax Distributors, Inc., 204 B.R. 492 (Bankr. N.D. Tex. 1996)
In re Norriss Brothers Lumber Company, Inc., 133 B.R. 599 (Bankr. N.D. Tex. 1991)
The Quilling firm agreed to take the case.

Rodney Alexander of Alexander Ricks PLLC was also approached to assist in the legal battle to continue Zeek Rewards. He also accepted the challenge. Mr. Alexander's bio describes an early commitment to public service and to pro bono service commitments which he has maintained throughout his career. From 1998 through May 2000, Mr. Alexander served as an Assistant District Attorney in Mecklenburg County, North Carolina. While serving in that capacity, Mr. Alexander honed his trial skills with more than forty felony jury trials and more than one hundred non-felony bench trials. But most significant, Rodney could serve as the local counsel in NC which the *net winners* and others needed.

The major thrust of the long legal battles was an effort to dispel the notion that Zeek Rewards was a security and that there was no Ponzi activity involved in paying the participates for the *"compounding points."* Although the *net winners* had a great deal of confidence in their *dream team* lawyers, the SEC prevailed.

MADOFF'S LAWYER, IRA LEE SORKIN, SAYS ZEEK REWARDS IS *"NO SECURITY"*

The position of the SEC had been from the inception that Zeek Rewards is a *"security"* or *"investment opportunity."* This position gave the SEC jurisdiction to intervene in the actions of the North Carolina Department of Justice and file a motion to seize the assets of Rex

Courtesy of Ira Lee Sorkin

Venture Group for the protection of the victims of a *"security fraud"* and a Ponzi scheme. Clearly if Zeek Rewards and Rex Venture Group did not sell *"unregistered securities"*, the SEC had no standing in Court and could not seize assets nor close Zeek Rewards. It was Ira Lee Sorkin's, Madoff's lawyer, contention that the SEC exceeded its authority and had no right to interfere with the business enterprise of Zeek Rewards or Rex Venture Group because a *"security"* was not involved. In his filing December 14, 2012 on behalf of *net winners* Trudy Gilmond and Kellie King, the following was submitted to the Court:

> *"This motion presents a matter of first impression: Whether parties which will be subject to claw back suits as a result of the Securities and Exchange Commission's (the "Commission" or "SEC") allegations that a corporation and its president engaged in a Ponzi and pyramid scheme, should be permitted to intervene for the purpose of*

arguing that the SEC never had jurisdiction to initiate this action because the alleged violative conduct did not involve a "security" as defined under §2(a)(1) of the Securities Act of 1933 ("Securities Act"). Should this Court grant intervention, as it should, the Proposed Interveners will establish that what the SEC has alleged is an "investment contract" is nothing of the sort. In fact, the purported i n v e s t o r s a r e not investing money in a common enterprise on the expectation that profits will be derived solely from the efforts of others. Rather, what the SEC purports are "investment contracts" are nothing more than contractual rights entitling independent contractors to a share of a company's profits in return for their efforts in promoting the company. Finally, because there is no "security" to justify the SEC's jurisdiction in bringing this action, the individual appointed at the SEC's request must be relieved of his duties, and the claw back suits must not go forward."[37]

The Receiver Moves Aggressively to Seize other Assets

In addition, other lawsuits[38] were filed by the Receiver to seize the assets of Zeek Rewards *"insiders"* who were involved in the promotion and/or management of the Company; namely:

- Paul Burks – Owner and Former Top Executive

---

[37] See the entire motion filed by Ira Lee Sorkin in Appendix Exhibit 6.
[38] See the entire motion filed by the Receiver to seize the assets of the Insiders in Appendix Exhibit 7.

- Dawn Wright-Olivares – Chief Operating Officer
- Daniel ("Danny") Olivares – Master Programmer
- Darryle Douglas – Affiliate Communications and Relations.
- Alexandre ("Alex") de Brantes – Executive Director of Training/Support Services
- Roger Plyler – Affiliate Relations

The Received filed a request to seize the monies received from the *"insiders"* based on their participation in the *"illegal"* scheme:

- Paul Burks--$10 million
- .Dawn Wright-Olivares--$7,800,000
- .Danny Olivares--3,100,000
- Mr. Plyler--$2,300,000
- Darryle Douglas--$1,975,000

The Receiver provided the following rationale for seizing the assets of the *Insiders*:

> *"Because Zeek's Insiders "won" or received (the victims') money in an unlawful Ponzi and pyramid scheme, they are not permitted to keep their winnings and must return the fraudulently transferred winnings back to the Receiver for distribution to Zeek's victims. In addition to "baiting the hook" by creating a number of net winners, the Insiders operated the scheme with the knowing, reckless or at least negligent assistance and encouragement of a number of managers and advisors that greatly enhanced the perceived legitimacy and resulting success of the*

*scheme. To the extent these individuals and
entities – many of whom profited from the
scheme – are not part of this action or
discussed specifically herein, they will be
subject to the future efforts of the Receiver to
recover damages and/or disgorgement of the
profits they received from the Zeek scheme."*

Early in the proceedings, SEC continued its
vigilant efforts to identify all of the assets of Zeek
Rewards and Rex Venture Group in its quest to return as
must money as possible to the *net losers*. The three
insiders who attracted the most attention with respect to
claw backs were Paul, Dawn and Daniel.

Initially, Paul filed a motion agreeing to turn over
the assets of Rex Venture Group d/b/a Zeek Rewards to
the authorities, [39] but shortly thereafter petitioned the
Court to exclude his personal assets[40]. All efforts to keep
his personal assets from the claw back procedures failed.

In a related criminal case, Dawn Wright-Olivares
and Danny Olivares pleaded guilty to securities fraud
and tax evasion:

*"On December 20, 2013, the United States
Attorney's Office for the Western District of North
Carolina filed a Bill of Information (the
"Information") against Dawn Wright-Olivares
and Danny Olivares alleging that they, with
others, engaged in an over $850 million Ponzi
scheme through Zeekler and ZeekRewards. Dawn
Wright-Olivares agreed to plead guilty to*

---

[39] The full text of the motion is in the Appendix Exhibit 8.
[40] The full text of the motion is in the Appendix Exhibit 9.

engaging in a securities fraud conspiracy and tax
evasion as charged in the Information. Danny
Olivares agreed to plead guilty to engaging in the
same securities fraud conspiracy as charged in the
Information."

Based on the above the guilty plea of Dawn and
Danny, the Courts attached millions of dollars to be
recovered from each for the benefit of the *net losers*.

A separate activity of the Receiver involved
reaching settlements with the *net winners*. As of October,
2013 it was reported on the Internet that at least 175 *net
winners* had pledged to return a combined $2.28 million
of their overall winnings of $4.06 million, or a 56.3
percent return. The Receiver continued the strategy to
locate *net winners* and work out settlements for the return
of an agreed-upon portion of the money.

NX Pay Systems was the US-based ewallet
Company used to process funds to and from Rex Venture
Group and was subject to the jurisdiction of the Receiver
in the seizure of assets. Accordingly, on September 7,
2012, NX Systems turned over, under seal, all monies in
Zeek Rewards participants' accounts.[41] Following the
receipt of the information, the Receiver moved to seize
the assets in the NX Systems ewallets of the *net winners*.
In a separate action filed in Court, three *net winners* had
their NX Systems accounts frozen:

*"Specifically, and apparently as a direct
result of the Receiver and/or the SEC sending the
Agreed Order to NxPay, the following accounts
owned exclusively by each of the Movants were*

---

[41]Case 3:12-cv-00519-GCM Document 25 filed 09/07/12

frozen and the Movants have had no access to the funds since that time:

Account	Institution	Amount
David	NxPay	$373,375.66
David	NxPay	$33,626.80
Mary	NxPay	$25,319.67

"42

The Receiver discovered that large sums of money were in various banks and ewallets in the United States and abroad. The following table shows the amounts of money identified in the various accounts that were subject to seizure:

---

42 See the entire motion filed by the Receiver to seize the assets of Sorrells and Kettner in Appendix Exhibit 10. Case 3:12-cv-00519-GCM Document 81 Filed 12/11/12 Page 6 of 18

Opening Balance		$322,701,285.52

RECEIPTS

Received From	Amount	
Bank Adjustments to deposits made in 2012	($200.00)	
ClickBank	$543.47	
Deposit of Affiliate-Investor financial instruments	$310,755.00	
Funds received from FXDD	$107,697.74	
Interest earned on Receiver's accounts	$80,340.07	
Seized Assets from Preferred Merchants	$982,301.00	
Settlements from Affiliate-Investors	$183,508.86	
Transfer of RVG funds held by American Express	$73,500.00	
Subtotal Receipts:		$1,738,446.14

DISBURSEMENTS

Expense Category	Amount	
2012 Withholding Tax	($29,440.20)	
Bank Fee	($6,882.53)	
Claims Process Implementation Expenses	($222,642.57)	
Claim Settlement with Internet Dynamo	($425,000.00)	
Forensic accounting services [1]	($381,067.20)	
Legal Services [1]	($709,486.17)	
Professional services [2]	($10,644.08)	
Process Service	($125.00)	
Service of complaint	($998.00)	
Service of subpoena	($180.87)	
Translation of Summons	($180.00)	
Website hosting	($75,660.00)	
Subtotal Disbursements:		($1,862,306.62)
Grand Total Cash on Hand:		$322,577,425.04

[1] Forensic Accounting services consist solely of a disbursement to FTI. Legal Services includes a $644,406.84 payment to MGW, as well as payments to various local counsel working on behalf of the Receiver.

[2] Professional Services consists solely of a disbursement to National Software Inc. as prepayment for the mailing of amended 1099s.

After numerous conferences and court hearings, the *net winners* lost their cases to (1) continue Zeek Rewards, (2) invalidate the order declaring Zeek Rewards a security, and/or (3) prevent the assets being seized by the SEC. The following announcement was published on the Receivership website announcing that the *net losers* would receive a 40% portion of the monies given to Zeek Rewards in excess of their payout amounts:

ANNOUNCEMENT FROM THE RECEIVER – August 1, 2014

> *On May 28, 2014, we filed a motion seeking to make an interim, partial distribution in amounts equal to 40% of each Affiliate's allowed claim using the "rising tide" method of calculation previously approved by the Court. Yesterday the Court approved this motion. You can read the Order here. In this distribution, Affiliates with allowed claims will receive an interim distribution of 40% of the amount of their cash membership fee in ZeekRewards, less any money received from ZeekRewards prior to my appointment as Receiver. If an affiliate holds an allowed claim, but received more than 40% of their cash membership fee in ZeekRewards from ZeekRewards prior to my appointment as Receiver, that Affiliate will not receive an interim distribution.*
>
> *We will make the first interim, partial distributions on allowed claims on September 30, 2014. The Court's order provides that August 15, 2014 is the date for determining whether a claim is allowed*

and payable on September 30, 2014. This means that if you are an Affiliate that holds an allowed claim on August 15, 2014, you received less than 40% of your cash membership fee in ZeekRewards prior to my appointment as Receiver, and would be entitled to a payment of in excess of $100.00, the first interim, partial distribution will be mailed to you on September 30, 2014.

In order for your claim to be allowed and eligible to receive a distribution, you must have received your claim determination, agreed to that claim determination (or resolved any objection you made to such claim determination and agreed to a claim determination), and provided the required release and OFAC certification requested on the claim portal. If you have received your claim determination, but have not agreed to the determination or have not provided the required release and OFAC certification, your claim is not yet allowed. Please submit this information as soon as possible. Without it, we are not permitted by the Court's orders to include you in the September 30, 2014 interim, partial distribution.

If you have not provided the tax information requested on the Claims Portal, I will be forced by applicable law to withhold taxes from your distribution.

Please submit your tax information so that I can distribute the maximum amount possible to you. Submitting your tax information does not necessarily mean you will owe taxes on your distribution. Please consult your professional tax advisor about your obligations, if any.

If your claim is not allowed or has not been determined before August 15, 2014, you will be eligible to receive your first interim, partial distribution on a later distribution date after your claim has been allowed. These later distribution dates will occur quarterly. You will receive distributions in the same total amount you would have received if your claim was allowed on August 15, 2014.

As of yesterday we have sent out approximately 160,000 letters of determination, leaving us with about 15,000 more claims to review. If you have not received your claim determination, please be patient; it is coming. If you have already received a claim determination, or when you do, I encourage you to respond as soon as you are able so that we can provide you with your first interim, partial distribution.

Let me emphasize that this is only a first distribution. I am entirely confident that we will make additional distributions. As you know, we have sued more than 9,000 individuals in the United States who took more money out of ZeekRewards than *they put in. This money rightfully belongs to affiliates with allowed claims. We will also sue foreign net winners in the near future. Also, I believe we will recover several millions of dollars more from financial institutions still holding Receivership assets. We also <u>continue</u> to eliminate overstated claims of Affiliates that allow us to release reserves. These reserve releases will fund additional distributions to Affiliates with allowed claims.*

The efforts on your behalf continue. Thank you for your continued support and patience.

Kenneth D. Bell, Receiver

Zeek Rewards attracted more than 500,000 foreign participates, many of whom were *net winners* and subject to seizure activities consistent with the motions filed in the courts in the United States. The Receiver confirmed that most of the foreign participates are citizens of countries that belong to the Hague Conference that allows for process of service in foreign countries in addition to assistance in collecting judgments. He vowed to aggressively pursue assets of foreigners who received in excess of $1,000 profit.

CONCLUSION

*T*he *Zeek Phenomenon*™ has taken you on a fascinating two-year journey of the alpha and omega of Zeek Rewards, the world's fastest growing MLM company where fortunes were made and lost by many ordinary people. As the author of this most extraordinary venture, I must reiterate, *"I am neutral with respect to whether or not Zeek Rewards should have met such a sudden and untimely death."*

The Zeek Rewards community is still recovering — and the wounds are very, very deep. It is evident that there are no clear *winners* or *losers* in the end. *The Zeek Phenomenon*™ will forever be remembered by many as one of the most enticing business ventures on the planet.

Epilogue

Will There Ever Be Another Zeek?

The answer to the question is, *"Most likely not."* You have seen there were so many factors that had to come together to make **The Zeek Phenomenon™** a reality. The likelihood of that happening again is *"slim to none."* I expect for years to come there will be groups that will try. Some will have a measure of success, but most will never feel the long arm of the law and implode before they ever reach their pinnacle.

I can say that there are good people and not so good people; but I believe that the average MLM entrepreneur is well meaning and willing to sacrifice self for others. *"The best rule of thumb is to obey the laws. To ensure that you are operating correctly, locate a quality legal team to help you create and explain your business model. When regulators come knocking, do not ignore them, treat them with the respect they deserve, and you may have an Amway model that will go on for years to come."*

Robert Craddock

APPENDIX

Exhibit 1

The Bowdoin Case Study #1

Around 2006 in Quincy, Florida; Thomas Anderson Bowdoin Jr[43], aka Andy Bowdoin started a company that allowed people to pay in to promote online advertising and earn a percentage of revenue from the monies the company received. This was known as Ad Surf Daily or ASD as the industry has come to know it as.

Andy Bowdoin started the company Ad Surf Daily Inc. a Florida for Profit Corporation on 05/23/2008, but had also been operating as a Nevada corporation from December 14, 2006 this is important because online and Government accounts say from August 2006, when in fact it was well into 2007 until his new business idea was off and running.

Andy Bowdoin is now 80 years old. On the Internet, ASD website promotes Andy as an astute businessman with a long and remarkable record of successes in numerous business ventures, but such successes are remarkably absent from his true work history.

Just prior to starting ASD, Bowdoin was arrested in Alabama for felony violations related to Fraud in Connection with the Offer and Sale of Securities by an Unregistered Agent. Bowdoin and several co-defendants were accused of having been promoters of a company called "Mobile International, Inc."

---

[43] http://investigativereportermikemason.blogspot.com/2009/08/ad-surf-daily-president-federal.html

The Alabama defendants said they had developed a mobile telephone system that was a cheaper alternative to the then-current cellular systems. That venture folded and Bowdoin with his co-defendants were charged with having sold unregistered securities to participants and with failing to state material facts to the participants that would have impacted the victims' decisions to invest.

In fact, Alabama officials asserted that Bowdoin instigated a scheme by which he took money from some victims to pay off prior participants. On October 6, 1997, in 1997, in Montgomery County, Bowdoin resolved this criminal matter by agreeing to enter Pre-Trial Diversion with three years of supervised probation and pay restitution of $15,000.

Andy Bowdoin completed his Pre-Trial requirements and the charges were dismissed. Additionally, on January 1 1, 1999, in Wilcox County, Bowdoin plead guilty to one count of sale of unregistered securities and was sentenced to 1 year in prison, however the sentence was suspended and he was placed on 3 years supervised probation and ordered to pay restitution of $75,000. What Andy did not expect was the attention he was soon going to receive. There were some key people that came to join him in his next venture Ad Surf Daily: Clarence Busby Jr. Dawn Stowers, Jerry Napier a well-respected network marketer, Todd Disner famous for starting Quiznos Sandwich shops[44], and Dawn Olivares.

These experienced network marketers knew they had a true race horse in the form of an online business opportunity and all they had to do was invite and hang on for the ride of their life. And quite simply, that is just what they did. Only problem was the ride was cut short by a person that did not

[44] http://en.wikipedia.org/wiki/Quiznos

fully understand the business model, Jack Arons[45], and when Jack complained to the Florida Attorney General office, not much happen.

Here is the irony, the state of Florida did not care what Andy was doing, and it had not pinged anyone's radar until Andy walked in their office to complain about the prior member Jack Arons and his threats. You see Andy did not feel he was doing anything wrong and it is quotes like this from US Department of Justice Senior Trial Attorney William R. Cohen stating *"Ad Surf Daily is a Ponzi [46]because it can only stay in business if new paying members join the company"* that confused Andy. Well correct me but is that not true with any company, if the customers stop coming or patronizing a company, the company will fold, so what a profound statement from a well-respected and trusted Government official. We would have to also ask William Cohen using his definition, if people stop going to McDonalds, and they close as a result, was McDonalds a Ponzi?

It was Andy going to the Florida Attorney General office that had someone there thinking *"there must be a lot of money at this company"* and yes there was about $53 million dollars in 15 accounts at Bank of America for the taking. You see this brings up one of the key reasons the Government agencies will act in the public interest, and again this is a true Oxymoron, the definition for this can be summed up in a simple paragraph Sometimes a pair of terms is claimed to be an oxymoron by those who hold the opinion that the two are mutually exclusive.

Now you may ask, what happens to the money captured by the Government. Is it held in an account and

[45] http://investigativereportermikemason.blogspot.com/2009/08/man-and-his-mission-to-take-down.html

[46] http://investigativereportermikemason.blogspot.com/2009/10/federal-prosecutor-of-asd-ponzi-case-is.html

distributed to the victims? The true answer is a little more complicated. This is where victims feel assaulted for a second time, in most cases the people/victims did not want the Government to step in, and in Zeek's case as well as ASD (Ad Surf Daily) the people did not want the Government to step in, but they hey did.

So after Andy made his business and the business model crystal clear to the Florida Attorney General office, the investigative process was now on. The US Secret Service gets in the act because there is a concern of a financial crime being committed, now we all remember the famous Madoff case where Bernie Madoff was accepting membership fee monies, investing them, delivering a return and all would be happy except Bernie Madoff used the funds for personal use, and took in new funds to pay false returns on prior participants, this is what is considered a Ponzi scheme, but Ad Surf Daily charged a fee for its advertising services and paid a commission for work performed. Just like Google in their ad sense program just without the MLM feature. However, Andy was charged with operating Ad Surf Daily as a Ponzi scheme and was jailed for committing that Federal crime.

The following lawsuit gives a bird's eye view of the Civil Forfeiture Procedure attached to a finding of guilty in a criminal case.

UNITED STATES DISTRICT COURT
FOR THE DISTRICT OF COLUMBIA

UNITED STATES OF AMERICA	:	Criminal No. 10-320 (RMC)
	:	
	:	
v.	:	
	:	
	:	
	:	
THOMAS ANDERSON BOWDOIN JR.,	:	
also known as "ANDY BOWDOIN,"	:	
	:	
Defendant.	:	

GOVERNMENT'S MOTION PURSUANT TO
TITLE 18, UNITED STATES CODE, § 3771

The United States, by and through its attorney, the United States Attorney for the District

of Columbia, respectfully submits this motion, pursuant to Title 18, United States Code, § 3771,

seeking entry of the attached proposed order which describes the procedures to be followed in

notifying potential victims of public proceedings to be held in this case.

Applicable Law

The Justice for All Act of 2004 (the "Act") expanded the rights of victims in federal

criminal proceedings and established certain requirements concerning the Government's

notification of victims. *See* 18 U.S.C. § 3771(a). The Act provides that crime victims have the

following rights: (1) the right to be reasonably protected from the accused; (2) the right to

reasonable, accurate, and timely notice of any public court proceeding, or parole proceeding,

involving the crime, or release of the defendant; (3) the right not to be excluded from any such

public court proceeding, unless the Court, after receiving clear and convincing evidence,

1

determines that testimony by the victim would be materially altered if the victim heard other testimony at that proceeding; (4) the right to be reasonably heard at any public proceeding in the district court involving release, plea, sentencing, or any parole proceeding; (5) the reasonable right to confer with the attorney for the Government in the case; (6) the right to full and timely restitution as provided in law; (7) the right to proceedings free from unreasonable delay; and (8) the right to be treated with fairness and with respect for the victim's dignity and privacy. *Id.* The Act defines a victim of a crime as "a person directly and proximately harmed as a result of the commission of a Federal offense or an offense in the District of Columbia." 18 U.S.C. § 3771(e).

Section 3771(b) requires the Court to ensure that crime victims are afforded the rights enumerated in the statute, and section 3771(c) obligates the Government to use "best efforts to see that crime victims are notified of, and accorded, the rights" provided. The Act does not set forth any specific notification procedures. In addition, the Act recognizes that in cases involving a large number of crime victims, it may be impracticable to accord all of the victims the rights identified in Section 3771(a). *See* 18 U.S.C. § 3771(d)(2).

Specifically, it provides that in such cases, "the court shall fashion a reasonable procedure to give effect to [the Act] that does not unduly complicate or prolong proceedings." *Id.* A number of courts have addressed the effect of the Act in cases involving large numbers of victims, particularly securities fraud prosecutions, and have approved procedures similar to those proposed and outlined below. *See, e.g., United States v. Mills et. al* 06-228 (ESH); *United States v. Madoff,* 09 Cr. 213 (S.D. N.Y.); *United States v. Rigas,* S1 02 Cr. 1236 (S.D.N.Y).

2

Discussion

On December 17, 2010, defendant Thomas Anderson Bowdoin Jr. also known as Andy Bowdoin ("Bowdoin") was arraigned on a seven count indictment charging him with wire fraud (18 U.S.C. § 1343), securities fraud (15 U.S.C. §§ 78j(b) and 78ff) and Unlawful Sale of Unregistered Securities (15 U.S.C. §§ 77e(a)(2) and 77(x)). This case involves charges arising from a scheme to defraud thousands of investors over more than two years. The criminal indictment alleges that the defendant, Thomas Anderson Bowdoin, Jr., ("Bowdoin"), perpetrated a scheme to defraud the members of AdSurfDaily Inc., ("ASD"). Specifically, the indictment alleges that Bowdoin solicited prospective customers to ASD based upon, among other things, his promise to use their funds to operate what was represented to be a profitable Internet advertising company capable of providing high returns on the funds they paid to ASD. Over the course of the two-year scheme Bowdoin made numerous misrepresentations and omissions in order to raise funds, including: (1) claiming to be operating a legitimate Internet advertising company; (2) asserting that ASD had independent revenue to pay member's the returns promised; (3) that Bowdoin's only run in with law enforcement authorities consisted of a traffic ticket, when in reality he had been convicted of criminal securities violations; (4) that the revenue methodology and numbers ASD published in support of its payouts were true and accurate, when in reality ASD was managing its revenue in order to ensure that it only paid out about 1% of a members investment each weekday and .5% on the weekends; (5) that ASD was not required to register its offering with the United States Securities and Exchange Commission, and (6) that Bowdoin was operating ASD far different than was described, essentially as his own piggy-bank.

3

As this Court is aware, in late July 2008, pursuant to seizure warrants, the government seized the proceeds of Bowdoin's fraudulent activity. Thereafter, the government filed two separate civil forfeiture cases against the seized property. Those cases were assigned to this Court (08-CV-1345 and 08-CV-2205). In January and March 2010, in both cases, this Court entered default judgments and final orders of forfeiture in favor of the government. Subsequently, the government established a remission program for victims to make claims of the seized property. The government has contracted with a claims administration firm to process claims from victims. The U.S. Secret Service and the Justice Department's Asset Forfeiture and Money Laundering Section are overseeing this program. Victims can make a claim by visiting a website on the Internet, http://www.adsurfdailyremission.com ; calling the phone number 1-888-398-8214; or by mail at address Ad Surf Daily Remission Administrator, P.O. Box 2353, Faribault, MN 55021-9053.

The potential victims in this case include individuals and entities who provided funds directly to ASD. The Government currently is aware of thousands of such individuals and entities; however, the Government does not know whether its information is complete. Moreover, potential victims reside outside the United States.

The government through its investigation obtained the ASD member database. That database has approximately 97,000 names in it. Those names include members who paid to join ASD, and who may have joined ASD for free. The government is not certain that this list is a complete list of all people who provided money to ASD and who potentially lost their money. It appears from the investigation that there may be members who provided funds to ASD but whose information ASD did not enter into its database.

4

To this juncture, the government has sent emails notifying approximately 40,000 known potential victims about the pending litigation and directing them to the Internet website of the Office of the United States Attorney for the District of Columbia: www.justice.gov/usao/dc/Victim_Witness_Assistance/.[1]   The government is in the process of sending out an additional email informing the names contained in the ASD database (who have not received an email already) about the website.

Given that there are thousands of potential victims in this case, and that as far as the Government is aware, there is no available accurate compilation of all such individuals and entities, the Government respectfully submits that it is impracticable to give individualized notice to each potential victim. Therefore, the Government requests a finding that, under these circumstances, the number of victims makes it impracticable to accord all of the victims the rights described in Section 3771(a). In order to give effect to the rights of the victims, however, the Government respectfully submits that the procedure outlined below is "reasonable" under Section 3771(d)(2).

Going forward, the Government will inform all potential victims of all public court proceeding by posting notice of those proceedings on the Internet website of the Office of the United States Attorney for the District of Columbia: www.justice.gov/usao/dc/Victim_Witness_Assistance/. In light of the fact that Bowdoin operated an Internet based scheme, it is reasonable to assume that victims will have access to the internet and will be able to easily access information on the government's website. Moreover,

---

[1] Those emails were sent to individuals who contacted the U.S. Attorney's Office directly and identified themselves as losing money in their ASD investment, members who agent's identified as potentially losing money with ASD and Golden Panda Ad Builder members.

5

the government will include on the remission website a link to the U.S. Attorney's Office's website for victims seeking information about public proceedings in the criminal case.

The Government respectfully submits that the proposed notice procedure is reasonable to give effect to the rights of the potential victims in this case, and requests that the Court enter the proposed order.

Conclusion

For the foregoing reasons, the Government respectfully requests that the Court enter the proposed order.

Respectfully submitted,

RONALD C. MACHEN JR.
United States Attorney
For the District of Columbia

By: s

VASU B. MUTHYALA
MICHAEL K. ATKINSON
Assistant United States Attorneys
Fraud and Public Corruption Section
555 4th Street, N.W.
Washington, D.C. 20530
202.252.7874 (Muthyala)
202.252.7914 (Atkinson)
Vasu.Muthyala@usdoj.gov
Michael.Atkinson2@usdoj.gov

DATED: January 10, 2010

6

96

Exhibit 2

The TelexFree Case Study #2

TelexFree's Brazilian operations were regarded as one of the largest financial frauds in Brazil's history, according to Brazil's Ministry of Justice and the Federal Public Ministry. The number of participants **(labeled as "promoters" by TelexFree)** had not yet been determined by the end of August 2013. Just after the companies' suspension, Company Director Carlos Roberto Costa said that the Company had 1,049,619 active *promoters* in Brazil. As of this printing, the Company is currently under investigation by Brazilian authorities. The Brazilian investigation prompted the Court to freeze the Company's and its owners' assets. Despite numerous appeals, the suspension of its operations in Brazil was maintained. TelexFree Brazil (Ympactus Comercial Ltda) denies the accusations, saying that it operates under a MLM structure, commercializing VoIP services (a specific telecommunications service). The final trial and judgment will likely be held sometime in 2014, and the Company assets will probably remain frozen until the final adjudication according to the Public Ministry of Acre State.

TelexFree was suspected of operating a Ponzi scheme, the same accusation as Zeek Rewards. TelexFree was featured among the top 10 most searched terms on Google during the year of 2013 in Brazil. TelexFree was ranked 2nd place.

On April 13, 2014, TelexFree LLC filed a petition for relief under the U.S. Bankruptcy Code[47]. During the same month, an investigation in the United States confirmed that TelexFree worked under a Ponzi scheme and handled more than **$1 billion worldwide**. This conclusion was made by SEC-MA, the Agency that regulates the financial transactions in the

---

[47] http://www.kccllc.net/TelexFree

Company's home state of Massachusetts. The SEC, in its Federal jurisdiction, also published a complaint against TelexFree INC, TelexFree LLC, the owners James Merril and Carlos Wanzeler, marketing director Steve Labriola, as well as TelexFree promoters Joseph Craft, Sanderley Rodrigues de Vasconcelos, Santiago de la Rosa, Randy N. Crosby and Faith R. Sloan. The case is still ongoing as of the printing of this book.

Exhibit 3

IN THE UNITED STATES DISTRICT COURT FOR THE
WESTERN DISTRICT OF NORTH CAROLINA
CHARLOTTE DIVISION

SECURITIES AND EXCHANGE COMMISSION,) Plaintiff,) vs.) REX VENTURE GROUP, LLC) d/b/a ZEEKREWARDS.COM, and) PAUL R. BURKS,) Defendant,))	Civil Action No. 3:12cv519

COMPLAINT

Plaintiff Securities and Exchange Commission ("Commission" or "SEC") alleges as follows:

SUMMARY OF ALLEGATIONS

1.   The Commission files this emergency action to halt the fraudulent unregistered offer and sale of securities in an unregistered investment contracts constituting securities in a combined Ponzi and Pyramid scheme perpetrated by Defendants Rex Venture Group, LLC ("Rex Venture") d/b/a

Case 3:12-cv-00519-GCM   Document 2   Filed 08/17/12   Page 1 of 21
Case 3:12-cv-00519-GCM   Document 52   Filed 10/08/12   Page 2 of 24

99

www.ZeekRewards.com ("ZeekRewards") and its principal, Paul Burks ("Burks") (collectively "Defendants").

2.   Defendants solicit investors through the internet and over interstate wires to participate in the ZeekRewards program, a self-described "affiliate advertising division" for the companion website, www.zeekler.com ("Zeekler"), through which Defendants operate penny auctions.

3.   Since approximately January 2011 through the present, the Defendants have raised more than $600 million from approximately 1 million investors nationwide and overseas by making unregistered offers and sales of securities through the ZeekRewards website in the form of Premium Subscriptions and VIP Bids.

4.   Unbeknownst to its investors, ZeekRewards is, in reality, a massive Ponzi and pyramid scheme.

5.   Approximately 98% of ZeekRewards' total revenues, and correspondingly the purported share of "net profits" paid to current investors, are comprised of funds received from new investors.

6.   Defendants currently hold approximately $225 million in investor funds in approximately 15 foreign and domestic financial institutions, and those funds are at risk of imminent dissipation and depletion.

2

Case 3:12-cv-00519-GCM   Document 2   Filed 08/17/12   Page 2 of 21
Case 3:12-cv-00519-GCM   Document 52   Filed 10/08/12   Page 3 of 24

100

7.   Defendants have violated, and unless enjoined will continue to violate, the antifraud and securities registration provisions of the federal securities laws. Unless restrained and enjoined, Defendants are likely to engage in future violations of the federal securities laws. Accordingly, the Commission (A) seeks to preserve investor funds through an asset freeze, (B) seeks orders (i) for an accounting, (ii) prohibiting the destruction of documents and (iii) appointing a temporary receiver over the Defendants' assets; and (C) seeks preliminary and permanent injunctions, disgorgement with prejudgment interest, and civil penalties against each of the Defendants.

JURISDICTION AND VENUE

8.   This Court has jurisdiction over this action pursuant to Sections 20(b), 20(d)(1) and 22(a) of the Securities Act of 1933 ("Securities Act") [15 U.S.C. §§ 77t(b), 77t(d)(1) & 77v(a)] and Sections 21(d)(1), 21(d)(3)(A), 21(e) and 27 of the Securities Exchange Act of 1934 ("Exchange Act") [15 U.S.C. §§ 78u(d)(1), 78u(d)(3)(A), 78u(e) & 78aa]. Defendants have, directly or indirectly, made use of the means or instrumentalities of interstate commerce, of the mails, or of the facilities of a national securities exchange, in connection with the transactions, acts, practices, and courses of business alleged in this complaint.

9.   Venue is proper in this district pursuant to Section 22(a) of the Securities Act [15 U.S.C. § 77v(a)] and Section 27 of the Exchange Act, 15 U.S.C.

3

Case 3:12-cv-00519-GCM   Document 2   Filed 08/17/12   Page 3 of 21
Case 3:12-cv-00519-GCM   Document 52   Filed 10/08/12   Page 4 of 24

§ 78aa, because certain of the transactions, acts, practices, and courses of conduct constituting violations of the federal securities laws occurred within this district. Both Defendant Burks and Defendant Rex Venture d/b/a/ ZeekRewards transacted business, and offered and sold the securities that are the subject of this action, to investors in this district.

DEFENDANTS

10.   **Paul R. Burks**, age 65, is a resident of Lexington, North Carolina. Burks is the sole owner of Rex Venture Group, LLC, and exercises control over ZeekRewards, Zeekler, and other affiliated websites.

11.   **Rex Venture Group, LLC** ("Rex Venture") is a Nevada limited liability company with its principal place of business in Lexington, North Carolina. Rex Venture wholly owns and operates ZeekRewards, an internet website (www.zeekrewards.com) with physical operations in Lexington, North Carolina, and internet customers and contacts throughout the United States and internationally.

4

Case 3:12-cv-00519-GCM   Document 2   Filed 08/17/12   Page 4 of 21
Case 3:12-cv-00519-GCM   Document 52   Filed 10/08/12   Page 5 of 24

102

FACTUAL ALLEGATIONS

ORIGINS OF ZEEKREWARS

12.   Since 1997, Burks has operated through Rex Venture (and its corporate predecessor) several online, multi-level marketing businesses.

13.   In 2010, Burks created Zeekler.com, a penny auction website offering items ranging from personal electronics to cash. Penny auctions require participants to pay a non-refundable fee to purchase and place each incremental bid (typically one cent) on merchandise sold via auction. The penny auctions were not particularly successful until Burks launched ZeekRewards in January 2011.

14.   ZeekRewards is the self-described "private, invitation-only, affiliate advertising division" of Zeekler. Bidders on Zeekler.com penny auctions can acquire bids by purchasing bids on Zeekler.com, but ZeekRewards and its affiliates also sell or give away free sample bids to be used in the penny auctions.

THE ZEEKREWARDS OFFERING

15.   Through publicly available websites that Defendants own, operate, control, or sponsor, Defendants solicit persons to become investors or "affiliates" in ZeekRewards.

16.   Through the ZeekRewards program, Defendants offer affiliates several ways to earn money, two of which involve the offer and sale of securities in the form of investment contracts: the "Retail Profit Pool" and the "Matrix."

5

Case 3:12-cv-00519-GCM   Document 2   Filed 08/17/12   Page 5 of 21
Case 3:12-cv-00519-GCM   Document 52   Filed 10/08/12   Page 6 of 24

103

17. From at least January 2011 through the present, via the ZeekRewards website, Defendants have raised at least $600 million through the offer and sale of securities (via the Retail Profit Pool and the Matrix) to more than 1 million domestic and international investors.

18. Defendants have not made any effort to determine if investors in fact have the financial wherewithal to invest, nor have they ever made any effort to determine if investors have any experience investing before investors commit any capital to ZeekRewards.

19. No registration statement has been filed or has been in effect with the Commission in connection with the securities the Defendants are offering and selling, and have offered and sold.

1. THE RETAIL PROFIT POOL

20. Defendants attracted new investors to ZeekRewards with the promise of daily profit-share awards distributed through a Retail Profit Pool, which operates as a Ponzi scheme. According to the ZeekRewards website, through the Retail Profit Pool the company shares "up to 50% of the daily net profits" with affiliates who meet certain qualifications ("Qualified Affiliates").

21. To become a Qualified Affiliate, investors must satisfy four criteria: (i) enroll in a monthly subscription plan requiring payments of $10, $50, or $99 per month; (ii) enroll new penny auction customers personally, through the

6

Case 3:12-cv-00519-GCM   Document 2   Filed 08/17/12   Page 6 of 21
Case 3:12-cv-00519-GCM   Document 52   Filed 10/08/12   Page 7 of 24

104

ZeekRewards co-op program, or through third-party businesses endorsed by ZeekRewards; (iii) sell at retail or purchase and give away as samples a minimum of ten Zeekler.com bids, earning Profit Points; and (iv) place one free ad daily for Zeekler.com and submit proof to ZeekRewards.

22.   The requirements to become a Qualified Affiliate constitute an investment in a common enterprise and require little or no investor effort.

23.   Qualified Affiliates have no role in ZeekRewards' operations. The Defendants alone created, update and operate the websites, handle all payments, manage the bank accounts and payment service providers, manage affiliate and customer accounts, manage all affiliate and customer services, oversee and disburse all bids, operate the auctions, create all advertisements, sponsor recruiting videos and calls, create the advertisements, and decide the daily payout percentages for the Retail Profit Pool.

24.   Investor funds paid are pooled and comingled in a handful of financial institutions. Investor funds also are commingled with ZeekRewards and the penny auction website's overall revenues from all company operations.

25.   Qualified Affiliates earn Profit Points by either (a) selling penny auction bid packages directly to retail customers ("Retail Bids"), or (b) purchasing "VIP Bids" and giving them away as samples to retail customers or to other personally-sponsored affiliates.

7

Case 3:12-cv-00519-GCM   Document 2   Filed 08/17/12   Page 7 of 21
Case 3:12-cv-00519-GCM   Document 52   Filed 10/08/12   Page 8 of 24

105

26. Most affiliates opt to simply purchase VIP Bids (up to a maximum $10,000 investment) and give them away as samples in order to earn Profit Points. Even then, affiliates need not exert any efforts in giving away the VIP Bids they purchase because Defendants have created automated programs, including the "Customer Co-Op" and the "5CC" programs, that generate or have generated purported customers to whom the bids can be given automatically without any further effort on the affiliates' part.

27. Earning daily dividends also requires that affiliates place one free internet advertisement daily for the company, but that exercise requires little or no effort. Affiliates may merely copy and paste free ads – created by Defendants without input from affiliates – from a company-sponsored program, which the ZeekRewards website boasts should take no more than five minutes per day. Affiliates also may employ a third-party program to generate ads automatically for them; affiliates must simply verify that they've placed the ad by submitting an internet link to ZeekRewards. Placing more or better ads does not enhance an individual's share of profits.

28. Qualified Affiliates are paid their share of net profits from the Retail Profit Pool in the form of daily "awards" or dividends on accumulated Profit Points, which function like shares of stock.

8

Case 3:12-cv-00519-GCM   Document 2   Filed 08/17/12   Page 8 of 21
Case 3:12-cv-00519-GCM   Document 52   Filed 10/08/12   Page 9 of 24

106

29.   The size of the each Qualified Affiliate's daily award is dependent solely on how many Profit Points that investor has accumulated, and is not based on rendering any significant service to ZeekRewards. Thus, buying and giving away more VIP Bids earns greater Profit Points, hence a larger daily profit share award, without any additional effort required.

30.   Qualified Affiliates have the option to receive their daily "award" that typically has approximated 1.5% per day as: (i) a cash payment; (ii) additional Profit Points ; or (iii) a combination of both.

31.   ZeekRewards encourages Qualified Affiliates to convert at least 80% of their daily award as additional Profit Points. Most Qualified Affiliates follow this suggested approach.

32.   The daily award has a compounding effect for those Qualified Affiliates who elect to receive the daily award as new Profit Points rather than cash.

33.   As a result of the compounding effect, Qualified Affiliates now have nearly 3 billion Profit Points outstanding. Based on the ZeekRewards current outstanding Profit Point balance, the company would be obligated to pay out approximately $45 million per day if all Qualified Affiliates elected to receive their daily award in cash.

9

Case 3:12-cv-00519-GCM   Document 2   Filed 08/17/12   Page 9 of 21
Case 3:12-cv-00519-GCM   Document 52   Filed 10/08/12   Page 10 of 24

107

34.   Qualified Affiliates have no role in ZeekRewards' operations. The
Defendants alone created, update and operate the websites, handle all payments,
manage the bank accounts and payment service providers, manage affiliate and
customer accounts, oversee and disburse all bids, operate the auctions, manage the
Customer Co-Op, manage the 5CC program, create all advertisements, sponsor
recruiting videos and calls, create the advertisements, and decide the daily payout
percentages for the Retail Profit Pool.

35.   Investor funds paid in the form of subscription payments and
purchases of VIP Bids are pooled and commingled in a handful of financial
institutions. Investor funds also are commingled with ZeekRewards and the penny
auction website's overall revenues from all company operations.

2. THE MATRIX

36.   ZeekRewards also employs a pyramid "Matrix" to reward its investors
for recruiting others to join the scheme. The company places each newly recruited
affiliate into a "2x5 forced-fill matrix," which is a multi-level marketing pyramid
with 63 positions that pools new investors' money and pays a bonus to affiliates
for every "downline" investor within each affiliate's personal matrix.

37.   Affiliates that have (i) enrolled in a monthly subscription plan
requiring payments of $10, $50, or $99 per month; and (ii) recruited at least two

10

Case 3:12-cv-00519-GCM   Document 2   Filed 08/17/12   Page 10 of 21
Case 3:12-cv-00519-GCM   Document 52   Filed 10/08/12   Page 11 of 24

108

other "Preferred Customers" (i.e., investors who have likewise enrolled in a monthly subscription plan) qualify to earn bonuses through the Matrix.

38.   Once qualified, an affiliate earns bonuses and commissions for every paid subscription within her downline 2x5 pyramid, whether or not she personally recruited everyone within the matrix. Furthermore, affiliates are rewarded merely for recruiting new investors without regard to any efforts by the affiliates to sell bids or otherwise support the retail businesses.

39.   The Defendants, not the investors, created, update, and operate the websites, handle all payments, manage the bank accounts and payment service providers, manage affiliate and customer accounts, create all advertisements, sponsor recruiting videos and calls, sponsor training videos and calls, and track and determine all Matrix bonus payments.

40.   Investor funds paid in the form of subscription payments are pooled and commingled in a handful of financial institutions along with all of Rex Venture's other revenues.

41.   Investors' Matrix bonuses and the Defendants' profits are both derived from the same source: the overall revenues generated from new investors to the ZeekRewards program and the penny auction website.

11

Case 3:12-cv-00519-GCM   Document 2   Filed 08/17/12   Page 11 of 21
Case 3:12-cv-00519-GCM   Document 52   Filed 10/08/12   Page 12 of 24

109

DEFENDANTS' OPERATION OF A FRAUDULENT PONZI AND PYRAMID SCHEME

42.   Defendants represent that through the Retail Profit Pool they will pay investors, or Qualified Affiliates, "up to 50%" of the company's daily net profits in the form of daily profit share awards.

43.   Burks is solely responsible for determining the amount of "net profits" to share in the Retail Profit Pool.

44.   Defendants represent that daily awards are calculated by dividing "up to 50%" of daily net profits by the number of Profit Points outstanding among all Qualified Affiliates. This calculation results in a daily dividend paid to each Qualified Affiliate that consistently has averaged approximately 1.5% per day.

45.   In fact, the dividend bears no relation to the company's net profits. Instead, Burks unilaterally and arbitrarily determines the daily dividend rate so that it averages approximately 1.5% per day, giving investors the false impression that the business is profitable.

46.   Despite encouraging affiliates to purchase and give away VIP Bids to promote and drive traffic to the Zeekler penny auction website, Defendants fail to disclose that almost none of the VIP Bids given away by Qualified investors are actually used on the Zeekler penny auction website. Of approximately 10 billion VIP Bids purchased by or awarded to investors, less than one-quarter of one

12

Case 3:12-cv-00519-GCM   Document 2   Filed 08/17/12   Page 12 of 21
Case 3:12-cv-00519-GCM   Document 52   Filed 10/08/12   Page 13 of 24

110

percent have been actually used in auctions on the Zeekler penny auction website. Thus, the VIP Bids do little or nothing to actually promote the retail business.

47.   Moreover, Defendants fail to disclose that more than 90% of all revenues (and hence net profits) are derived from new investor deposits (in the form of VIP Bid purchases and subscription fees) rather than actual retail revenues.

48.   Defendants also fail to disclose that without new investor deposits (in the form of VIP Bid purchases and subscription fees), revenues would dwindle substantially as less than 10% of daily revenues come from actual retail sales, and the scheme would likely collapse immediately.

49.   Based on the average 1.5% daily dividend on 3 billion Profit Points outstanding, ZeekRewards would owe nearly $45 million per day in profit share awards to investors – ZeekRewards Qualified Affiliates – if investors requested cash rewards instead of points. The company's actual daily revenues, which in July 2012 averaged approximately $5 million per day, cannot support the daily awards that have been consistently been "paid" or awarded at an average of approximately 1.5% per day.

50.   Defendants fail to disclose to investors that the company would quickly become insolvent if more Qualified Affiliates elected to take daily awards in cash from the Retail Profit Pool rather than converting their awards into ever-increasing accumulated Profit Points.

13

Case 3:12-cv-00519-GCM   Document 2   Filed 08/17/12   Page 13 of 21
Case 3:12-cv-00519-GCM   Document 52   Filed 10/08/12   Page 14 of 24

111

51.   Defendants also fail to inform investors of the substantial risk that the Matrix is prone to collapse if the promoters are unable to recruit ever-increasing numbers of paid affiliates into the Matrix pyramid, because without new investors there will be no source of revenue to pay existing participants in the scheme.

52.   Although to date ZeekRewards has paid out nearly $375 million to Qualified Affiliates through the Retail Profit Pool and the Matrix, the company has only approximately $225 million in deposits, which is insufficient to satisfy future awards based on outstanding Profit Points and Matrix commissions and bonuses.

RISK OF FURTHER DISSIPATION OF INVESTOR FUNDS

53.   ZeekRewards' current investor payouts are approaching, and may soon exceed, total incoming revenue. In July 2012, total revenue for ZeekRewards was approximately $162 million, while total investor cash pay-outs were approximately $160 million. If more Qualified Affiliates in the Retail Profit Pool elect to receive cash payouts for daily awards rather than reinvestment into more VIP Points, ZeekRewards' cash outflows would eventually exceed total revenue.

54.   Burks has withdrawn approximately $11 million while operating Rex Venture and ZeekRewards, of which approximately $4 million remains in his possession, custody or control.

55.   Burks distributed approximately $1 million of the funds garnered from ZeekRewards to family members.

14

Case 3:12-cv-00519-GCM   Document 2   Filed 08/17/12   Page 14 of 21
Case 3:12-cv-00519-GCM   Document 52   Filed 10/08/12   Page 15 of 24

112

56. Defendant Rex Venture currently hold approximately $225 million in investor funds in approximately 15 financial institutions. These funds are in danger of rapid depletion.

57. Approximately $40 million of those investor funds are held in the accounts of online payment service providers, of which approximately $30 million are held outside the United States. The vast majority of these funds are being held by the payment processors as reserves against potential credit card "charge-backs" (i.e., claims for refunds for transactions involving fraud).

58. The Retail Profit Pool's viability hinges on investors continuing to accept daily rewards in points instead of cash. With approximately 3 billion VIP Points outstanding in the Retail Profit Pool, if Defendants continue to pay daily awards at their historical average rate of approximately 1.5%, and investors seek cash awards instead of points, investor claims for cash withdrawals could increase to approximately $45 million per day. With only approximately $225 million on hand, the company would quickly be rendered insolvent.

FIRST CLAIM FOR RELIEF

UNREGISTERED OFFER AND SALE OF SECURITIES

Violations of Sections 5(a) and 5(c) of the Securities Act

59. The Commission realleges and incorporates by reference the foregoing paragraphs.

15

Case 3:12-cv-00519-GCM   Document 2   Filed 08/17/12   Page 15 of 21
Case 3:12-cv-00519-GCM   Document 52   Filed 10/08/12   Page 16 of 24

113

60.   Defendants, by engaging in the conduct described above, directly or indirectly, made use of means or instruments of transportation or communication in interstate commerce or of the mails, to offer to sell or to sell securities, or to carry or cause such securities to be carried through the mails or in interstate commerce for the purpose of sale or for delivery after sale.

61.   No registration statement has been filed with the Commission or has been in effect with respect to any of the offerings or sales alleged herein.

62.   By engaging in the conduct described above, Defendants violated, and unless restrained and enjoined will continue to violate, Sections 5(a) and 5(c) of the Securities Act [15 U.S.C. §§ 77e(a) and 77e(c)].

SECOND CLAIM FOR RELIEF

FRAUD IN THE OFFER OR SALE OF SECURITIES

Violations of Section 17(a) of the Securities Act

63.   The Commission realleges and incorporates by reference the foregoing paragraphs.

64.   Defendants, and each of them, by engaging in the conduct described above, directly or indirectly, in the offer or sale of securities by the use of means or instruments of transportation or communication in interstate commerce or by use of the mails:

16

Case 3:12-cv-00519-GCM   Document 2   Filed 08/17/12   Page 16 of 21
Case 3:12-cv-00519-GCM   Document 52   Filed 10/08/12   Page 17 of 24

114

a.   with scienter, employed devices, schemes, or artifices to

defraud;

b.   obtained money or property by means of untrue statements of a

material fact or by omitting to state a material fact necessary in

order to make the statements made, in light of the

circumstances under which they were made, not misleading; or

c.   engaged in transactions, practices, or courses of business which

operated or would operate as a fraud or deceit upon the

purchaser.

65.   By engaging in the conduct described above, Defendants violated, and

unless restrained and enjoined will continue to violate, Section 17(a) of the

Securities Act [15 U.S.C. § 77q(a)].

THIRD CLAIM FOR RELIEF

FRAUD IN CONNECTION WITH THE PURCHASE OR SALE OF SECURITIES

Violations of Section 10(b) of the Exchange Act and Rule 10b-5 Thereunder

66.   The Commission realleges and incorporates by reference paragraphs 1

through 64 above.

67.   Defendants, and each of them, by engaging in the conduct described

above, directly or indirectly, in connection with the purchase or sale of a security,

17

Case 3:12-cv-00519-GCM   Document 2   Filed 08/17/12   Page 17 of 21
Case 3:12-cv-00519-GCM   Document 52   Filed 10/08/12   Page 18 of 24

115

by the use of means or instrumentalities of interstate commerce, of the mails, or of the facilities of a national securities exchange, with scienter:

a.   employed devices, schemes, or artifices to defraud;

b.   made untrue statements of a material fact or omitted to state a material fact necessary in order to make the statements made, in the light of the circumstances under which they were made, not misleading; or

c.   engaged in acts, practices, or courses of business which operated or would operate as a fraud or deceit upon other persons.

68.   By engaging in the conduct described above, Defendants violated, and unless restrained and enjoined will continue to violate, Section 10(b) of the Exchange Act [15 U.S.C. § 78j(b)], and Rule 10b-5 thereunder [17 C.F.R. § 240.10b-5].

PRAYER FOR RELIEF

WHEREFORE, Plaintiff Securities and Exchange Commission respectfully requests that the Court:

I.

Issue findings of fact and conclusions of law that Defendants committed the alleged violations described hereinabove.

II.

Issue judgments, in a form consistent with Fed. R. Civ. P. 65(d),

permanently enjoining Defendants and their officers, agents, servants, employees,

and attorneys, and those persons in active concert or participation with any of

them, who receive actual notice of the judgment by personal service or otherwise,

and each of them, from violating, directly or indirectly, Sections 5(a), 5(c) and

17(a) of the Securities Act [15 U.S.C. §§ 77e(a), 77e(c), and 77q(a)], and Section

10(b) of the Exchange Act [15 U.S.C. § 78j(b)], and Rule 10b-5 thereunder [17

C.F.R. § 240.10b-5].

III.

Issue, in a form consistent with Fed. R. Civ. P. 65, as to all Defendants, a

permanent injunction freezing the assets of Rex Venture and any entity affiliated

with it, directing that all financial or depository institutions comply with the

Court's Order, appointing a temporary receiver over the assets of Rex Venture,

prohibiting each of the Defendants from destroying documents, requiring

accountings from each of the Defendants, and ordering expedited discovery.

IV.

Order that Defendants, and any employees or agents of Rex Venture, be

restrained and enjoined from destroying, removing, mutilating, altering,

concealing, or disposing of, in any manner, any of their books, records and

19

Case 3:12-cv-00519-GCM   Document 2   Filed 08/17/12   Page 19 of 21
Case 3:12-cv-00519-GCM   Document 52   Filed 10/08/12   Page 20 of 24

documents relating to the matters set forth in the Complaint, or the books, records

John J. Bowers (NC Bar No. 23950)
Stephen L. Cohen
J. Lee Buck, II
Brian M. Privor
Alfred C. Tierney
U.S. Securities and Exchange Commission
100 F Street, N.E.
Washington, DC 20549-xxxx
Telephone: (202) 551-4645 (Bowers)
Facsimile: (202) xxx-xxxx
Email: BowersJ@sec.gov

Attorney for Plaintiff
Securities and Exchange Commission

21

Case 3:12-cv-00519-GCM   Document 2   Filed 08/17/12   Page 21 of 21
Case 3:12-cv-00519-GCM   Document 52   Filed 10/08/12   Page 22 of 24

118

JS 44 (Rev. 09/11)

CIVIL COVER SHEET

The JS 44 civil cover sheet and the information contained herein neither replace nor supplement the filing and service of pleadings or other papers as required by law, except as provided by local rules of court. This form, approved by the Judicial Conference of the United States in September 1974, is required for the use of the Clerk of Court for the purpose of initiating the civil docket sheet. *(SEE INSTRUCTIONS ON NEXT PAGE OF THIS FORM.)*

I. (a) PLAINTIFFS	DEFENDANTS
UNITED STATES SECURITIES AND EXCHANGE COMMISSION	REX VENTURE GROUP, LLC d/b/a ZEEKREWARDS.COM and PAUL R. BURKS
(b) County of Residence of First Listed Plaintiff _____ *(EXCEPT IN U.S. PLAINTIFF CASES)*	County of Residence of First Listed Defendant Davidson *(IN U.S. PLAINTIFF CASES ONLY)* NOTE: IN LAND CONDEMNATION CASES, USE THE LOCATION OF THE TRACT OF LAND INVOLVED.
(c) Attorneys *(Firm Name, Address, and Telephone Number)* See attachment	Attorneys *(If Known)* See attachment

II. BASIS OF JURISDICTION *(Place an "X" in One Box Only)*

☒ 1 U.S. Government Plaintiff
☐ 3 Federal Question *(U.S. Government Not a Party)*
☐ 2 U.S. Government Defendant
☐ 4 Diversity *(Indicate Citizenship of Parties in Item III)*

III. CITIZENSHIP OF PRINCIPAL PARTIES *(Place an "X" in One Box for Plaintiff and One Box for Defendant)* *(For Diversity Cases Only)*

	PTF	DEF		PTF	DEF
Citizen of This State	☐ 1	☐ 1	Incorporated or Principal Place of Business In This State	☐ 4	☐ 4
Citizen of Another State	☐ 2	☐ 2	Incorporated and Principal Place of Business In Another State	☐ 5	☐ 5
Citizen or Subject of a Foreign Country	☐ 3	☐ 3	Foreign Nation	☐ 6	☐ 6

IV. NATURE OF SUIT *(Place an "X" in One Box Only)*

CONTRACT	TORTS	FORFEITURE/PENALTY	BANKRUPTCY	OTHER STATUTES
☐ 110 Insurance	**PERSONAL INJURY** / **PERSONAL INJURY**	☐ 625 Drug Related Seizure of Property 21 USC 881	☐ 422 Appeal 28 USC 158	☐ 375 False Claims Act
☐ 120 Marine	☐ 310 Airplane / ☐ 365 Personal Injury - Product Liability	☐ 690 Other	☐ 423 Withdrawal 28 USC 157	☐ 400 State Reapportionment
☐ 130 Miller Act	☐ 315 Airplane Product Liability / ☐ 367 Health Care/			☐ 410 Antitrust
☐ 140 Negotiable Instrument	☐ 320 Assault, Libel & Slander / Pharmaceutical Personal Injury		**PROPERTY RIGHTS**	☐ 430 Banks and Banking
☐ 150 Recovery of Overpayment & Enforcement of Judgment	☐ 330 Federal Employers' Liability / Product Liability		☐ 820 Copyrights	☐ 450 Commerce
☐ 151 Medicare Act	☐ 340 Marine / ☐ 368 Asbestos Personal Injury Product Liability		☐ 830 Patent	☐ 460 Deportation
☐ 152 Recovery of Defaulted Student Loans (Excl. Veterans)	☐ 345 Marine Product Liability	**LABOR**	☐ 840 Trademark	☐ 470 Racketeer Influenced and Corrupt Organizations
☐ 153 Recovery of Overpayment of Veteran's Benefits	☐ 350 Motor Vehicle / **PERSONAL PROPERTY** ☐ 370 Other Fraud	☐ 710 Fair Labor Standards Act	**SOCIAL SECURITY**	☐ 480 Consumer Credit
☐ 160 Stockholders' Suits	☐ 355 Motor Vehicle Product Liability / ☐ 371 Truth in Lending	☐ 720 Labor/Mgmt. Relations	☐ 861 HIA (1395ff)	☐ 490 Cable/Sat TV
☐ 190 Other Contract	☐ 360 Other Personal Injury / ☐ 380 Other Personal Property Damage	☐ 740 Railway Labor Act	☐ 862 Black Lung (923)	☒ 850 Securities/Commodities/Exchange
☐ 195 Contract Product Liability	☐ 362 Personal Injury - Med. Malpractice / ☐ 385 Property Damage Product Liability	☐ 751 Family and Medical Leave Act	☐ 863 DIWC/DIWW (405(g))	☐ 890 Other Statutory Actions
☐ 196 Franchise		☐ 790 Other Labor Litigation	☐ 864 SSID Title XVI	☐ 891 Agricultural Acts
		☐ 791 Empl. Ret. Inc. Security Act	☐ 865 RSI (405(g))	☐ 893 Environmental Matters
REAL PROPERTY	**CIVIL RIGHTS** / **PRISONER PETITIONS**		**FEDERAL TAX SUITS**	☐ 895 Freedom of Information Act
☐ 210 Land Condemnation	☐ 440 Other Civil Rights / ☐ 510 Motions to Vacate Sentence		☐ 870 Taxes (U.S. Plaintiff or Defendant)	☐ 896 Arbitration
☐ 220 Foreclosure	☐ 441 Voting / **Habeas Corpus:**		☐ 871 IRS—Third Party 26 USC 7609	☐ 899 Administrative Procedure Act/Review or Appeal of Agency Decision
☐ 230 Rent Lease & Ejectment	☐ 442 Employment / ☐ 530 General			☐ 950 Constitutionality of State Statutes
☐ 240 Torts to Land	☐ 443 Housing/ Accommodations / ☐ 535 Death Penalty		**IMMIGRATION**	
☐ 245 Tort Product Liability	☐ 445 Amer. w/Disabilities - Employment / ☐ 540 Mandamus & Other	☐ 462 Naturalization Application		
☐ 290 All Other Real Property	☐ 446 Amer. w/Disabilities - Other / ☐ 550 Civil Rights	☐ 465 Other Immigration Actions		
	☐ 448 Education / ☐ 555 Prison Condition / ☐ 560 Civil Detainee - Conditions of Confinement			

V. ORIGIN *(Place an "X" in One Box Only)*

☒ 1 Original Proceeding
☐ 2 Removed from State Court
☐ 3 Remanded from Appellate Court
☐ 4 Reinstated or Reopened
☐ 5 Transferred from another district *(specify)*
☐ 6 Multidistrict Litigation

VI. CAUSE OF ACTION
Cite the U.S. Civil Statute under which you are filing *(Do not cite jurisdictional statutes unless diversity)*:
15 U.S.C. §§ 77e(a), 77e(c), 77q(a), 78j(b) and 17 C.F.R. § 240.10b-5
Brief description of cause:
Action for securities fraud and unregistered offering and sale of securities

VII. REQUESTED IN COMPLAINT:
☐ CHECK IF THIS IS A CLASS ACTION UNDER F.R.C.P. 23
DEMAND $ _____
CHECK YES only if demanded in complaint:
JURY DEMAND: ☐ Yes ☒ No

VIII. RELATED CASE(S) IF ANY *(See instructions)*:
JUDGE _____   DOCKET NUMBER _____

DATE 8/17/12

SIGNATURE OF ATTORNEY OF RECORD _____

FOR OFFICE USE ONLY

RECEIPT # _____   AMOUNT _____   APPLYING IFP _____   JUDGE _____   MAG. JUDGE _____

Case 3:12-cv-00519-GCM Document 2-1 Filed 08/17/12 Page 1 of 2

Case 3:12-cv-00519-GCM Document 52 Filed 10/08/12 Page 23 of 24

Exhibit 4

The Dehkos Case Study #2

Courtesy of the Dehko's

Terry Dehko and his daughter Sandy Dehko operated a traditional business, a supermarket. Imagine heading to your bank to make a withdrawal and finding your account empty. Next, imagine finding out that your identity hasn't been stolen, your banking information hasn't been compromised, but rather the Federal Government has emptied your account, on purpose. And there's nothing you can do about it. **Well this is totally true** and, that's what happened. Just Google the story and see for yourself!

The Dehkos owned and operated the Schott's Market[48], a small grocery store in Fraser, Michigan for 35 years, a city of less than 15,000. It's a family run business that the Dehkos have run since 1978.

In January 2013, the Federal Government seized all of the money [49]that the Dehkos had in their store bank account, and for what reason? The Federal Government alleged that the Dehkos were violating Federal money-laundering rules. They were accused of structuring their deposits in order to avoid

---

[48] http://www.ij.org/michigan-civil-forfeiture-background

[49] http://www.ij.org/michigan-civil-forfeiture-media-advisory-2-19-14

being subject to bank-reporting rules. You can hear more about their story below.

Under federal law, banks are required to report any transactions (cash deposits or withdrawals) to the Treasury which total more than $10,000 in any single day. This information is included on a Currency Transaction Report (CTR). The purpose of the CTR is to help the Government track large transactions and prevent money laundering. Money laundering works this way: the bad guys get money through illegal activities – like drugs or theft. It's important to get rid of that "bad" cash and replace it with more legitimate funds. The easiest way, of course, is to run the cash through a bank or other financial institution and replace those dollars with new ones. In order to prevent this, Federal laws require that large transactions be reported.

One of the ways that folks try to get around the law is to break down really large transactions into smaller ones, an act called structuring or sometimes, smurfing. So, if you had $100,000 in bad funds that you wanted to get rid of, rather than putting it all in at once, you would break it down into smaller transactions: say, 11 deposits of $9,091 in a number of different accounts or on a number of different days. The folks who make those deposits are sometimes called "runners" or "smurfs" (yes, after the little blue guys from the 1980s cartoons). And what they do – smurfing or structuring, is illegal. It's important to note that the actual practice of making cash deposits of less than $10,000 is not illegal under 18 U.S.C. § 5324(a); it only violates the law when the transactions are structured "for the purpose of evading" those reporting requirements.

This is what the Federal Government alleged the Dehkos were doing: structuring deposits in order to avoid reporting requirements. The Dehkos have consistently denied any wrongdoing. Instead, they insist that the deposits were generally less than $10,000 because their insurance policy covers the theft of cash only up to that sum. As a result, they do not let their employees carry more than $10,000 at any time, including walking deposits to the local bank.

That didn't stop the Feds from seizing the Dehkos' remaining funds. Using a process called civil forfeiture, the Federal Government can seize assets on the basis of suspicion: there is no requirement for firm evidence nor are the property owners entitled to notice. The Government didn't ask the Dehkos about their deposits or they would have found out about the insurance policy.

Months after the seizure, prosecutors had never offered any evidence to prove that the Dehkos were engaged in money laundering or that they were avoiding income tax. In fact, a Bank Secrecy Act examination from last year resulted in a notice stating that "no violations were identified". And the Internal Revenue Service had not indicated that there were any concerns about taxes. IRS had not assessed any delinquent taxes or penalties on the Dehkos.

The Government's case, as filed in Federal Court, is not actually against the Dehkos. It is, by law, filed against the Dehkos' property. The official case name is **United States of America v. Thirty Five Thousand Six Hundred and Fifty-One Dollars and Eleven Cents ($35,651.11) In U.S. Currency from PNC Bank Account Number XXXXXX6937.** That's the case for all such seizure matters, referred to as civil asset forfeiture. Seizures don't have to be in cash, they can be real estate or other real property. **All of it done without notice and without a timely hearing.**

As is often the case with these matters, months after the seizure, there had been no hearing. The Dehkos were still out of pocket. So they decided to fight back.

On September 25, 2013, the Dehkos, with the attorneys at the Institute for Justice (IJ), filed a constitutional lawsuit challenging the Federal Government's use of civil forfeiture in their case. The complaint in that case, TARIK DEHKO; SANDRA THOMAS; and DEHKO FOODS, INC. d/b/a SCHOTT'S SUPERMARKET v. ERIC H. HOLDER, Jr., in his official capacity as Attorney General of the United States; DANIEL I. WERFEL, in his official capacity as Acting Internal Revenue Service Commissioner; and BARBARA L. McQUADE, in her official capacity as United States Attorney for the Eastern District of Michigan.

In the complaint, the Dehkos asked for their money back. They also requested a Federal Court ruling declaring that property owners are entitled to a prompt hearing either before or immediately after their property is seized, something that isn't the case now. The lawsuit also asks the cCourt to confirm that law-abiding businesses that make frequent cash deposits for legitimate business purposes are not in violation of the Federal Statute.

In September, a Federal judge scheduled a hearing for the Dekhos-- they would finally get their day in court. The hearing was scheduled for December 4, nearly one year after their funds were seized. IJ Senior Attorney Clark Neily said, about the ruling:" *The fact that it took nearly a year for them to get that hearing highlights the due process problems with Civil Forfeiture law. No American should have to wait so long without an opportunity to challenge the seizure of their property.*"

The Dehkos won't have to wait until December, because once the IRS saw the challenge coming, the IRS filed motions to voluntarily dismiss their forfeiture actions against the Dehkos. As a result, the money which was seized without warning nearly a year ago from their bank accounts was returned. A dismissal was also filed for a similar case: Mark Zaniewski of Sterling Heights, Michigan, who is also represented by the IJ. He will get his money back too. It appears the IRS and other Government agencies that practice the art of taking your money without notice did not want a ruling coming down that would have impacted that practice.

That doesn't mean that the plaintiffs are ready to walk away. Their attorney, Neily, said, about the cases: *The IRS should not be raiding the bank accounts of innocent Americans, and it should not take a team of lawyers to put a stop to this behavior. We are thrilled that Terry, Sandy, and Mark will finally get their money back"*.

Exhibit 5

KENNETH D. BELL, in his capacity as court-appointed Receiver for Rex Venture Group, LLC d/b/a ZeekRewards.com,
 	
       Plaintiff,
 	
  vs.
 	
TODD DISNER, in his individual capacity and in his capacity as trustee for Kestrel Spendthrift Trust; TRUDY GILMOND; TRUDY GILMOND, LLC; JERRY NAPIER; DARREN MILLER; RHONDA GATES; DAVID SORRELLS; INNOVATION MARKETING, LLC; AARON ANDREWS; SHARA ANDREWS; GLOBAL INTERNET FORMULA, INC.; T. LEMONT SILVER; KAREN SILVER; MICHAEL VAN LEEUWEN; DURANT BROCKETT; DAVID KETTNER; MARY KETTNER; P.A.W.S. CAPITAL MANAGEMENT LLC; LORI JEAN WEBER; and a Defendant Class of Net Winners in ZEEKREWARDS.COM;
 	
       Defendants.
	Civil Action No. 3:14-cv-'

COMPLAINT

Kenneth D. Bell (the "Receiver"), as Receiver for Rex Venture Group, LLC

("RVG") d/b/a www.ZeekRewards.com ("ZeekRewards" or "Zeek"), alleges as follows:

SUMMARY OF CLAIMS

1.   RVG operated a massive Ponzi and pyramid scheme through ZeekRewards

from at least January 2011 until August 2012 in which over 700,000 participants lost over

$700 million dollars. This lawsuit is one of several steps the Receiver is taking to recapture the money paid to the scheme's winners so that it can be returned to RVG's victims.

2. As part of the scheme, RVG promised substantial payouts or outsized returns to all participants, but few actually benefitted. The largest "net winners" (those who received more money from Zeek than they paid in to Zeek) each received well over a million dollars, and many others received hundreds of thousands of dollars. Each of the net winners sued by name in this action won in excess of $900,000 (either individually or together with another family member or through their shell corporation). And, each member of the Defendant class of net winners won more than $1,000. In total, the class comprises approximately 9,000 net winners.

3. Like all classic Ponzi and pyramid schemes, the vast majority of the Zeek winners' money came from the Zeek losers rather than legitimate business profits. At least $845 million was paid in to Zeek. No more than $6.3 million (less than 1%) came from retail bid purchases by non-participants. In total, the Zeek database records show that over 92% of the money paid in to Zeek came from net losers, and Zeek's net winners received over $283 million in net winnings.

4. Because Zeek's net winners "won" (the victims') money in an unlawful combined Ponzi and pyramid scheme, the net winners are not permitted to keep their winnings and must return the fraudulently transferred winnings back to the Receiver for distribution to Zeek's victims.

2

THE PARTIES

The Receiver

5. Kenneth D. Bell is the Receiver appointed by this Court in *Securities and Exchange Commission v. Rex Venture Group, LLC d/b/a ZeekRewards.com and Paul Burks*, Civil Action No. 3:12 cv 519 (the "SEC Action") for and over the assets, rights, and all other interests of the estate of Rex Venture Group, LLC, d/b/a ZeekRewards.com and its subsidiaries and any businesses or business names under which it does business (the "Receivership Entities").

The Receivership Entities

6. Rex Venture Group, LLC is a Nevada limited liability company with its former principal place of business in Lexington, North Carolina. RVG wholly owns and operated ZeekRewards, an internet website (www.zeekrewards.com) with a physical location for operations in Lexington, North Carolina, and internet customers and contacts in this judicial district and throughout the United States and internationally. RVG also owns and operated Zeekler.com, an online auction business.

7. Paul R. Burks was the owner and former top executive of RVG. He was the acknowledged leader of Zeek. Dawn Wright-Olivares was RVG's Chief Operating Officer and the Chief Marketing Officer of ZeekRewards. Together with Burks, Dawn Wright-Olivares developed the ZeekRewards scheme.

8. Other key employees of RVG included Daniel ("Danny") Olivares, Dawn Wright-Olivares' stepson who was responsible for designing and running RVG's websites and databases with Burks; Alexandre ("Alex") de Brantes, Dawn Wright-

3

Olivares' then-fiancée who had the title of Executive Director of Training and Support Services; Roger Plyler, who handled "affiliate relations"; and Darryle Douglas, who was a member of RVG's senior-level management.

9. Burks, Dawn Wright-Olivares, Danny Olivares, de Brantes, Plyler and Douglas were the primary operators and insider beneficiaries of the ZeekRewards scheme. Collectively, these individuals may be referred to as RVG's "Insiders." The Insiders are not named defendants in this action; however, the Receiver has filed a separate action against them in this Court asserting claims for breach of fiduciary duty, conversion, unjust enrichment, avoidance of fraudulent transfers and other relief.

10. On or about December 20, 2013, the United States Attorney's Office for the Western District of North Carolina filed a Bill of Information (the "Information") against Dawn Wright-Olivares and Danny Olivares alleging that they, with others, engaged in an over $850 million Ponzi scheme through Zeekler and ZeekRewards.

11. Dawn Wright-Olivares agreed to plead guilty to engaging in a securities fraud conspiracy and tax evasion as charged in the Information. Danny Olivares agreed to plead guilty to engaging in the same securities fraud conspiracy as charged in the Information.

The Defendants

12. Todd Disner is, upon information and belief, a resident of Miami, Florida. He is a former ZeekRewards "affiliate" and was a "net winner" of more than $1,875,000 under one or more usernames, including "tdisner," using Kestrel Spendthrift Trust as the

4

nominal payee for his payments. Upon information and belief, Todd Disner is the trustee for the Kestrel Spendthrift Trust.

13.   Trudy Gilmond is, upon information and belief, a resident of St. Albans, Vermont. She is a former "field liaison" in the ZeekRewards' scheme, a ZeekRewards "affiliate" and a "net winner" of more than $1,750,000 under one or more usernames, including "trudygilmond," and using Trudy Gilmond, LLC, a shell company, as the nominal payee.

14.   Jerry Napier is, upon information and belief, a resident of Owosso, Michigan. He is a former ZeekRewards "affiliate" and was a "net winner" of more than $1,745,000 under one or more usernames, including "napier."

15.   Durant Brockett is, upon information and belief, a resident of Las Vegas, Nevada. He is a former ZeekRewards "affiliate" and was a "net winner" of more than $1,720,000 under one or more usernames, including "DBA."

16.   Darren Miller is, upon information and belief, a resident of Coeur d'Alene, Idaho. He is a former ZeekRewards "affiliate" and was a "net winner" of more than $1,635,000 under one or more usernames, including "djmiller742."

17.   Rhonda Gates is, upon information and belief, a resident of Nashville, Tennessee. She is a former ZeekRewards "affiliate" and was a "net winner" of more than $1,425,000 under one or more usernames, including "cybernetcentral."

18.   Michael Van Leeuwen, also known as "CoachVan," is upon information and belief a resident of Fayetteville, North Carolina. He is a former ZeekRewards

5

"affiliate" and was a "net winner" of more than $1,400,000 under one or more usernames, including "coachvan78" and "coachvan."

19.   David Sorrells is, upon information and belief, a resident of Scottsdale, Arizona. He is a former ZeekRewards "affiliate" and was a "net winner" of more than $1,000,000 under one or more usernames, including "davidsorrells."

20.   T. Le Mont Silver Sr. is, upon information and belief, a resident of Orlando, Florida. He was a "field liaison" in the ZeekRewards scheme, a former ZeekRewards "affiliate" and "net winner" of more than $773,000 under one or more usernames, including "LKW" and "shnookput."

21.   Mr. Silver also used Global Internet Formula, Inc., which is, upon information and belief, incorporated in Florida, as a shell company through which he was a ZeekRewards "net winner" of more than $943,000 under one or more usernames, including "mentor."

22.   Karen Silver is, upon information and belief, T. Le Mont Silver's wife and resides with him or is a resident of Orlando, Florida. She is a former ZeekRewards "affiliate" and was a "net winner" of more than $600,000 under one or more usernames, including "tlksilver.

23.   Aaron and Shara Andrews are, upon information and belief, residents of Lake Worth, Florida. Innovation Marketing is, upon information and belief, incorporated in Florida, and a shell company through which Aaron and Shara Andrews were ZeekRewards "net winners" of more than $1,000,000 under one or more usernames, including "aaronandshara."

6

24.   David and Mary Kettner are, upon information and belief, residents of Peoria, Arizona. They are former ZeekRewards "affiliates" and "net winners" of more than $930,000 under one or more usernames, including "mypennyauctions" and "pennyauctionbids," using the shell companies named Desert Oasis International Marketing, LLC and Kettner & Associates, LLC as nominal payees.

25.   Lori Jean Weber is, upon information and belief, a resident of Land O'Lakes, Florida. P.A.W.S. Capital Management, LLC is, upon information and belief, incorporated in Florida, and a shell company through which Lori Jean Weber was a ZeekRewards "net winner" of more than $1,940,000 under one or more usernames, including "snook" and "billyboy."

JURISDICTION, VENUE AND STANDING

26.   On August 17, 2012, the Securities and Exchange Commission filed the SEC Action in this District pursuant to Sections 20(b), 20(d)(1) and/or 22(a) of the Securities Act of 1933 ("Securities Act") [15 U.S.C. §§ 77t(b), 77t(d)(1) & 77v(a)] and Sections 21(d)(1), 21(d)(3)(A), 21(e) and/or 27 of the Securities Exchange Act of 1934 ("Exchange Act") [15 U.S.C. §§ 78u(d)(1), 78u(d)(3)(A), 78u(e) & 78aa to halt the ZeekRewards Ponzi and pyramid scheme, freeze RVG's assets, and seek the appointment of a receiver for RVG.

27.   On the same date, in an Agreed Order Appointing Temporary Receiver and Freezing Assets of Defendant Rex Venture Group, LLC (the "Agreed Order"), this Court authorized and directed Mr. Bell as RVG's Receiver to institute actions and legal proceedings seeking the avoidance of fraudulent transfers, disgorgement of profits,

7

imposition of constructive trusts and any other legal and equitable relief that the Receiver deems necessary and appropriate to preserve and recover RVG's assets for the benefit of the Receivership Estate.

28.   Within 10 days of his reappointment on December 4, 2012, the Receiver filed the original Complaint and Agreed Order in the SEC Action in all of the United States District Courts pursuant to 28 U.S.C. § 754 giving this Court jurisdiction over RVG's property in every federal district.

29.   As an action brought by the Receiver in furtherance of his appointment and in the performance of his duties as directed by this Court, this action is within the ancillary jurisdiction of this Court.

30.   This action is also within the ancillary jurisdiction of this Court because this action concerns RVG's property and assets, which are now under this Court's exclusive jurisdiction.

31.   This Court has subject matter jurisdiction over this matter pursuant to its common law ancillary jurisdiction as set forth above.

32.   Also, this Court has subject matter jurisdiction under 28 U.S.C. § 1367 because this action is directly related to the claims in the SEC Action, concerns property within this Court's exclusive control and/or is in furtherance of the duties given to the Receiver by this Court.

33.   Further, this Court has subject matter jurisdiction over this matter pursuant to 28 U.S.C. § 1332(d) as a class action in which the amount in controversy exceeds $5,000,000, numerous members of the net winner class are residents of different states

8

than the Receiver, and far fewer than two-thirds of the net winner class are residents of North Carolina.

34.   This Court has personal jurisdiction over the Defendants pursuant to 28 U.S.C. § 754 and 28 U.S.C. § 1692.

35.   This Court also has personal jurisdiction over the Defendants pursuant to N.C. Gen. Stat. §1-75.4 because, *inter alia*, this action relates to money or other things of value sent from North Carolina to Defendants at their order or direction. By voluntarily participating in the ZeekRewards scheme, including numerous communications with RVG and/or meetings in North Carolina, the Defendants created a substantial connection to North Carolina such that the exercise of personal jurisdiction over them is fair and just.

36.   Venue is proper in this District under 28 U.S.C. § 1391(b)(2) because a substantial portion of the acts and transfers alleged herein giving rise to this action occurred in this District.

37.   The Receiver has standing to bring the claims made in this action pursuant to his authority and the direction of this Court and additionally has standing to bring the fraudulent transfer claims pursuant to N.C. Gen. Stat. § 39-23.7.

38.   Pursuant to the Agreed Order, the Receiver has obtained the permission of this Court to file this action.

DEFENDANT CLASS ALLEGATIONS

39.   The Receiver brings a portion of this action as a defendant class action pursuant to Federal Rules of Civil Procedure 23(a) and (b)(1)(A) and (B) against a class consisting of all persons or entities who were "Net Winners" in ZeekRewards (as defined

9

below) in an amount in excess of one thousand dollars ($1,000) (the "Net Winner Class"). Excluded from the Net Winner Class in this action are persons or entities that have entered into a settlement agreement approved by this Court or who resided outside the United States at the time of their participation in ZeekRewards.[1]

40. For the purposes of inclusion in the Net Winner Class, a "Net Winner" is a participant in ZeekRewards who received more money from RVG/ZeekRewards (as "profit payments," "commissions," "bonuses" or any other payments) than was paid in to RVG/ZeekRewards for the purchase of "bids," monthly "subscriptions," "memberships," or other fees.

41. Payments to or from third parties other than RVG/ZeekRewards are not included in the calculation of the amount of a ZeekRewards participant's net winnings for this purpose.

42. The members of the Net Winner Class are so numerous that joinder of all members is impracticable. Upon information and belief, there are approximately 9,000 Net Winner Class members.

43. There are questions of law and fact that are common to the Net Winner Class. These questions include, but are not limited to, whether ZeekRewards was operated as a Ponzi and/or pyramid scheme and whether the payments from ZeekRewards to class members are fraudulent transfers that must be repaid under applicable law.

---

[1] Claims against Net Winners who resided outside the United States at the time of their participation in ZeekRewards will be brought in a separate action.

44.   The named individual defendants above, who were among the largest net winners of the ZeekRewards scheme and are already parties to this action, should be appointed, without cost to the class or the Receivership, as representatives of the Net Winner Class (the "Class Representatives").

45.   The claims against and anticipated defenses of the Class Representatives are typical of the claims against and anticipated defenses of the unnamed members of the Net Winner Class. Like the Class Representatives, each of the unnamed members of the Net Winner Class voluntarily participated in the ZeekRewards scheme as affiliates and received more money from RVG than they paid in to RVG during the course of their participation. The claims for return of "net winnings" against all the Net Winners are the same and should be calculated the same way for all class members. The nature of the defenses that may be asserted by the Class Representatives also would be the same, as liability for repayment of the fraudulent transfers made by RVG to the Net Winner Class does not depend on the personal circumstances of particular affiliates (other than in the mathematical calculation of the amount of their liability, which will be resolved independently of the determination of liability).

46.   The Class Representatives will be adequate and appropriate representatives of the Net Winner Class in the course of and by virtue of their own defense to the same claims. Because they have substantially more (or certainly at least as much) incentive to vigorously defend against the Receiver's claims as any unnamed class member, these defendants will fairly and adequately protect and represent the interests of the unnamed members of the Net Winner Class.

11

47.   Moreover, several of the named Defendants – Trudy Gilmond, David Sorrells, David Kettner and Mary Kettner – have already engaged counsel and filed motions in the SEC Action challenging various aspects of the receivership.

48.   Prosecuting separate actions against individual class members would create a risk of inconsistent judgments with respect to individual class members. If multiple actions against net winners resulted in, for example, different determinations on whether ZeekRewards was a Ponzi and/or pyramid scheme then that would establish incompatible standards for the Receiver in seeking the repayment of net winnings from the various net winners.

49.   Further, as a practical matter, the cost and difficulty of defending against separate suits following the adjudication of the common questions of fact and law related to ZeekRewards and the liability of net winners to repay their net winnings as fraudulent transfers would be dispositive of or substantially impair the interests of the unnamed class members.

PONZI AND PYRAMID SCHEMES

50.   Legitimate business and investment opportunities are based on the expectation of a return from or portion of the profits of an actual business enterprise.

51.   In contrast, a Ponzi scheme is a fraudulent scheme in which returns to participants are not financed through the success of the underlying business venture. Instead, the money to pay returns comes from the payments made by other (usually later) participants in the scheme.

52.   Typically, participants are led to believe they will receive unrealistically high returns for their payments. Then, money from the scheme is used to pay high returns to early participants in order to create the (false) appearance of profitability and attract new participants to perpetuate the scheme.

53.   The scheme inevitably collapses when the flow of money from new participants is insufficient to pay the expected returns to existing participants or the fraud is discovered.

54.   Thus, a Ponzi scheme is established, *inter alia*, by evidence that (1) participants put money into a company because they are led to believe that they will receive large returns for their payments, (2) initial participants are actually paid the high returns, which attracts additional participants, (3) the underlying business venture, if any, is exaggerated and yields insufficient funds to pay for expenses and provide the expected returns to participants, and (4) the source of payments to earlier participants is cash infused by later participants.

55.   Other potential indications of a Ponzi scheme include, but are not limited to, the promise of large, unrealistic returns with little or no risk; the promise of consistent returns; false or non-existent books, records, financial statements and communications with the participants and the public; and the lack of transparency, secrecy, exclusivity and/or the complexity of the scheme.

56.   A pyramid scheme is a scheme in which a participant pays for the chance to receive compensation for recruiting new persons into the scheme as well as for when those new persons themselves recruit new participants. In unlawful pyramid schemes,

13

compensation rewards are not primarily paid based on the sale of products to ultimate users.

57.   An intent to defraud future participants can be inferred from the mere fact that a person or company is running a Ponzi and/or pyramid scheme. Indeed, no other reasonable inference is possible. A Ponzi and/or pyramid scheme cannot work forever. The investor pool is a limited resource and will eventually run dry. The perpetrator must know that the scheme will eventually collapse as a result of the inability to attract new investors. He or she must know all along, from the very nature of the activities, that investors at the end of the line will lose their money. This knowledge that future investors will not be paid is sufficient to establish an actual intent to defraud them.

FACTS SUPPORTING THE RECEIVER'S CLAIMS

ZeekRewards and Zeekler's Operations

58.   Beginning at least as far back as 1997, Paul Burks operated a number of generally unsuccessful multi-level marketing businesses through Rex Venture Group, LLC (and related entities) with names such as Go-Go Hub, Free Store Club, My Bid Shack, New Net Mail and Signed and Numbered International.

59.   In 2010, RVG launched Zeekler.com, a so-called "penny auction" website where items ranging from personal electronics to cash were auctioned to bidders.

60.   A "penny auction" does not work like a typical auction. In a normal auction, it costs nothing to bid, and the auction price rises based on the amount of the bid until there is no higher bid or the amount of time set for the auction expires. In a "penny auction," bids must be *purchased* by bidders, and each incremental bid placed raises the

14

amount of the total price of the auction item only by $0.01. Penny auctions have a timer, but unlike a typical auction, each new bid at the end of the timer resets the bid clock, usually for 30 seconds to a minute. The penny auction ends when the bid clock expires with no new bid. The winner then pays the auction price (plus the cost of bids used), which is theoretically well below the retail price. However, the unsuccessful bidders lose all the money they spent to purchase bids.

61.   During 2010, the Zeekler penny auctions were not very successful. Indeed, Burks was forced to borrow money from Roger Plyler, then a business partner, to keep the business going.

62.   RVG's fortunes changed in 2011. In January 2011, RVG launched a new money-making scheme – ZeekRewards. RVG promoted ZeekRewards as Zeekler.com's "private, invitation-only affiliate advertising division." In reality, ZeekRewards was just a multi-level marketing scheme grafted onto the Zeekler business. It purported to pay a portion of the profits from the Zeekler penny auction business to participants who earned bid balances or points, primarily by buying auction bids. RVG told potential participants, "Zeekler tallies total sales and pays a percentage to all active ZeekRewards members." Also, participants in ZeekRewards, often called "Affiliates," were paid for recruiting other participants in a pyramid "multi-level" sales format.

63.   Bidders on the Zeekler penny auctions could purchase bids at retail for $0.65, or they could acquire bids as ZeekRewards affiliates (or as free samples from RVG or an affiliate). ZeekRewards affiliates paid $1 for what RVG referred to as "compounding," "sample" or "VIP" bids. The retail bids and the compounding / sample /

15

VIP bids all had the same effect in the auctions – placing a bid raised the price of an auction item by one cent. However, bids bought through ZeekRewards rather than as retail bids were much more valuable because what were really being purchased were points that entitled Affiliates to a portion of the profits from the business. This was the real reason Affiliates paid $1 for auction bids they could buy for $.65.

64.   As one Affiliate told Burks, "I know how the system works mathematically and you know I know. Whether you call the bids bids or hamburgers makes no difference. People are not joining Zeek to get hamburgers, or auction bids; they are joining Zeek to make money...."

65.   ZeekRewards emphasized that the offer to pay Affiliates for purchasing compounding / sample / VIP "bids" distinguished those bids from the simple purchase of retail bids to participate in the Zeekler auctions. In the "About us" section of the ZeekRewards website, the company wrote: "PLEASE NOTE: To qualify for the 125% reward points you MUST buy the bids in the ZeekRewards back office. Bids purchased on the Zeekler Penny Auction site are 'retail customer' bids and do not qualify."

66.   Further, ZeekRewards made clear that even though bids bought through ZeekRewards could be used in the auctions, that fact was irrelevant to the multi-level marketing scheme. Affiliates were told that using the bids in the auction would have no effect on their all-important bid or points balance ("Each time you buy a Compounding Bid in your ZeekRewards Back Office a bid is added to the Compounding bucket. *Spending the bid in an auction does not remove it from the bucket.*") (emphasis added).

16

67.   Not surprisingly, even though a largely bogus "bid giveaway requirement" was added later in the scheme, relatively few ZeekRewards participants or "bid giveaway" recipients used their sample/VIP bids in the Zeekler auctions. Prior to shutdown, RVG estimated that only approximately 19 million VIP bids were used in auctions out of over 7 billion VIP bids created – less than 1/3 of 1%.

68.   From the beginning, RVG intended to use "bids" in ZeekRewards not as a product but as a proxy for money deposited into the program. Dawn Wright-Olivares was very clear about the plan, telling Danny Olivares on January 21, 2011: "We're just going to use bids as currency." On another occasion, Dawn Wright-Olivares referred to the compounding bids as "Monopoly money."

69.   Quickly, RVG's focus changed from Zeekler to ZeekRewards, which was the source of nearly all the company's income. Relative to ZeekRewards, little or no money was made in the Zeekler "penny auction" business.

70.   The sale of compounding / sample / VIP bids in ZeekRewards dwarfed the sale of "retail" bids. According to the ZeekRewards database, ZeekRewards sold approximately $820 million in compounding / sample / VIP bids, but only about $10 million in retail bids were sold.

71.   While over $400 million dollars was paid out to ZeekRewards Affiliates over the course of the scheme, the money used to fund ZeekRewards' distributions to Affiliates came almost entirely from new participants rather than income from the Zeekler penny auctions. Only about $10 million dollars in retail bids were sold (of which $3.6 million reflected purchases by net losing Affiliates). So, the "profit" from the penny

17

auction business, if there was any at all, was too small to support even 3% of the total payments made to participants.

72.   Burks and the other Insiders were aware that the payouts to Affiliates would be funded by new participants rather than retail profits from the penny auctions. Dawn Wright-Olivares excitedly told Burks early in the scheme, "I think we can blow this OUT together- we've already attracted a great many big fishes."

ZeekRewards Compensation Plan

73.   ZeekRewards succeeded because it promoted a lucrative "compensation plan," offering large amounts of passive income to entice individuals to participate in the scheme.

74.   The participants in the ZeekRewards scheme invested money in the scheme by buying so-called "bids/points," "memberships," "subscriptions," customer names, and other items related to the scheme.

75.   ZeekRewards was a common enterprise in that the participants relied on Burks and RVG to run the "penny auction" business, which was claimed to be the source of profits for the company. The participants in ZeekRewards expected that they would receive profits from the Zeekler penny auction or other Zeek efforts.

76.   The compensation plan consisted primarily of two components: (1) the "Compounder," also known as the "Retail Profit Pool" or "RPP," which supposedly allowed participants to collectively share up to 50% of Zeek's net retail profits and receive a 125% return on investment; and (2) the "Matrix," which was a multi-level marketing commission program.

18

142

77.   Initially, ZeekRewards promised a 125% return on a passive investment, describing the program as follows: "What if you found a very simple and quick way to earn 125% profit on the dollars you spend with us without ever having to sell a thing or recruit a soul?"

78.   In a pitch entitled "Latest Zeek Compounder News" on January 10, 2011, RVG wrote: "ZeekRewards is a new kind of loyalty program that gives a limited number of early adopters the opportunity to compound up to 125% of each bid purchased," and went on to say that there is "no recruiting, . . . your money [is] compounding for you daily." Other recruiting emails claimed, "the minimal requirement is to simply place one free ad *somewhere* each day" and "if you do then the company will rebate you up to 125% of each bid purchased." (emphasis in original email).

79.   Another pitch touted the income participants would receive: "I found something I believe is absolutely out of this world . . . it's called the 'Compounder' and "grows income for you by compounding it daily;" . . . "the new system [lets] you earn every 24 hours and can generate for you 4 or 5 figures or more per month . . . ." "[I]f you've ever wanted to earn 5 figures or more monthly, passively, then this is your chance." Similarly, de Brantes boasted that by participating in ZeekRewards: "Many are currently receiving $2,000 to $3,000 per month PASSIVELY." (emphasis in original).

80.   Early ZeekRewards participants were told to expect profit shares of .5% to 4% *daily*. The first day the Compounder share percentage was allocated to participants was January 20, 2011, and the share percentage was 3.24%.

81.   As the scheme progressed, participants continued to be told to expect large, consistent daily returns. On May 14, 2011, Paul Burks told Michael VanLeeuwen ("Coach Van") that "our goal has always been 1% Mon-Thurs and 1/2% weekends, Fri-Sun. We have always maintained those averages and exceeded them often."

82.   And, even after counsel advised against publicly promoting a 125% return, RVG continued to tell Affiliates and prospects to expect large returns. For example, de Brantes told an affiliate in July 2011:

> [O]ur average has been between 1.6–1.8% which would actually be a great deal more than 125%. The attorneys our [sic] advising us on what we can and can't say and now it's our job to figure out how much we need to pay daily to get everyone exactly what we intend to give (it makes it a little tricky but it is our intention to maintain a system that pays 125% without saying it anywhere on the site). It's my understanding that to reach 125% we'll need to pay 1.38% per day. Our programmers and strategists are working around the clock to land on the right method, percentages, and presentation for all of this. Right now we're still working on the 125% cap system. We just aren't saying 125%.

83.   Therefore, Affiliates paid and invested money into ZeekRewards with the expectation that they would profit from their payments based on the success of the company's operations.

84.   All the income received by ZeekRewards and Zeekler, regardless of source, was pooled and comingled in a cast of financial institutions that changed as the scheme evolved or as financial companies refused to work with RVG.

85.   Although the specifics and the terminology of the ZeekRewards "Compensation Plan" changed from time to time as Burks and the other Insiders tried to prolong and prop up the scheme, the two pillars of the plan for most Affiliates were

20

always: (1) "profit" sharing (first called the Compounder then later the Retail Profit Pool (or "RPP")) and (2) the multi-level marketing pyramid that paid Affiliates a "commission" on the membership fees paid by recruited "downline" Affiliates (known as the Matrix).

The Compounder a/k/a Retail Profit Pool

86.   ZeekRewards' Affiliates' primary money making tool was the "Compounder." To participate in the Compounder, Affiliates purchased "compounding" bids, which earned Affiliates one point for each "compounding" bid that they purchased from the company.

87.   To become an Affiliate "qualified" to receive points required little or no effort, despite the bogus claim that Affiliates "earned" points. As discussed in more detail below, Affiliates were required to place daily one free digital ad (prepared by the company) for Zeekler.com. Later, Affiliates were told they needed to "give away" the bids in order to obtain points, although in practice this so-called "requirement" was easily met: Affiliates could simply pay extra to have the company "give away" the bids for them. This, in turn, was yet another revenue source for the company.

88.   As the inducement to purchase these "compounding" bids, ZeekRewards told Affiliates that the company would give a portion of the company's daily earnings or profits (often claimed to be 50%) to point-holding Affiliates. The size of the daily "profit sharing" payment each affiliate received through the Compounder was based upon the number of points the affiliate held in his or her account.

89.   The size of each Affiliate's daily award depended only on the Affiliate's point total and was not based on the amount of services provided to ZeekRewards. Thus, regardless of the Affiliates' efforts, buying more points resulted in a larger profit share, just like having more shares of stock results in a larger dividend for a stockholder.

90.   ZeekRewards described the "Compounder" process as follows: "At the end of each business day (7days a week) the company determines its daily overall profitability and rebates a percentage back to its Active Advertising Affiliates based on each individual Premium Members Compounder Bid Balance."

91.   Each day, affiliates had a choice to be paid all or a portion of the so-called "profit" award in cash or to use the "cash" award to buy more bids/points, which then added to the bid / points balance and "compounded" as the daily percentage awards were made.

92.   Burks and the other insiders understood that the compensation plan would be unsustainable in both the short run and the long run because there would not be enough new participants to support full daily cash payments to a growing number of existing Affiliates.

93.   Prior to the shutdown of ZeekRewards, there were over 3 billion VIP bid points in the ZeekRewards system. Based on the actual average daily "profit" percentage of 1.43% used during the scheme, the daily "profit" award to Affiliates would be over $40,000,000 on 3 billion points. The amount of money paid in to ZeekRewards daily was far less than $40 million. Therefore, if RVG had been required to pay the daily awards supposedly available to Affiliates in cash, ZeekRewards would have quickly collapsed.

94.   Specifically, during the last month ZeekRewards operated (July 16, 2012 to August 15, 2012) the daily average RPP award was $38,237,036, but the daily receipts (from all sources, not just retail auctions) were much smaller, averaging approximately $8,850,000. Thus, not only were the ZeekRewards payouts made from the money put in by other participants, but the so-called "profit" awards greatly exceeded total receipts, which, of course, was unsustainable.

95.   So, to maintain the program for as long as possible and generate the most income, ZeekRewards actively discouraged Affiliates from requesting actual payment of all their profit awards in cash. Instead, Affiliates were encouraged to let their balances "compound" and only take 20% or less of their "earnings."

96.   Dawn Wright-Olivares explained and promoted the plan in a Skype chat as follows:

> Here's a scenario here where you could be receiving $3,000 per month RESIDUALLY. Let's use a 1% daily cash-back figure in this example (Please note: This is only an example and the actual amount will vary day to day). When you reach 50,000 points in your account, then you could start doing an 80/20 cash-out plan. Pay close attention? When you hit 50,000 points in your account, if the daily cash-back percentage is 1%, ZeekRewards will be awarding you with $500.00 each day. First of all, did you catch that? ... you're making $500 per day ... it's your money! Ok, the 80/20 plan works like this, take 80% of that $500 (or $400) and purchase more VIP bids to give away to new customers as samples to continue growing your points balance. Then, keep doing what you've been doing every day, which primarily consists of giving free bids away as samples and placing one free ad per day for Zeekler.com's penny auctions and submitting into your ZeekRewards back office. Then, pull out 20% of the $500 (or $100) and request a check weekly. That's $700 per week, or about $3,000 per month in residual income! And keep in mind, these amounts can continue to grow day after day and month after month.

23

97.   ZeekRewards eventually changed the name of the Compounder to the "Retail Profit Pool," or "RPP." In addition, they changed the name of compounding bids to "VIP bids" or "sample bids." However, while the names changed, the essential nature of the "profit" sharing scheme remained the same.

98.   In one email, when referring to compounding bids being renamed VIP bids, Wright-Olivares wrote, "wherever you see a (compounding) next to VIP – you will know that these terms are interchangeable," and she later wrote that "no change has been made in how they operate, qualify or earn."

99.   Indeed, Wright-Olivares admitted that she thought the name changes were a joke. In a June 15, 2011 email to O.H. Brown, an RVG advisor whose company created marketing videos for ZeekRewards, about a company webinar script, she said: "you'll see where I started to say Retail Profit Pool (lol) instead of Compounder…. We're going to call compounding bids – VIP bids."

100.   However, whether it was called the Compounder or the Retail Profit Pool, the program was a fraud because the payments had no relation to actual "retail" profits nor were they calculated from real receipts or expenses.

101.   Instead, the alleged "profit percentage" was nothing more than a number made up by Burks or one of the other Insiders. Most days, Burks made up the number. As Danny Olivares explained to RVG's internet provider, "Paul [Burks] goes in nightly and opens up adm_displayCompunder3.asp and enters a decimal percentage." Sometimes, the number was made up by Dawn Wright-Olivares or Danny Olivares.

24

102.   Rather than reflecting the typical variances that might be expected in a company's profits, the alleged profits paid in ZeekRewards were remarkably consistent, falling nearly always between 1% and 2% on Monday through Thursday and between .5% and 1% on the weekends, Friday through Sunday. The goal of this fake consistency was to project the appearance of a stable source of income to entice new participants and to encourage existing Affiliates to allow their bid balances to compound rather than request payment of their daily award in cash.

103.   With RVG's knowledge, Affiliates regularly touted the consistent payments in their recruiting of new participants. For example, "Coach Van's" email footer said: "It has been going like clockwork for over 220 days, 7 days per week."....
"EVERYONE...GETS...PAID...FIRST...DAY!" . . . This works every time with just one minute per day! If you're not getting paid every single day for 1 minute of work, . . . [sic] why not?" . . . "100 percent of our active members are paid daily 100 percent of the time within their first 24 hours without any referrals."

104.   The payouts were so consistent that when a mistake was made (such as when an extra decimal place was added to the "profit" percentage or the lower "weekend" percentage was used on a "weekday") Affiliates would immediately complain. For example, on August 3, 2012, de Brantes sent Danny Olivares a Skype message saying, the "Thursday [RPP] commission's % are running like a weekend commission % and everyone is going crazy." Olivares replies that, he is "working on it."

105.   And, the Insiders realized that not paying Affiliates, even once, was not an option if they wanted to keep the scheme going. On May 20, 2012, there were problems

25

with payments to affiliates. Dawn Wright-Olivares texted Danny Olivares and instructed him to post an update letting affiliates know their payments would eventually be processed and commissions would be paid, telling him, "[t]he fastest way to get charge [sic] as a Ponzi scheme is for distributors to claim they are not getting paid."

106. Burks deliberately evaded affiliate questions asking how the RPP was calculated. In a Skype chat with an affiliate, he said: "[a] proprietary system is used to determine the amount of profit sharing that is done each day. We do not divulge the details of how those numbers are determined. Our stated target of minimum of 1% weekdays (Mon-Thur) and .5% weekends (Fri-Sun) has always been met and exceeded. It is clearly not directly tied to the number of auctions in a particular day. It is the overall average that counts."

107. Behind the scenes, the insiders were not even subtle about the fake earnings numbers. Often, the company simply used the previous week's daily RPP percentages. For example, on one occasion, Danny Olivares sent a text message to multiple insiders stating, "Need a % for rpp when you can." Dawn Wright-Olivares responded, "Do whatever was last Monday." Or, from Paul Burks: "Hey Dan. Sorry about last night. What percent did you use?" Danny Olivares: "Same as last Friday. 0.009."

108. On another occasion, Burks wrote in a Skype message to Olivares that the RPP would be ".0089 unless you have already grabbed last week[']s :)."

109. Sometimes, Burks even told Danny Olivares *in advance* what a day's profit number would be, such as on September 14, 2011, when in the early morning Burks told

26

him "to start the RPP run shortly after 7p.m. using .00179 as the percentage" because Burks was not going to be able to run it himself.

110.   Even if the Insiders had intended to calculate actual profits (which they plainly did not), RVG did not maintain financial records sufficient to allow Burks or anyone else to calculate a daily retail profit for the company.

ZeekRewards' "Advertising" Requirement

111.   In an unsuccessful effort to avoid the obvious legal infirmity of Affiliates simply buying points in return for the expectation of a share of the profits (like a stock purchase), ZeekRewards told Affiliates that in order to supposedly "earn" their points, they were required to place a short, free digital ad each day on one of the many free classified websites available on the internet.

112.   Affiliates were told to merely copy and paste free ads created by ZeekRewards into a free digital classified ad website. Affiliates then submitted the ad's internet link to ZeekRewards to verify that they had placed the ad. Placing more ads or better ads did not change an Affiliate's share of the profits in any way.

113.   And, the ad "requirement" was not imposed on all Affiliates. Burks even wrote a computer program that allowed a number of Affiliates who managed multiple accounts to avoid placing the ads altogether. As Burks wrote in an email to Danny Olivares on January 23, 2011, "This allows us to defer to some of our major people like Agnita Solomon who manage dozens of accounts so that they don'e [sic] have to place so many ads every day."

114.	The ad process was intended to be very simple and was widely advertised as taking only 3-5 minutes each day. For example, Burks routinely told Affiliates: "Placing an ad takes three to five minutes a day and can be done from anywhere there is an Internet connection."

115.	Indeed, because of how minimal the task was, Burks was irritated by Affiliates who complained when they were not paid: "I am afraid I don't have a lot of patience anymore for people who are making hundreds of dollars a day for placing an ad and they get mad when their card declines and they miss a day. Tough luck."

116.	The company did not believe that these digital ads made any material difference in the success of the Zeekler auctions and did no research to determine if the ads were successful.

117.	In reality, the ads were just an attempt to manufacture a cover for what was nothing more than the investment of money by Affiliates with the expectation of receiving daily "profit" distributions.

ZeekRewards' Bid "Give Away" Requirement

118.	In a further effort to justify the Affiliates' investments of money, beginning in August 2011, ZeekRewards purportedly required Affiliates to "give away" their purchased VIP bids to earn points. The claimed intent of this "requirement" was to promote use of the auctions by new retail customers who received these free bids.

119.	However, Burks and the insiders knew that in practice the bid "give away" program (like the free ads) had no material impact on the success of the penny auctions.

120.   First, the company made little or no attempt to determine if bids had in fact been given to legitimate prospective retail customers. Many Affiliates simply listed fake email addresses, addresses of other existing Affiliates or those planning to be affiliates, family members, and other non-productive locations for where the bids had been given away. In some cases, the company just agreed not to require the affiliate to give away their bids to earn points.

121.   Also, both as a way to minimize any real effort by Affiliates and a way to make more money, Affiliates were given the opportunity to pay to have the company (supposedly) give the bids away on behalf of the affiliate. Points were earned when the bids were given to the company (supposedly) to be given away.

122.   In fact, the company did not find prospective retail customers to whom it could give away all the bids, so millions of bids remained in the company unused. But, ZeekRewards did make an additional $2.00 - $2.50 per customer "sold" to Affiliates. And, because there were alleged limits on the number of bids that could be given away to any one person based on the Affiliate's membership level, tying the "give away" of bids to the accrual of points drove "upgrades" in membership levels which increased revenues even more.

123.   Danny Olivares explained the process of how VIP bids were automatically given away to accrue points for Affiliates as follows: After a VIP bid is purchased, the "Company pool automates the process of giving bids away as samples. Giving the bids away as samples is what generates VIP points. Which the rpp uses to calculate your award. So we come full circle."

124.   Burks told Affiliates that the company-wide Bid Pool would "take ALL of the sting out of the whole bid-give requirement! . . . [Y]ou will be able to automatically give your bids each day" and "you will automatically receive the VIP points as soon as you receive your daily RPP award each day. . . . All you'll have to do is select the "Give my bids to the Zeek bid pool" option and the system will automatically give your bids to your customers and every customer that registers @ Zeekler.com that wants free bids! If you do not have any customers then you simply purchase them as you need them from the customer co-op, and that will be automated as well!"

125.   Later, Affiliates were not allowed to simply pay the company to "give away" the bids for them, but they were allowed to pay third parties to do so. ZeekRewards made no effort to determine if these bids were in fact given to legitimate potential retail customers.

The Matrix

126.   The second broad component of the ZeekRewards compensation plan was paying Affiliates to recruit other Affiliates in a pyramid-style payment system. ZeekRewards referred to this system as the "Matrix."

127.   The Matrix pyramid was initially a "2x21" matrix in which Affiliates made multi-level marketing commissions for 21 levels down in their "organization." Later, ZeekRewards used a "2x5 forced-fill matrix," which is a pyramid with 63 positions that paid a bonus to Affiliates for every "downline" investor within each affiliate's personal matrix, plus a "matching bonus" for every 5th level where certain qualifiers were met, so in effect the commissions could be earned indefinitely.

30

128. To get bonuses through the Matrix, Affiliates just had to (1) enroll in a monthly subscription plan requiring payments of $10, $50, or $99 per month; and (2) recruit at least two other "Preferred Customers" (i.e., investors who also enrolled in a monthly subscription plan).

129. Once qualified, affiliates earned bonuses and commissions for every paid subscription within their "downline" pyramid, whether or not they personally recruited everyone within the matrix. Simply put, Affiliates were rewarded merely for recruiting new investors without regard to any efforts by the Affiliates to sell bids or products or otherwise materially support the Zeekler retail business.

130. The funds raised through the Matrix were commingled with the money raised through the Compounder / Retail Profit Pool (and what little money came in from the retail auction business), so nearly all the money used to pay the pyramid commissions came from other investors in the scheme.

131. While some commissions were available to Affiliates on customers' purchases of retail bids for use in the Zeekler auctions, Affiliates did not need to sell retail bids to customers in order to receive commissions through the Matrix. Furthermore, overall commissions from the sale of retail bids to end-user customers were miniscule. These retail commissions, referred to by RVG as "Zap Commissions," were merely incidental to the overall commissions earned through the Matrix for downline subscription payments and through the Compounder/RPP.

132. As with the Compounder, the Insiders changed the terminology for the Matrix, but they never changed the real essence of the scheme. Dawn Wright-Olivares

31

155

explained the cosmetic changes to the Matrix this way: "you [will] in effect be paid on levels 5-10".... "but we can't SAY that. Deep matrices get shut down. So instead...we say that you are getting a matching bonus on all of the 2x5's on your 5th level. It's semantics, but semantics mean a great deal with regulators." ... "[I] don't really understand how they can say they have levels 10, 15, etc. when it's a 2x5, but if we can get away with it this way - then it's my vote to leave it alone."

133. Similarly, Keith Laggos, a ZeekRewards advisor, emailed Dawn Wright-Olivares (copying Burks) in July 2011: "when talking about matching bonuses, you are showing being paid on 1 to 10, 1 to 15 and 1 to 20 levels. This defeats what we did by going to a 2x5 matrix. You should say a 100% matching on all your 5th, 15th and 20th level affiliates' 2 x 5 matrixes. I know you want to show they get paid on 20 levels in a 2 by 20 matrix, but that is when you can get a pyramid investigation or charge."

The "Sweet 16"

134. In addition to the Compounder/RPP and the Matrix, a select group of individuals was allowed an additional revenue source, referred to as the "Sweet 16."

135. The Sweet 16 was another means by which RVG made payments on a passive investment. It did not involve the sale of a product, nor did it require a member to recruit other participants into the program.

136. As RVG advertised in late 2010 or early 2011, the Sweet 16 was a program where participants received "a 1/16 share at the diamond level" on paid subscriptions in the then-2x21 matrix "across the entire width of the matrix."

137. Participation in the Sweet 16 cost a one-time fee of $999.

138. Each month, RVG totaled commissions from all diamond subscription renewals for the entire Matrix and divided a portion of those commissions among the Sweet 16 members.

139. On information and belief, Sweet 16 payments to investors totaled more than $4.7 million over the life of the scheme.

The "Row of 16"

140. In addition to the Sweet 16, two insiders were allowed payments through a revenue source referred to as the "Row of 16."

141. Dawn Wright-Olivares and Danny Olivares were the only two members of the Row of 16.

142. These Row of 16 payments were generally calculated as sixteen times the highest Sweet 16 payment amount.

143. The Row of 16 was nothing more than a gift or bonus to these two individuals.

144. As with the other "compensation" payments made to Affiliates, these payments were made with money received from Affiliates purchasing VIP bids or subscription renewals, not from a legitimate retail activity.

145. Dawn Wright-Olivares and Daniel Olivares received more than $5.8 million in Row of 16 payments over the life of the scheme.

33

146.   RVG's insiders often worried about being caught and sought to make the unlawful scheme seem legitimate in many ways.

147.   As described above, the changing of terminology or the rules of the game, but not the substance of the scheme, was a common practice. Throughout 2011 and 2012, Burks and the Insiders regularly changed the names of the program elements or demanded that Affiliates stop using certain words, which accurately described the scheme but highlighted its illegality.

148.   For example, on July 26, 2011, de Brantes emailed an Affiliate with a list of things the Affiliate can and cannot say, including: "compounder, compound, compounded, compounding, 125%, Members, Interest, Investment, Mature." On the list of sanitized things the Affiliate could say: "You make a purchase and re-purchase; You earn bids; The bids retire on a 90 day timeline averaging 1.5% a day; You get cash rewards; Retail Profit Pool; Everyone is an Affiliate and they own business center subscriptions; Your Bid balance can increase as oppose to mature."

149.   Also, RVG employees openly discussed the words that could and could not be said, even adding a bit of black humor as the scheme headed towards its inevitable demise. On June 8, 2012, de Brantes and others discussed "training" Affiliates on "the top 10 or 12 words that every Affiliate should erase from their vocabulary". The list included "investment, put money in, roi [return on investment], fund, passive income, passive returns, returns and points are not dollars." In response to this list, Ken Kilby (a

34

supposed "compliance officer") suggested adding: "BBB, Attorney General, FBI, FTC,

Report, turn you in."

150.   Beyond the shifting terminology, Burks and the Insiders tried to bolster the

perception of the legitimacy of the scheme by running "Compliance" courses for

Affiliates. As with the advertising or bid give-away "requirements," the "compliance"

courses were just an effort to obscure the fraud and wrap it in a cloak of propriety, while

making even more money in the process.

FIRST CLAIM FOR RELIEF

Fraudulent Transfer of RVG Funds in Violation of
the North Carolina Uniform Fraudulent Transfer Act
(Against all named Defendants and the Net Winner Class)

151.   The Receiver realleges and incorporates by reference the foregoing

paragraphs.

152.   In the course of operating the ZeekRewards scheme, Burks and others –

through RVG – made numerous "profit payments," "commission" payments, bonuses and

other payments to the Defendants and members of the Net Winner Class as described

above in excess of the amount of money paid by these Defendants and the members of

the Net Winner Class to RVG. These excess payments are collectively referred to as the

"Transfers."

153.   The Transfers were made within four years before the date of this action.

154.   Each of the Transfers constitutes a "transfer" of an asset or an interest in an

asset within the meaning of N.C. Gen. Stat. §39-23.1(12).

155. All of the Transfers occurred during the course of a Ponzi and/or pyramid scheme, when participant money was commingled and the Receivership Entities were effectively insolvent.

156. Each of the Transfers was to, or for the benefit of, one or more of the Defendants or a member of the Net Winner Class.

157. Each of the Transfers was made with money misappropriated from one or more of the Receivership Entities. At all times relevant herein, the Receivership Entities had a claim to the funds used for the Transfers.

158. Each of the Transfers was made without receipt of reasonably equivalent value from the Defendants or the members of the Net Winner Class.

159. Each of the Transfers was made by Burks and others to further the Ponzi and/or pyramid scheme and was made with the actual intent to hinder, delay or defraud some or all of the Receivership Entities' then existing creditors.

160. In the alternative, at the time of each of the Transfers, the Receivership Entities were insolvent or became insolvent as a result of the Transfer; were engaged in a business or transaction, or were about to engage in a business or transaction, for which the remaining assets of the Receivership Entities were unreasonably small in relation to the business or transaction; or intended to incur, or believed that they would incur, debts that would be beyond their ability to pay as such debts became due.

161. The Transfers constitute fraudulent transfers avoidable by the Receiver pursuant to N.C. Gen. Stat. §39-23.4(a)(1), N.C. Gen. Stat. §39-23.4(a)(2) or N.C. Gen.

36

Stat. §39-23.5 and recoverable from the Defendants and the members of the Net Winner Class pursuant to N.C. Gen. Stat. §39-23.7 and N.C. Gen. Stat. §39-23.8.

162. Pursuant to N.C. Gen. Stat. §39-23.4(a)(1), N.C. Gen. Stat. §39-23.7, N.C. Gen. Stat. §39-23.8 and 28 U.S.C. §2201, the Receiver is entitled to a Judgment: (1) avoiding the Transfers; and (2) recovering the Transfers, or the value thereof, from the Defendants and the members of the Net Winner Class for the benefit of the Receivership Estate.

SECOND CLAIM FOR RELIEF
Common Law Fraudulent Transfer
(Against all named Defendants and the Net Winner Class)

163. The Receiver realleges and incorporates by reference the foregoing paragraphs.

164. The Transfers were made within three years before the date of this action.

165. Each of the Transfers constitutes a transfer of an asset or an interest in an asset of the Receivership Entities.

166. All of the Transfers occurred during the course of a Ponzi and/or pyramid scheme, when participant money was commingled and the Receivership Entities were insolvent.

167. Each of the Transfers was to, or for the benefit of, one or more of the Defendants or a member of the Net Winner Class.

37

168. Each of the Transfers was made with money misappropriated from one or more of the Receivership Entities. At all times relevant herein, the Receivership Entities had a claim to the funds used for the Transfers.

169. Each of the Transfers was made without receipt of reasonably equivalent value from the Defendants or the members of the Net Winner Class.

170. At the time of each of the Transfers, the Receivership Entities were insolvent, or became insolvent, as a result of the Transfer.

171. The Transfers constitute fraudulent transfers avoidable by the Receiver and recoverable from the Defendants and the members of the Net Winner Class.

172. Accordingly, pursuant to 28 U.S.C. §2201, the Receiver is entitled to a Judgment: (1) avoiding the Transfers; and (2) recovering the Transfers, or the value thereof, from the Defendants and the members of the Net Winner Class for the benefit of the Receivership Estate.

THIRD CLAIM FOR RELIEF
Constructive Trust
(Against all named Defendants and the Net Winner Class)

173. The Receiver realleges and incorporates by reference the foregoing paragraphs.

174. As alleged above, the assets of the Receivership Entities have been wrongfully diverted as a result of fraudulent transfers to the Defendants and the Net Winner Class for their individual interests and enrichment.

175. The Receiver has no adequate remedy at law.

38

176.   Because of the fraudulent transfers, the Receiver is entitled to the imposition of a constructive trust with respect to any transfer of funds, assets, or property from the Receivership Entities, as well as any assets received by Defendants in the past or on a going forward basis as a result of those transfers from the Receivership Entities.

177.   The Receiver is entitled to and demands title, possession, use and enjoyment of the foregoing property for the benefit of the Receivership Estate.

PRAYER FOR RELIEF

WHEREFORE, the Receiver respectfully requests that the Court:

1.   Enter a declaratory Judgment against the Net Winner Class determining that the net winnings they received were fraudulent transfers from RVG, ordering that the net winnings of each of the Net Winner Class members are Receivership Property and subject to a constructive trust for the benefit of the Receivership Estate and ordering the repayment of those net winnings back to RVG.

2.   Enter Judgment against each of the named Defendants in the amount of their net winnings from the ZeekRewards scheme.

3.   Enter an injunction against the named Defendants and the Net Winner Class prohibiting each of them from dissipating their assets pending satisfaction of the Judgment against them.

4.   Order that each Net Winner Class member be notified of the proposed amount of their net winnings according to RVG records and be given an opportunity to respond to that calculation in a fair, efficient and cost-effective manner to be determined by the Court.

39

5.   Enter Judgment against each Net Winner Class member in the amount

determined to be their net winnings through the process set by the Court.

6.   Award prejudgment and post-judgment interest, costs and such other and

further relief against all Defendants and the Net Winner Class as the Receiver is entitled

to recover.

Dated: February 28, 2014   Respectfully submitted,

                                            /s/ Irving M. Brenner
                                            Kenneth D. Bell, Esq., Receiver
                                            Irving M. Brenner (NC Bar No. 15483)
                                            Jennifer L. King (NC Bar No. 34158)
                                            Susan Rodriguez (NC Bar No. 40035)
                                            Matthew E. Orso (NC Bar No. 42409)
                                            McGuireWoods LLP
                                            201 North Tryon Street, Suite 3000
                                            Charlotte, North Carolina 28202
                                            (704) 373-4620
                                            (704) 373-8836 (fax)
                                            kbell@mcguirewoods.com
                                            ibrenner@mcguirewoods.com
                                            jlking@mcguirewoods.com
                                            srodriguez@mcguirewoods.com
                                            morso@mcguirewoods.com

Exhibit 6

SECURITIES AND EXCHANGE COMMISSION	Civil Action No. 3:12-cv-00519-GCM
Plaintiff,	**MOTION TO INTERVENE AND FOR**
	AN ORDER DISSOLVING THE
-vs-	**APPOINTMENT OF A TEMPORARY**
	RECEIVER AND MEMORANDUM
REX VENTURE GROUP, LLC d/b/a	**IN SUPPORT THEREOF**
ZEEKREWARDS.COM, and PAUL R. BURKS,	
Defendants.	

Trudy Gilmond and Kellie King (collectively "Proposed Intervenors") file this Motion to Intervene seeking an Order Dissolving the Appointment of a Temporary Receiver. This Motion is based on the accompanying Memorandum of Law in support thereof.

MEMORANDUM OF LAW OF PROPOSED INTERVENORS IN SUPPORT
OF THEIR MOTION TO INTERVENE AND FOR AN ORDER
DISSOLVING THE APPOINTMENT OF A TEMPORARY RECEIVER

TABLE OF AUTHORITIES

i

ii

Trudy Gilmond and Kellie King (collectively, "Proposed Intervenors"), by and through their undersigned counsel, respectfully submit this Memorandum of Law in Support of their Motion to Intervene and for an Order Dissolving the Appointment of a Temporary Receiver.

PRELIMINARY STATEMENT

This motion presents a matter of first impression: Whether parties which will be subject to clawback suits as a result of the Securities and Exchange Commission's (the "Commission" or "SEC") allegations that a corporation and its president engaged in a ponzi and pyramid scheme, should be permitted to intervene for the purpose of arguing that the SEC never had jurisdiction to initiate this action because the alleged violative conduct did not involve a "security" as defined under §2(a)(1) of the Securities Act of 1933 ("Securities Act"). Should this Court grant intervention, as it should, the Proposed Intervenors will establish that what the SEC has alleged is an "investment contract" is nothing of the sort. In fact, the purported investors are not investing money in a common enterprise on the expectation that profits will be derived solely from the efforts of others. Rather, what the SEC purports are "investment contracts" are nothing more than contractual rights entitling independent contractors to a share of a company's profits *in return for their efforts in promoting the company*. Finally, because there is no "security" to justify the SEC's jurisdiction in bringing this action, the individual appointed at the SEC's request must be relieved of his duties, and the clawback suits must not go forward.

FACTUAL BACKGROUND

On August 17, 2012 the SEC filed this "emergency action" to purportedly "halt the fraudulent unregistered offer and sale of securities" through "unregistered investment contracts" in "an alleged combined Ponzi and Pyramid scheme perpetrated by Defendants Rex Venture Group, LLC ('Rex Venture') d/b/a www.ZeekRewards.com ('ZeekRewards') and its principal, Paul Burks ('Burks') (collectively, 'Defendants')." Complaint ¶1. The SEC alleges that in 2010

1

Burks "created Zeekler.com, a penny auction website offering items ranging from personal electronics to cash." Id. ¶13. Penny auctions require participants to pay a non-refundable fee to purchase and place each incremental bid (typically one cent) on merchandise sold in the auction. Id. Affiliated with Zeekler.com is ZeekRewards, which is the advertising division of Zeekler.com. Through the ZeekRewards program, the Defendants offered affiliates several ways to *earn* money, two of which the SEC alleges involve "the offer and sale of securities in the form of investment contracts," the Retail Profit Pool and the Matrix. Id. ¶16.

The SEC has alleged that the Retail Profit Pool – through which ZeekRewads would share up to 50% of the company's daily net profits with affiliates who met four qualifications ("Qualified Affiliates") -- operated as a Ponzi scheme. Id. ¶20. The four qualifications are as follows: First, each Qualified Affiliate had to enroll in a monthly subscription plan which required payments of $10, $50, or $99 per month. Id. ¶21. Second, each Qualified Affiliate had to enroll new penny auction customers personally, either through the ZeekRewards co-op program, or through third-party businesses endorsed by ZeekRewards. Id. Third, each Qualified Affiliate had to sell at retail, or purchase and give away as samples, a minimum of ten Zeekler.com bids, which in turn earned them Profit Points. Id. Finally, each Qualified Affiliate had to place one free ad daily for Zeekler.com. Id.

The SEC alleges that the "requirements to become a Qualified Affiliate constitute an investment in a common enterprise" that requires "little or no" effort. Id. ¶22. To support this claim, the SEC has alleged that the Qualified Affiliates "have no role in ZeekRewards' operations" because the Defendants "alone created, update and operate the websites, handle all payments, manage the bank accounts and payment service providers," and perform a number of related tasks. Id. ¶23.

2

While Defendants may have operated ZeekRewards, just as management operates any company, the SEC's conclusion that the "requirements to become a Qualified Affiliate" requires "little or no" effort is simply incorrect. To begin, the SEC's own allegations establish that the Qualified Affiliates put forth substantial effort in building up Profit Points. Indeed, to earn Profit Points the Qualified Affiliates had to either (1) sell penny auction bid packages directly to retail customers ("Retail Bids"), or (2) purchase "VIP Bids" and give them away as samples to retail customers or to other personally-sponsored affiliates. Id. ¶25. This was a time-consuming task that the Qualified Affiliates, including the Proposed Intervenors, spent a substantial amount of time performing. See Declaration of Trudy Gilmond in Support of Motion to Intervene and For an Order Dissolving the Appointment of a Temporary Receiver ("Gilmond Decl.") and Declaration of Kellie King in Support of Motion to Intervene and For an Order Dissolving the Appointment of a Temporary Receiver ("King Decl."). Ms. Gilmond spent upwards of twelve to fourteen hours per day performing tasks to help market and grow ZeekRewards. See Gilmond Decl.

The SEC has alleged that the Qualified Affiliates "are paid their share of net profits from the Retail Profit Pool in the form of daily 'awards' or dividends on accumulated Profit Points, which function like shares of stock." Id. ¶28. Despite the SEC's self-serving re-labeling, the daily "awards" were *not* dividends and the Profit Points were nothing like shares of stock. Each Qualified Affiliate would accumulate Profit Points based on how many penny auction bid packages they sold to retail customers, or how many VIP bids they gave away as samples to retail customers or sponsored affiliates. While the SEC's claim that the "size of . . . each Qualified Affiliate's daily award is dependent solely on how many Profit Points that investor has accumulated," is correct, the SEC's qualification that the accumulation of Profit Points is "not

3

based on rendering any significant service to ZeekRewards" is incorrect. Indeed, the Qualified Affiliate's efforts in selling penny auction bid packages to retail customers, purchasing VIP bids to give away, enrolling in monthly subscription plans, enrolling new penny auction customers personally, and placing ads for Zeekler.com all reflect *substantial* effort. Without their efforts, the Qualified Affiliates would not *earn* Profit Points.

As the SEC explains, Qualified Affiliates have the option to receive the daily "award" that typically has approximated 1.5% per day as (i) a cash payment, (ii) additional Profit Points, or (iii) a combination of both. Id. ¶30. If the Qualified Affiliate agrees to accept the average 1.5% payout as additional Profit Points, the Profit Points have an accumulating effect. For example, if Qualified Affiliate John Doe has 10,000 Profit Points, and the company's daily "award" is 1.5%, John Doe has the option of receiving 150 additional Profit Points, $150 in cash, or a combination of both. If for ten consecutive days the company's daily award was 1.5% and John Doe opted to receive additional Profit Points, he would have 11,433.89 Profit Points by the end of the ten-day period, and his 1.5% allocation would yield him $171.51. Similarly, assuming the 1.5% allocation was consistent throughout, if John Doe went thirty (30) straight days accumulating Profit Points his balance would be 15,399.76, entitling him to a $231 payout. The way ZeekRewards operated, Qualified Affiliates were encouraged to accumulate Profit Points. The critical point, however, is that to originally *earn* the Profit Points the Qualified Affiliates had to perform the necessary tasks to become and maintain Qualified Affiliate status.

The SEC has alleged that as a result of this compounding effect, "Qualified Affiliates now have nearly 3 billion Profit Points outstanding." Id. ¶33. From this figure, the SEC concludes that the "company would be obligated to pay out approximately $45 million per day if all Qualified Affiliates elected to receive their daily award in cash." Id. The SEC's reasoning

4

does not follow. As the SEC itself concedes, through the Retail Profit Pool, ZeekRewards "shares 'up to 50% of the daily *net profits*' with affiliates who meet certain qualifications." Id. ¶20 (emphasis added). As such, if ZeekRewards *did not* make any profits on a particular day, it would not have to pay out *anything* to Qualified Affiliates. See Gilmond Decl. and King Decl. The SEC's allegation that Burks "unilaterally and arbitrarily determine[d] the daily dividend rate so that it average[d] approximately 1.5% per day" (id. ¶45), even if true, does not alter the analysis. Indeed, the fact that a Qualified Affiliate holds Profit Points does not, in and of itself, entitle the Qualified Affiliate to any money, nor does it grant the Qualified Affiliate any equity interest in the company, as a share of stock would. Gilmond Decl. and King Decl. In fact, if ZeekRewards was to go ninety straight days without earning any profit, the Qualified Affiliate in the above example would not be entitled to *any* payout. Further, the Profit Points expired in a ninety day period, further distinguishing them from shares of stock. Id.

ZeekRewards also operated a pyramid "Matrix" to reward Qualified Affiliates for recruiting others to participate in the penny auction website. Id. ¶36. As the SEC has alleged, ZeekRewards "place[d] each newly recruited affiliate into a '2X5 forced-fill matrix,' which is a multi-level marketing pyramid with 63 positions that pools new investors' money and pays a bonus to affiliates for every 'downline' investor within each affiliate's personal matrix." Id. To qualify to earn bonuses through the Matrix, one must be an affiliate that has (i) enrolled in a monthly subscription plan requiring payments of $10, $50, or $99 per month, and (ii) recruited at least two other "Preferred Customers," i.e. customers who had likewise enrolled in a monthly subscription plan. Id. ¶38. While the SEC attempts to trivialize the fact that affiliates were rewarded "*merely* for recruiting new investors without regard to any efforts by the affiliates to sell bids or otherwise support the retail businesses" (emphasis added) (Id. ¶38.), the act of

5

172

recruiting new individuals to the ZeekRewards business was not ministerial, but extremely time-consuming. See Gilmond Decl. and King Decl.

PROCEDURAL HISTORY

Simultaneous with the filing of the SEC's complaint on August 17, 2012, this Court entered an "Agreed Order Appointing Temporary Receiver and Freezing Assets of Defendant Rex Venture Group, LLC" ("Order Appointing Temporary Receiver") (Dkt. No. 4). The Order Appointing Temporary Receiver appointed Kenneth Bell as the receiver ("Receiver") for the Rex Venture Group/ZeekRewards estate ("Receivership Defendant"). This Court also froze all of the Receivership Defendant's assets (id. ¶4), and granted the Receiver the authority to "take custody, control and possession of all Receivership Property and records relevant thereto from the Receivership Defendant" and "to sue for and collect, recover, receive and take into possession from third parties all Receivership Property and records relevant thereto." Id. ¶7(B). To accomplish this goal, the Receiver was given the authority to "issue subpoenas for documents and testimony consistent with the Federal Rules of Civil Procedure." Id. ¶7(H). The Receiver was also "authorized, empowered and directed to develop a plan for the fair, reasonable, and efficient recovery and liquidation of all remaining, recovered, and recoverable Receivership Property (the 'Liquidation Plan')." Id. ¶52.

On October 8, 2012 the Receiver filed his Preliminary Liquidation Plan (Dkt. No. 51), in which he represented that he would pursue "'clawback' claims under applicable fraudulent transfer statutes against those who ran the operations and 'net-winner' participants, i.e. those who received back more (of other Affiliate-Investor's money) than they paid into the Receivership Defendant." Id. at 20. Consistent with that plan, the Receiver has sent subpoenas to certain Qualified Affiliates purporting that they owe the balance between what they withdrew

6

versus what they paid into ZeekRewards. For example, Ms. Gilmond received the following letter attached to her defective subpoena[1]:

> You are receiving this subpoena because you have been identified as an 'affiliate,' participant, agent or employee in the ZeekRewards operation who received significantly more money from ZeekRewards than you put into the operation. As alleged . . . ZeekRewards was an unlawful Ponzi and pyramid scheme that used money from later participants to pay 'profits' (really just other people's money) to earlier participants and/or those higher up on the pyramid. My goal is to recover these unlawful 'winnings' from the alleged scheme for the benefit of the hundreds of thousands of victims who lost money. The preliminary ZeekRewards records that we have reviewed show that you received $1,367,850.10 from ZeekRewards but paid in only $3,105.00. Therefore, you received $1,364,745.10 of the money lost by victims that must be returned to the Receivership estate. See Gilmond Decl. at Exh. A.

The Proposed Intervenors are "net winners" as that term is defined by the Receiver, and each has received notice from the Receiver that she likely will be subject to a "clawback" action. Gilmond Decl. and King Decl.

ARGUMENT

THE PROPOSED INTERVENORS ARE ENTITILED TO INTERVENE BECAUSE THEY MEET ALL THE REQUIREMENTS OF FED.R.CIV.P. 24

The Proposed Intervenors seek to intervene in this action to establish that there is no "investment contract" between ZeekRewards and the Qualified Affiliates, and thus the SEC never had jurisdiction over this case and the appointment of the Receiver must be dissolved. See United Housing Foundation, Inc. et al. v. Forman, et al., 421 U.S. 837, 859 (1975) (holding that there was no federal jurisdiction because there was no underlying security to sustain the federal claim). The Proposed Intervenors are entitled to intervene in this action pursuant to Federal Rule of Civil Procedure 24 because this (i) motion has been timely filed, (ii) the Proposed Intervenors

---

[1] The subpoena served on Ms. Gilmond was defective because it failed to comply with Fed.R.Civ.P. 45.

7

have a property interest in this action because they are likely subjects of a clawback suit, (iii) the Proposed Intervenors have no other forum in which to assert their claims, and (iv) none of the existing parties to the suit currently represent the Proposed Intervenors' interests. Further, Section 21(g) of the Securities Exchange Act of 1934 ("Exchange Act"), 15 U.S.C. § 78u(g), does not prohibit intervention even though the SEC initiated this action because the Proposed Intervenors do not seek to consolidate or coordinate this action with another, nor do they seek to assert any cross-claims, counterclaims, or third-party claims.

Federal Rule Civil Procedure 24 Authorizes Intervention

Pursuant to Fed. R. Civ. P. 24(a)(2), intervention *as of right* is authorized on timely motion by any party who "claims an interest relating to the property or transaction that is the subject of the action, and is so situated that disposing of the action may as a practical matter impair or impede the movant's ability to protect its interest, unless existing parties adequately represent that interest." See also Richman v. First Woman's Bank, 104 F.3d 654, 659 (4th Cir. 1997) (listing the elements as follows: "First, the intervenor must submit a timely motion to intervene in the adversary proceeding. Second, he must demonstrate a 'direct and substantial interest' in the property or transaction. Third, he has to prove that the interest would be impaired if intervention was not allowed. Finally, he must establish that the interest is inadequately represented by existing parties.") The Proposed Intervenors meet each of these requirements.

First, the Proposed Intervenors' motion is timely filed. "With respect to timeliness, courts may consider factors such as 'how far the suit has progressed, the prejudice that delay might cause other parties, and the reason for the tardiness in moving to intervene.'" Diagnostic Devices, Inc. v. Taidoc Tech. Corp., 257 F.R.D 96, 98 (W.D.N.C. 2009) (quoting Wright v. Krispy Kreme Doughnuts, Inc., 231 F.R.D. 475, 478 (M.D.N.C. 2005)). Although a consent judgment has been entered against Rex Ventures Group and Paul Burks, that was done

8

simultaneously with the filing of the Complaint. Further, although a Receiver has been appointed, a Final Liquidation plan has not been filed, and clawback suits, as far as undersigned counsel is aware, have not been initiated. Thus, while the Proposed Intervenors acknowledge that this suit is not in its infancy, it is certainly not too late to challenge the SEC's jurisdiction and the Receiver's authority.

Further, there will be minimal prejudice to the Receiver and SEC if the Proposed Intervenors' motion is granted. The primary issue is whether there is an "investment contract" or "security" anywhere in this case to justify the SEC's jurisdiction in this matter. The parties can readily brief this issue at this stage of the litigation. Indeed, the parties may actually be in a *better* position to brief this issue now that the Receiver has had access to the Receivership Defendant's books and records.

Any "tardiness" by Proposed Intervenors in moving to intervene is justified by the fact that the Receiver only recently sent notice that he was seeking to "clawback" the legitimate money the Proposed Intervenors earned. See Gilmond Decl. and King Decl. Upon receipt of her subpoena, Proposed Intervenor Gilmond contacted undersigned counsel, who then performed the necessary research and due diligence to determine whether the Receiver's stated position was justified. Within due course, Gilmond referred Ms. King to undersigned counsel, who brought this motion.

Second, the Qualified Affiliates have an interest in the property which is the subject of this action because the Receiver has put each of them on notice that he intends to assert "claw-back" claims against them because they are purported "net-winner" participants (see Dkt. No. 51 at 20). See e.g. Gilmond Decl. at Exh. A ("The preliminary ZeekRewards records that we have reviewed show that you received $1,367,850.10 from ZeekRewards but paid in only $3,105.00.

Therefore, you received $1,364,745.10 of the money lost by victims that must be returned to the Receivership estate."); see also King Decl. at Exh. A ("The preliminary ZeekRewards records that we have reviewed show that you received $206,672.92 from ZeekRewards but paid in only $1,492.00. Therefore, you received $205,180.92 of the money lost by victims that must be returned to the Receivership estate.")

Third, and most critical, disposing of this action without the participation of the Proposed Intervenors would impede their ability to protect their interests because they would have no other forum in which to challenge the SEC's, or the Receiver's, jurisdiction over ZeekRewards. Indeed, the Proposed Intervenors are challenging the Receiver's authority to seek clawbacks on the grounds that the Qualified Affiliates did not enter into "investment contracts" with ZeekRewards, and thus the SEC did not have jurisdiction to initiate this case in the first instance, or seek appointment of a receiver. This argument could only be presented in this Court and in this action, and failure to do so exposes the Proposed Intervenors and all the similarly situated Qualified Affiliates to over a of million dollars in clawback suits without affording them an opportunity to challenge the Receiver's authority to seek such clawbacks.

SEC v. Flight Transportation, 699 F.2d 943 (8th Cir. 1983) offers persuasive precedent on this issue. In *Flight Transportation*, a Minnesota holding company and its two subsidiaries which provided aircraft-charter and other general aviation services were the subject of an SEC action alleging that they violated and aided and abetted violations of the anti-fraud, reporting, and record keeping provisions of the federal securities laws. 699 F.2d at 945. The district court appointed a receiver to take control of the corporation and its subsidiaries, and stayed all court actions regarding the proceeds of the corporation's public offerings of securities, proceeds which comprised substantially all of the corporation's assets. Greyhound Leasing and Financial

Corporation ("Greyhound"), which leased two airplanes to the corporation at an approximate monthly cost of $75,000, sought to intervene after the receiver took possession of both planes. Id. at 946. The District Court denied Greyhound's motion to intervene, and the 8th circuit reversed, reasoning that because "virtually all [the corporation's] assets are in the hands of the receiver and may be subject to an order of 'disgorgement' or constructive trust by the District Court," Greyhound's ability to protect its interests would be impaired unless it was permitted to intervene. Id. at 948.

By analogy, a similar result is warranted here. If this Court's Order Appointing a Temporary Receiver is allowed to stand, the Proposed Intervenors may be foreclosed from arguing, in another court, that the Receiver is not authorized to seek "clawbacks" because the SEC never had jurisdiction in the first instance. Similar to how Greyhound could only adequately protect its interests in property held by the receiver by intervening in the underlying action, the Proposed Intervenors could only adequately protect their interests by arguing *in this court* that the Receiver's authority to handle the Receivership Estate must be revoked.

Finally, none of the existing parties to this suit currently represent the Proposed Intervenors' interests. As this Court has previously held, "an intervenor's burden of showing inadequacy of representation is 'minimal.'" Diagnostic, 257 F.R.D. at 99 (citation omitted); see also Flight Transportation, 699 F.2d at 948 (finding that the proposed intervenor had "met the 'minimal' burden of showing that its interests may not be adequately represented by existing parties.") (citing Trbovich v. United Mine Workers, 404 U.S. 528, 538 n.10 (1972)). To begin, because the Receiver seeks to clawback money from the Proposed Intervenors, his interests are diametrically opposed to the interests of the Proposed Intervenors. Further, because the Proposed Intervenors are challenging the SEC's jurisdiction in this matter, the SEC's interests

11

are diametrically opposed to the Proposed Intervenors' interests as well. Finally, neither Rex Ventures Group nor Paul Burks is going to represent the Proposed Intervenors' interests, as both have consented to judgments finding them liable for violating the federal securities laws. See Dkt. Nos. 6, 8. As such, no party represents the Proposed Intervenors' interests.

Notably, even if this Court found that the Proposed Intervenors were not permitted to intervene as of right, permissive intervention is appropriate under Fed. R. Civ. P. 24(b)(1)(B) ("On timely motion, the court may permit anyone to intervene who . . . has a claim or defense that shares with the main action a common question of law or fact.") Of course, the Proposed Intervenors have common issues of law with this matter, principally, whether the SEC had jurisdiction to bring the underlying action in the first instance. Further, permissive intervention here would "help avoid inconsistent results and promote judicial economy." Diagnostic Devices, 257 F.R.D. at 100 (citing Mahurin's Constr. Co. v. Granite RE, Inc., 2004 WL 2249489, *1 (D. Kan. 2004) (holding that permissive intervention is appropriate to promote judicial efficiency). Indeed, this Court may even permit permissive intervention by the Proposed Intervenors for the sole purpose of determining whether the SEC had jurisdiction to file this case, and thus whether the Receiver should be authorized to seek clawbacks. See Broth of Railroad Trainmen v. Baltimore & Ohio R. Co., 331 U.S. 519, 524 (1947) ("restrictive conditions may be appropriately placed on a permissive intervenor.")

Section 21(g) of the Securities Exchange Act of 1934 ("Exchange Act") Does Not Prohibit Intervention because The Proposed Intervenors are Not Seeking to Consolidate or Coordinate this Action with Another, Nor do They Seek to Assert any Counterclaim, Cross-claim or Third-Party Claim

Section 21(g) of the Exchange Act provides as follows:

No action for equitable relief instituted by the Commission pursuant to the securities laws shall be consolidated or coordinated with other actions not brought by the Commission, even though

12

> such other actions may involve common questions of fact, unless
> such consolidation is consented to by the Commission.

Because the Proposed Intervenors do not seek to "consolidate" or "coordinate" this action with another, Section 21(g), by its plain terms, is not implicated. Despite the statute's plain terms, however, the Commission's blanket practice has been to oppose intervention on the grounds that Section 21(g) of the Exchange Act operates as an "impenetrable wall" to intervention. See SEC v. Kings Real Estate Investment Trust, et al. ("REIT"), 222 F.R.D. 660, 662 (D. Kan. 2004) ("REIT") ("The S.E.C. opposes [intervenor's] motion to intervene on the grounds that there is an 'impenetrable wall' to intervention under 15 U.S.C. § 78u(g)"); SEC v. Cogley, No. 98cv802, 2001 WL 1842476, *3 (S.D. Ohio March 21, 2001) ("First, the SEC argues that Section 21(g) of the Exchange Act . . . bars the Trustee's intervention without the SEC's consent"); SEC v. Novus Tech., LLC, et al., No. 2:07-cv-0235 DB, 2008 WL 115114, *1 (D. Utah Jan. 10, 2008) ("The SEC opposes Chase's attempt to intervene arguing that [S]ection 21(g) of the Securities Exchange Act of 1934 is an absolute bar to intervention.") Critically, a number of federal courts throughout the country have rejected the SEC's argument. See Flight Transportation, 699 F.2d at 950 (permitting intervention and noting that "the purpose of [Section 21(g)] is simply to exempt the Commission from the compulsory consolidation and coordination provisions applicable to multidistrict litigation"); REIT, 222 F.R.D. at 664 ("[T]he Court concludes that Section 21(g) does not serve as an impenetrable wall to intervention.")

Admittedly, while there is a "split of authority across the country regarding the SEC's position concerning Section 21(g)" (Novus, 2008 WL 115114 at *1), neither the Fourth Circuit nor this Court has addressed the scope of Section 21(g). Notably, even courts which have prohibited intervention because of Section 21(g) have generally done so when the proposed intervening party sought to assert *private* cross-claims, counter-claims, and third-party claims.

13

180

See SEC v. Prudential Securities Inc., 171 F.R.D. 1, 3 (D.D.C. 1997) (noting that "there is significant authority which suggests that section 21(g) bars all private cross-claims, counter-claims, and third-party claims to SEC enforcement actions to which SEC does not consent"); SEC v. Allison, 1981 WL 1667 (N.D. Cal. Aug. 7, 1981) (holding that cross-claims are expressly prohibited by section 21(g)); SEC v. Sprecher, 81 F.3d 1147 (D.C. Cir. Apr. 9, 1996) (denying counterclaim based on section 21(g)); SEC v. Thrasher, 1995 WL 456402 (S.D.N.Y. Aug. 2, 1995) (Section 21(g) bars third-party claims in SEC actions seeking both equitable relief and civil penalties). Critically, Section 21(g) is *not* a bar to intervention when the proposed intervening party (i) seeks to protect its interest in the underlying property that is in dispute with the receiver, (ii) does not seek to consolidate or coordinate the underlying action with another action, and (iii) does not assert any counterclaim, cross-claim or third party claim. See REIT, 222 F.R.D. at 662, 666 (permitting intervention where proposed intervenor had to intervene to protect his investment which was now in the possession of the receiver, and rejecting SEC's claim that intervention was prohibited).

While the scope of Section 21(g) is a matter of first impression before this Court, Proposed Intervenors respectfully submit that this Court should interpret Section 21(g) according to its plain text and legislative purpose, and hence find that it does not prohibit intervention in this instance. Indeed, the first step in interpreting any statute is to look at the plain meaning of the text. See Landreth Timber Co. v. Landreth et al., 471 U.S. 681, 685 (1985) ("It is axiomatic that the starting point in every case involving construction of a statute is the language itself.") (internal citation/quotation omitted). Here, the plain text of Section 21(g) states that no action brought by the Commission "shall be *consolidated* or *coordinated* with other actions not brought by the Commission." (emphasis added). Section 21(g) does not make any mention of prohibiting

14

intervention by third parties who otherwise comply with the dictates of Fed. R. Civ. P. 24. See Flight Transportation, 699 F.2d at 950 (noting that Section 21(g) "does not say that no one may intervene in an action brought by the SEC without its consent" and "does not mention Fed. R. Civ. P. 24, nor does Rule 24 contain any clause giving special privileges to the SEC"); Novus Tech., 2008 WL 115114 at *3 ("[T]he Court finds no support for the proposition that Congress, by including only the words 'coordinate' and 'consolidate' in the language of Section 21(g), meant for that provision to apply to all possible interventions in S.E.C. enforcement actions . . . ."); SEC v. Credit Bancorp., Ltd., 194 F.R.D. 457, 466 (S.D.N.Y. 2000) (noting that the "specific language of Section 21(g) [does] not apply, on its face, to intervention[.]")

The legislative history behind Section 21(g) similarly does not support a finding that Section 21(g) was meant to prohibit all intervention. As one federal court has noted, "Congress enacted Section 21(g) in response to the SEC's concern that its enforcement actions were being hindered by the consolidation provisions governing multidistrict litigation under 28 U.S.C. § 1407." REIT, 222 F.R.D. at 663. For example, the Senate report specifically provided that Section 21(g) would "'exempt law enforcement actions brought by the Commission from the operation of the judicial procedures provided by the Congress in 1968 to transfer, for coordinated or consolidated pretrial procedures, civil actions pending in different judicial districts that have one or more common questions of fact.'" Id. (quoting S. Rep. No. 94-74 (1975)). That same Senate report also noted "that multidistrict litigation rules compelling consolidation of civil cases were particularly harmful in the context of injunctive enforcement suits by the Commission because the delay associated with a complex pretrial phase of a consolidated suit interfered with the Commission's ability to enjoin the potentially fraudulent conduct, leading to further fraudulent acts and new losses to investors." Id. After conducting a detailed review of the

15

legislative history, the *REIT* court concluded that "the Senate report supports the conclusion that Section 21(g) was designed to safeguard S.E.C. enforcement actions against the application of multidistrict litigation rules, rather than to preclude all intervention in such cases." Id. at 664.

Here, neither the plain meaning of Section 21(g), nor its closely consistent legislative history, prohibits intervention. For instance, the Proposed Intervenors are not intervening for the purpose of consolidating or coordinating this action with another action, which would be strictly prohibited by the plain text of the statute. See Cogley, 2001 WL 1842476 at *3 (prohibiting intervention because "the Trustee's intervention . . . would require th[e] Court to 'coordinate' the present action with a case 'not brought by the Commission,' but that is pending before the Bankruptcy Court"), but compare REIT, 222 F.R.D. at 666 (permitting intervention in part because the proposed intervenor "ha[d] no lawsuit pending anywhere" and the only place where the proposed intervenor "would be allowed to bring suit against the Receiver would be in this Court.") Here, the Proposed Intervenors are intervening to directly challenge the Receiver's authority to marshal assets of the ZeekRewards estate, authority derived from the previously unchallenged (and faulty) presumption that the SEC had jurisdiction over ZeekRewards' alleged violations of the Securities Act and Exchange Act. Proposed Intervenors do not have any related lawsuit pending anywhere.

Further, the legislative history which shines light on the purpose behind Section 21(g) similarly does not prohibit intervention. In passing Section 21(g), the Senate Committee expressed its concern that "when Commission injunctive actions are subject to being transferred for coordinated or consolidated pretrial proceedings, delay in the prosecution of the Commission action may ensue which is potentially damaging to the public interest in securing prompt relief from illegal practices and preventing such practices in the future." S. Rep. No. 94-74, at 77

16

(1975), 1975 U.S.C.C.A.N. 179, 255. Indeed, in *REIT*, the District of Kansas found that because the SEC had secured injunctive relief against all defendants immediately upon filing of the lawsuit, "the primary concern of the United States Congress that led to the enactment of Section 21(g) [was] no longer implicated[.]" REIT, 222 F.R.D. at 666. A similar result is warranted here -- because the SEC has already secured injunctive relief against Rex Ventures and its related entities, and the alleged ponzi and pyramid scheme has been enjoined, the primary concern behind Section 21(g) is no longer present (even though the Proposed Intervenors contest whether such injunctive relief was proper).

THE SEC DOES NOT HAVE JURISDICTION OVER ZEEKREWARDS BECAUSE THERE IS NO INVESTMENT CONTRACT

Contrary to the SEC's assertions, neither the Retail Profit Pool nor the Matrix amounts to an "investment contract" between ZeekRewards and the Qualified Affiliates because the Qualified Affiliates did not expect to profit solely from the efforts of ZeekRewards or a third party, but rather from their own efforts in marketing and growing ZeekRewards. Additionally, the Profit Points did not amount to "shares of stock" because the Profit Points were non-negotiable, could not be pledged, did not confer voting rights, and did not have the capacity to appreciate in value.

The Retail Profit Pool and the Matrix are Not Investment Contracts

Section 2(1) of the Securities Act defines the term "security," in part, as an "investment contract." While the term "investment contract" is not defined in the Securities Act, in the landmark case *SEC v. Howey*, 328 U.S. 293, 298 (1946), the Supreme Court defined an "investment contract" for purposes of the Securities Act as "a contract, transaction, or scheme whereby a person invests his money in a common enterprise and is led to expect profits *solely from the efforts of the promoter or third party*, it being immaterial whether the shares in the

17

enterprise are evidenced by formal certificates or by nominal interests in the physical assets employed in the enterprise." See Forman, 421 U.S. at 852 (emphasis added) (noting that the "touchstone" of an investment contract "is the presence of an investment in a common venture premised on a reasonable expectation of profits to be derived from the entrepreneurial or managerial efforts *of others*.") (emphasis added). Notably, the Supreme Court has held that Congress intended the application of the Securities Act and Exchange Act "to turn on the economic realities underlying a transaction, and not on the name appended thereto." Forman, 421 U.S. at 849.

Here, the SEC alleges that the Retail Profit Pool and the Matrix purportedly involve the offer and sale of securities "in the form of investment contracts[.]" Complaint ¶16; see also id. at ¶17 ("From at least January 2011 through the present, via the ZeekRewards website, Defendants have raised at least $600 million through the offer and sale of securities to more than 1 million domestic and international investors.") The SEC further alleges that the four requirements to become a Qualified Affiliate -- (i) enrolling in a monthly subscription plan, (ii) enrolling new penny auction customers, (iii) selling at retail or purchasing and giving away Zeekler.com bids, and (iv) placing one free ad daily for Zeekler.com -- constituted "an investment in a common enterprise and require[d] little or no investor effort." Id. ¶22.

As to the Matrix, the SEC notes that ZeekRewards paid Qualified Affiliates for "recruiting others" to join ZeekRewards as an affiliate. Complaint ¶36. Specifically, ZeekRewards "place[d] each newly recruited affiliate into a '2X5 forced-fill matrix,'" with 63 positions that permitted Qualified Affiliates that recruited new affiliates to ZeekRewards to receive bonuses for doing so. Admittedly, while Qualified Affiliates had to recruit the first two

18

positions on each down line, the Qualified Affiliate would also receive credit for any additional affiliates recruited by the Qualified Affiliate's first two recruits.

Neither the Retail Profit Pool nor the Matrix establish "investment contracts" between Qualified Affiliates and ZeekRewards because the Qualified Affiliates have to *earn* the Profit Points through the Retail Profit Pool and the bonuses through the Matrix by performing a number of time-consuming tasks. See Forman, 421 U.S. at 849 (application of the Securities Act and Exchange Act turns "on the economic realities underlying a transaction[.]") As the SEC itself concedes, a Qualified Affiliate *must* first enroll in a monthly subscription plan which costs him or her either $10, $55, or $99 per month. Complaint ¶21. Second, the Qualified Affiliate must enroll new penny auction customers personally either through the ZeekRewards co-op program, or through third-party businesses endorsed by ZeekRewards. Id. Contrary to the SEC's attempt to downplay this requirement, Qualified Affiliates spent an inordinate amount of time trying to recruit customers to the penny auction portion of ZeekRewards. See Gilmond Decl. (attesting that she spent twelve to fourteen hours each day working for ZeekRewards, including recruiting new penny auction customers). The concept was actually quite simple: If Qualified Affiliates helped drive additional traffic, i.e., customers, to ZeekRewards' website which exhibited the penny stock auction, this would increase revenue for ZeekRewards.

Third, Qualified Affiliates were required to either (a) sell penny auction bid packages directly to retail customers, i.e. Retail Bids, or (b) purchase VIP Bids and give them away as samples to retail customers or to other personally-sponsored affiliates. Complaint ¶25. Either method earned the Qualified Affiliate Profit Points. This was simply a method for ZeekRewards to share with the Qualified Affiliate a portion of the additional revenue which the Qualified Affiliate brought to the company. If the company was profitable, the Qualified Affiliate would

19

186

receive a payout on the Profit Points. Alternatively, if a Qualified Affiliate purchased "VIP Bids" and distributed them to new customers, this also brought revenue into ZeekRewards *and* raised the potential for a new customer to participate in the company's penny auctions. In this context, the Qualified Affiliates were essentially independent contractors of ZeekRewards, a point further supported by the fact that the Qualified Affiliates received 1099 forms reflecting ordinary *income* earned from the company (when cash was distributed against the Profit Points), rather than capital gains.

Finally, the Qualified Affiliates had to place one free ad daily for Zeekler.com and submit proof to ZeekRewards. Complaint ¶21. As the SEC notes, the affiliates could copy and paste free ads from company-sponsored programs, which the ZeekRewards website stated would take no more than five minutes per day. Id. ¶27. While this task may not have been time consuming, it provided value to ZeekRewards because it promoted the company. Further, this task should not be viewed in isolation from the additional tasks the Qualified Affiliates were required to perform.

On these facts, it is clear that the Qualified Affiliates *did not* invest money with the expectation that profits would come solely from the efforts of others, a necessary requirement to find that an investment contract exists. See Howey, 328 U.S. at 301 ("The test is whether the scheme involves an investment of money in a common enterprise with profits to come solely from the efforts of others.")[2] In fact, the Qualified Affiliates did not even have to invest money

---

[2] Admittedly, there is some precedent in the Fourth Circuit for the principle that "the Supreme Court has endorsed relaxation of the requirement that an investor rely solely on others' efforts, by omitting the word 'solely' from its restatement of the *Howey* test." Robinson v. Glynn, 349 F.3d 166, 170 (4th Cir. 2003) (citing Int'l Bhd. Of Teamsters v. Daniel, 439 U.S. 551, 561 (1979)). Critically, however, the Fourth Circuit has noted that this was done to avoid excluding "from the protection of the securities laws any agreement that involved even *slight* efforts from investors themselves." Id. (emphasis added). Here, of course, the Proposed Intervenors had to put forth *substantial* effort to earn money. Indeed, the *Robinson* court continued that the test was whether, "as a result of the investment agreement itself or the factual circumstances that surround it," the investor "is unable to exercise meaningful control over his investment." Id. Because the Proposed Intervenors *did* exercise meaningful control over how their profits

to make money. Except for the monthly subscription plan (for which a Qualified Affiliate had to pay), a Qualified Affiliate could sell penny auction bid packages to new customers and earn Profit Points that way, without ever committing new capital to ZeekRewards. See Forman, 421 U.S. at 858 ("What distinguishes a security transaction . . . is an investment where one *parts with his money* in the hope of receiving profits from the efforts of others . . . .") (emphasis added).

For these same reasons, the Matrix also does not reflect an investment contract between ZeekRewards and the Qualified Affiliates. To begin, the Qualified Affiliate does not have to invest any additional money to be a part of the Matrix (beyond the same monthly subscription plan). Forman, 421 U.S. at 858. Further, before the Qualified Affiliate could receive any profit from the Matrix, he or she had to recruit *two* Preferred Customers (i.e., customers who have likewise enrolled in a monthly subscription plan). Complaint ¶37. Without the investment of money to make money or a reliance on others to grow one's investment, the Matrix cannot qualify as an investment contract.

The Profit Points Do Not Amount to Shares of Stock

In *Forman*, the Supreme Court stated that the "characteristics traditionally associated with stock" are their negotiability, ability to be pledged or hypothecated, and the fact that they confer voting rights in proportion to the number of shares owned, and appreciate in value. Id.; see also Landreth Timber Co. v. Landreth, 471 U.S. 681, 686 (1985) (re-affirming that the "characteristics usually associated with common stock" are "(i) the right to receive dividends contingent upon an apportionment of profits; (ii) negotiability; (iii) the ability to be pledged or hypothecated; (iv) the conferring of voting rights in proportion to the number of shares owned; and (v) the capacity to appreciate in value.") The SEC alleges that Profit Points -- which are

---

were earned, this is yet another factor supporting a finding that the Proposed Intervenors did not enter into "investment contracts" with ZeekRewards.

21

earned by either (a) selling penny auction bid packages directly to retail customers, i.e., Retail Bids, or (b) purchasing "VIP Bids" and giving them away as samples to retail customers or to other personally-sponsored affiliates -- amount to "shares of stock" because 50% of the company's daily profit is distributed against the number of Profit Points. Id. at ¶28. When tested against the characteristics traditionally associated with stock, however, it becomes abundantly clear that Profit Points carry none of the same characteristics.

First, the Profit Points are not negotiable, and cannot be pledged or hypothecated. Indeed, Qualified Affiliates such as Proposed Intervenors cannot trade Profit Points among one another, sell them into a securities exchange or to the investing public. Further, the Profit Points cannot be "pledged" or "hypothecated" to a bank, financial institution, or broker dealer as collateral for cash, margin, or other shares of stock. In fact, the Profit Points have no inherent value, do not entitle the holder to an equity piece of ZeekRewards, and are only of value to its holder if the company is profitable. Finally the Profit Points expire in ninety days. See Gilmond Decl. and King Decl.

Second, the Profit Points do not confer any voting rights whatsoever, let alone in proportion to the number of shares one owns. See Gilmond Decl. and King Decl.

Third, Profit Points do not have the potential to increase or decrease in value in manner similar to how traditional shares of stock increase or decrease in value. Admittedly, on the one hand, a Profit Point could be considered more "valuable" if ZeekRewards' profits are increasing because that single Profit Point would entitle its holder to a larger cash payout; similarly, if ZeekRewards' profits were decreasing or non-existent, that same Profit Point would entitle its holder to a smaller cash payout, or none at all. But this is not how shares of stock increase or decrease in value. Rather, shares of stock increase for a variety of reasons if a company

22

189

performs well, because the holder of the stock *has an equity interest in the company*. Thus, the share of stock is *inherently* more valuable. Indeed, a share of stock may rise in value regardless of whether the company was more profitable that quarter or year, for example, if the company was expected to increase its market share. In other words, a share of stock's increase or decrease in value is not tied, as a Profit Point is, *solely* to a company's daily profitability. For this reason, Profit Points do *not* increase or decrease in value similar to how shares of stock increase or decrease in value.

Admittedly, a Profit Point does entitle its holder to receive "an apportionment of profits." Landreth, 471 U.S. at 686. Again, however, there is a significant difference between how a share of stock entitles its holder to receive an apportionment of profits through a dividend, and how a Profit Point entitles its holder to profits. With a stockholder, company management controls whether to issue a dividend to distribute a portion, or all, of the company's profits. A share of stock *does not* entitle its holder to *demand* a dividend reflecting a proportionate share of the company's profits. To the contrary, a Profit Point holder is *entitled* to a percentage of ZeekRewards' profits. Again, this demonstrates how a Profit Point is nothing more than a contractual right to receive a percentage of a company's profits, and *not* a share of stock. This contractual right is a form of payment for the Qualified Affiliate's efforts as, essentially, an independent contractor promoting ZeekRewards.

CONCLUSION

For the above stated reasons, Proposed Intervenors respectfully submit that Motion to Intervene and for an Order Dissolving the Appointment of a Temporary Receiver be granted in its entirety.

23

Respectfully submitted, this 14th day of December, 2012.

LOWENSTEIN SANDLER PC
By: __/s/ Ira Lee Sorkin__
    Ira Lee Sorkin, Esq.*
    Amit Sondhi, Esq.*
    1251 Avenue of the Americas
    New York, New York 10020
    (212) 262-6700

    pending admission pro hac vice

and

NEXSEN PRUET, PLLC

By: /s/ William R. Terpening
    William R. Terpening, Esq.
    N.C. Bar No. 36418
    wterpening@nexsenpruet.com
    Matthew S. DeAntonio
    N.C. Bar No. 39625
    mdeantonio@nexsenpruet.com
    227 West Trade Street, Suite 1550
    Charlotte, North Carolina 28202
    (704) 338-5358

    Attorneys for Trudy Gilmond and
    Kellie King

24

191

CERTIFICATE OF SERVICE

I certify that on December 14, 2012, I served the foregoing **MOTION TO NTERVENE AND FOR AN ORDER DISSOLVING THE APPOINTMENT OF A TEMPORARY RECEIVER AND MEMORANDUM IN SUPPORT THEREOF** upon all counsel of record by filing the same on the Court's online CM/ECF system, and by U.S. Mail as to the *pro se* party, addressed as follows:

C. Melissa Owen
cmowen@tinfulton.com
Jacob H. Sussman
jsussman@tinfulton.com
Jeremy Drew Freeman
jfreeman@mcguirewoods.com
Noell P. Tin
ntin@tinfulton.com
Sarah Elizabeth Bennett
sbennett@tinfulton.com
Attorneys for Defendant Rex Venture Group, LLC

C. Melissa Owen
cmowen@tinfulton.com
Jacob H. Sussman
jsussman@tinfulton.com
Noell P. Tin
ntin@tinfulton.com
Sarah Elizabeth Bennett
sbennett@tinfulton.com
Attorneys for Defendant Paul R. Burks

Kenneth D. Bell
kbell@mcguirewoods.com
Irving M. Brenner
ibrenner@mcguirewoods.com
Jennifer L. King
jlking@mcguirewoods.com
Attorneys for Receiver for Rex Ventures Group, LLC

Nathanial Woods
216 S.W. 11th Avenue
Ocala, FL 34471
Pro Se

John J. Bowers
bowersj@sec.gov
Attorney for the Securities and Exchange Commission

/s/ Matthew S. DeAntonio
Matthew S. DeAntonio

25

192

Exhibit 7

KENNETH D. BELL, in his capacity as court-appointed Receiver for Rex Venture Group, LLC d/b/a ZeekRewards.com,
 	
        Plaintiff,
 	
  vs.
 	
PAUL R. BURKS, DAWN WRIGHT-OLIVARES, DANIEL OLIVARES, ALEXANDRE DE BRANTES, DARRYLE DOUGLAS, and BETH C. PLYLER AND JAMES L. QUICK in their capacity as Co-Trustees of the Roger A. Plyler Revocable Trust and Co-Administrators of the Estate of Roger Anthony Plyler,
 	
        Defendants.
	Civil Action No. 3:14-cv-89

COMPLAINT

Kenneth D. Bell (the "Receiver"), as Receiver for Rex Venture Group, LLC

("RVG") d/b/a www.ZeekRewards.com ("ZeekRewards" or "Zeek"), alleges as follows:

SUMMARY OF CLAIMS

1.   RVG operated a massive Ponzi and pyramid scheme through ZeekRewards

from at least January 2011 until August 2012 in which over 700,000 participants lost over

$700 million dollars. This lawsuit is one of several steps the Receiver is taking in his

continuing effort to force those who were responsible to repay the losses caused by their unlawful conduct and to recapture money paid to the scheme's insiders so that it can be returned to RVG's victims.

2.	This scheme was created and primarily implemented by Paul Burks, Dawn Wright-Olivares, Daniel ("Danny") Olivares, Darryle Douglas, Alexandre ("Alex") de Brantes and Roger Plyler (collectively the "Insiders"). In perpetrating this fraud and enjoying the fruits of their dishonest labor, the Insiders breached their fiduciary duties and corporate obligations to RVG, converted and wasted corporate assets, were unjustly enriched and were the beneficiaries of fraudulent transfers from RVG.

3.	Like all classic Ponzi and pyramid schemes, the vast majority of the Zeek Insiders and winners' money came from the Zeek losers rather than legitimate business profits. At least $845 million was paid in to Zeek. No more than $6.3 million (less than 1%) came from retail bid purchases by non-participants. In total, the Zeek database records show that over 92% of the money paid in to Zeek came from net losers, and Zeek's net winners received over $283 million in net winnings.

4.	On or about December 20, 2013, the United States Attorney's Office for the Western District of North Carolina filed a Bill of Information (the "Information") against Dawn Wright-Olivares and Danny Olivares alleging that they, with others, engaged in an over $850 million Ponzi scheme through Zeekler and ZeekRewards.

5.	Dawn Wright-Olivares agreed to plead guilty to engaging in a securities fraud conspiracy and tax evasion as charged in the Information. Danny Olivares agreed to plead guilty to engaging in the same securities fraud conspiracy as charged in the Information.

2

6. Because Zeek's Insiders "won" or received (the victims') money in an unlawful Ponzi and pyramid scheme, they are not permitted to keep their winnings and must return the fraudulently transferred winnings back to the Receiver for distribution to Zeek's victims.

7. In addition to "baiting the hook" by creating a number of net winners, the Insiders operated the scheme with the knowing, reckless or at least negligent assistance and encouragement of a number of managers and advisors that greatly enhanced the perceived legitimacy and resulting success of the scheme. To the extent these individuals and entities – many of whom profited from the scheme – are not part of this action or discussed specifically herein, they will be subject to the future efforts of the Receiver to recover damages and/or disgorgement of the profits they received from the Zeek scheme.

THE PARTIES

The Receiver

8. Kenneth D. Bell is the Receiver appointed by this Court in *Securities and Exchange Commission v. Rex Venture Group, LLC d/b/a ZeekRewards.com and Paul Burks*, Civil Action No. 3:12 cv 519 (the "SEC Action") for and over the assets, rights, and all other interests of the estate of Rex Venture Group, LLC, d/b/a ZeekRewards.com and its subsidiaries and any businesses or business names under which it does business (the "Receivership Entities").

The Receivership Entities

9. Rex Venture Group, LLC is a Nevada limited liability company with its former principal place of business in Lexington, North Carolina. RVG wholly owns and

3

operated ZeekRewards, an internet website (www.zeekrewards.com) with a physical location for operations in Lexington, North Carolina, and internet customers and contacts in this judicial district and throughout the United States and internationally. RVG also owns and operated Zeekler.com, an online auction business.

The Defendants

10.   Paul R. Burks is, upon information and belief, a resident of Lexington, North Carolina and the owner and former top executive of RVG. He was the acknowledged leader of Zeek. Paul Burks received in excess of $10 million from RVG.

11.   Dawn Wright-Olivares is, upon information and belief, a resident of Clarksville, Arkansas and the former Chief Operating Officer of RVG and Chief Marketing Officer of ZeekRewards. Together with Burks, Dawn Wright-Olivares developed the ZeekRewards scheme. Dawn Wright-Olivares received more than $7,800,000 from Zeek under her own name, one or more usernames, including "hippiediva," and one or more entities she controlled.

12.   Daniel ("Danny") Olivares is, upon information and belief, a resident of Clarksville, Arkansas and is Dawn Wright Olivares' stepson. He is a computer programmer and was responsible for designing and running RVG's websites and databases with Burks. Danny Olivares received more than $3,100,000 from Zeek under his own name or one or more usernames, including "dcolive."

13.   Roger Plyler was, upon information and belief, a resident of Charlotte, North Carolina and handled "affiliate relations" for Zeek. Mr. Plyler received more than $2,300,000 from Zeek under one or more usernames, including "roger." Beth C. Plyler

4

is, upon information and belief, a resident of Charlotte, North Carolina and a Co-Trustee of the Roger A. Plyler Revocable Trust and Co-Administrator of the Estate of Roger Anthony Plyler. James L. Quick is, upon information and belief, a resident of Mint Hill, North Carolina and a Co-Trustee of the Roger A. Plyler Revocable Trust and Co-Administrator of the Estate of Roger Anthony Plyler.

14. Alexandre ("Alex") de Brantes is, upon information and belief, a resident of Clarksville, Arkansas and is Dawn Wright-Olivares' husband. He had the title of Executive Director of Training and Support Services at Zeek.

15. Darryle Douglas is, upon information and belief, a resident of Orange, California and was part of Zeek's senior level management involved with affiliate communications and relations. Prior to Zeek, he worked with Burks in other multi-level marketing businesses. Mr. Douglas received more than $1,975,000 from Zeek under one or more usernames, including "dd."

JURISDICTION, VENUE AND STANDING

16. On August 17, 2012, the Securities and Exchange Commission filed the SEC Action in this District pursuant to Sections 20(b), 20(d)(1) and/or 22(a) of the Securities Act of 1933 ("Securities Act") [15 U.S.C. §§ 77t(b), 77t(d)(1) & 77v(a)] and Sections 21(d)(1), 21(d)(3)(A), 21(e) and/or 27 of the Securities Exchange Act of 1934 ("Exchange Act") [15 U.S.C. §§ 78u(d)(1), 78u(d)(3)(A), 78u(e) & 78aa to halt the ZeekRewards Ponzi and pyramid scheme, freeze RVG's assets, and seek the appointment of a receiver for RVG.

5

17.   On the same date, in an Agreed Order Appointing Temporary Receiver and Freezing Assets of Defendant Rex Venture Group, LLC (the "Agreed Order"), this Court authorized and directed Mr. Bell as RVG's Receiver to institute actions and legal proceedings seeking the avoidance of fraudulent transfers, disgorgement of profits, imposition of constructive trusts and any other legal and equitable relief that the Receiver deems necessary and appropriate to preserve and recover RVG's assets for the benefit of the Receivership Estate.

18.   Within 10 days of his reappointment on December 4, 2012, the Receiver filed the original Complaint and Agreed Order in the SEC Action in all of the United States District Courts pursuant to 28 U.S.C. § 754 giving this Court jurisdiction over RVG's property in every federal district.

19.   As an action brought by the Receiver in furtherance of his appointment and in the performance of his duties as directed by this Court, this action is within the ancillary jurisdiction of this Court.

20.   This action is also within the ancillary jurisdiction of this Court because this action concerns RVG's property and assets, which are now under this Court's exclusive jurisdiction.

21.   This Court has subject matter jurisdiction over this matter pursuant to its common law ancillary jurisdiction as set forth above.

22.   Also, this Court has subject matter jurisdiction under 28 U.S.C. § 1367 because this action is directly related to the claims in the SEC Action, concerns property

6

within this Court's exclusive control and/or is in furtherance of the duties given to the Receiver by this Court.

23. This Court has personal jurisdiction over the Defendants pursuant to 28 U.S.C. § 754 and 28 U.S.C. § 1692.

24. This Court also has personal jurisdiction over the Defendants pursuant to N.C. Gen. Stat. §1-75.4 because, *inter alia*, the defendants worked for RVG in North Carolina, are residents of North Carolina, and/or this action relates to money or other things of value sent from North Carolina to Defendants at their order or direction. By working for RVG and operating and/or participating in the ZeekRewards scheme, including numerous communications with RVG and/or meetings in North Carolina, the Defendants created a substantial connection to North Carolina such that the exercise of personal jurisdiction over them is fair and just.

25. Venue is proper in this District under 28 U.S.C. § 1391(b)(2) because a substantial portion of the acts and transfers alleged herein giving rise to this action occurred in this District.

26. The Receiver has standing to bring the claims made in this action pursuant to his authority and the direction of this Court and additionally has standing to bring the fraudulent transfer claims pursuant to N.C. Gen. Stat. § 39-23.7.

27. Pursuant to the Agreed Order, the Receiver has obtained the permission of this Court to file this action.

PONZI AND PYRAMID SCHEMES

28.   Legitimate business and investment opportunities are based on the expectation of a return from or portion of the profits of an actual business enterprise.

29.   In contrast, a Ponzi scheme is a fraudulent scheme in which returns to participants are not financed through the success of the underlying business venture. Instead, the money to pay returns comes from the payments made by other (usually later) participants in the scheme.

30.   Typically, participants are led to believe they will receive unrealistically high returns for their payments. Then, money from the scheme is used to pay high returns to early participants in order to create the (false) appearance of profitability and attract new participants to perpetuate the scheme.

31.   The scheme inevitably collapses when the flow of money from new participants is insufficient to pay the expected returns to existing participants or the fraud is discovered.

32.   Thus, a Ponzi scheme is established, *inter alia*, by evidence that (1) participants put money into a company because they are led to believe that they will receive large returns for their payments, (2) initial participants are actually paid the high returns, which attracts additional participants, (3) the underlying business venture, if any, is exaggerated and yields insufficient funds to pay for expenses and provide the expected returns to participants, and (4) the source of payments to earlier participants is cash infused by later participants.

8

33.   Other potential indications of a Ponzi scheme include, but are not limited to, the promise of large, unrealistic returns with little or no risk; the promise of consistent returns; false or non-existent books, records, financial statements and communications with the participants and the public; and the lack of transparency, secrecy, exclusivity and/or the complexity of the scheme.

34.   A pyramid scheme is a scheme in which a participant pays for the chance to receive compensation for recruiting new persons into the scheme as well as for when those new persons themselves recruit new participants. In unlawful pyramid schemes, compensation rewards are not primarily paid based on the sale of products to ultimate users.

35.   An intent to defraud future participants can be inferred from the mere fact that a person or company is running a Ponzi and/or pyramid scheme. Indeed, no other reasonable inference is possible. A Ponzi and/or pyramid scheme cannot work forever. The investor pool is a limited resource and will eventually run dry. The perpetrator must know that the scheme will eventually collapse as a result of the inability to attract new investors. He or she must know all along, from the very nature of the activities, that investors at the end of the line will lose their money. This knowledge that future investors will not be paid is sufficient to establish an actual intent to defraud them.

FACTS SUPPORTING THE RECEIVER'S CLAIMS

ZeekRewards and Zeekler's Operations

36.   Beginning at least as far back as 1997, Paul Burks operated a number of generally unsuccessful multi-level marketing businesses through Rex Venture Group,

9

LLC (and related entities) with names such as Go-Go Hub, Free Store Club, My Bid Shack, New Net Mail and Signed and Numbered International.

37.   In 2010, RVG launched Zeekler.com, a so-called "penny auction" website where items ranging from personal electronics to cash were auctioned to bidders.

38.   A "penny auction" does not work like a typical auction. In a normal auction, it costs nothing to bid, and the auction price rises based on the amount of the bid until there is no higher bid or the amount of time set for the auction expires. In a "penny auction," bids must be *purchased* by bidders, and each incremental bid placed raises the amount of the total price of the auction item only by $0.01. Penny auctions have a timer, but unlike a typical auction, each new bid at the end of the timer resets the bid clock, usually for 30 seconds to a minute. The penny auction ends when the bid clock expires with no new bid. The winner then pays the auction price (plus the cost of bids used), which is theoretically well below the retail price. However, the unsuccessful bidders lose all the money they spent to purchase bids.

39.   During 2010, the Zeekler penny auctions were not very successful. Indeed, Burks was forced to borrow money from Roger Plyler, then a business partner, to keep the business going.

40.   RVG's fortunes changed in 2011. In January 2011, RVG launched a new money-making scheme – ZeekRewards. RVG promoted ZeekRewards as Zeekler.com's "private, invitation-only affiliate advertising division." In reality, ZeekRewards was just a multi-level marketing scheme grafted onto the Zeekler business. It purported to pay a portion of the profits from the Zeekler penny auction business to participants who earned

10

bid balances or points, primarily by buying auction bids. RVG told potential participants, "Zeekler tallies total sales and pays a percentage to all active ZeekRewards members." Also, participants in ZeekRewards, often called "Affiliates," were paid for recruiting other participants in a pyramid "multi-level" sales format.

41.   Bidders on the Zeekler penny auctions could purchase bids at retail for $0.65, or they could acquire bids as ZeekRewards affiliates (or as free samples from RVG or an affiliate). ZeekRewards affiliates paid $1 for what RVG referred to as "compounding," "sample" or "VIP" bids. The retail bids and the compounding / sample / VIP bids all had the same effect in the auctions – placing a bid raised the price of an auction item by one cent. However, bids bought through ZeekRewards rather than as retail bids were much more valuable because what were really being purchased were points that entitled Affiliates to a portion of the profits from the business. This was the real reason Affiliates paid $1 for auction bids they could buy for $.65.

42.   As one Affiliate told Burks, "I know how the system works mathematically and you know I know. Whether you call the bids bids or hamburgers makes no difference. People are not joining Zeek to get hamburgers, or auction bids; they are joining Zeek to make money...."

43.   ZeekRewards emphasized that the offer to pay Affiliates for purchasing compounding / sample / VIP "bids" distinguished those bids from the simple purchase of retail bids to participate in the Zeekler auctions. In the "About us" section of the ZeekRewards website, the company wrote: "PLEASE NOTE: To qualify for the 125%

11

reward points you MUST buy the bids in the ZeekRewards back office. Bids purchased on the Zeekler Penny Auction site are 'retail customer' bids and do not qualify."

44.   Further, ZeekRewards made clear that even though bids bought through ZeekRewards could be used in the auctions, that fact was irrelevant to the multi-level marketing scheme. Affiliates were told that using the bids in the auction would have no effect on their all-important bid or points balance ("Each time you buy a Compounding Bid in your ZeekRewards Back Office a bid is added to the Compounding bucket. *Spending the bid in an auction does not remove it from the bucket*.") (emphasis added).

45.   Not surprisingly, even though a largely bogus "bid giveaway requirement" was added later in the scheme, relatively few ZeekRewards participants or "bid giveaway" recipients used their sample/VIP bids in the Zeekler auctions. Prior to shutdown, RVG estimated that only approximately 19 million VIP bids were used in auctions out of over 7 billion VIP bids created – less than 1/3 of 1%.

46.   From the beginning, RVG intended to use "bids" in ZeekRewards not as a product but as a proxy for money deposited into the program. Dawn Wright-Olivares was very clear about the plan, telling Danny Olivares on January 21, 2011: "We're just going to use bids as currency." On another occasion, Dawn Wright-Olivares referred to the compounding bids as "Monopoly money."

47.   Quickly, RVG's focus changed from Zeekler to ZeekRewards, which was the source of nearly all the company's income. Relative to ZeekRewards, little or no money was made in the Zeekler "penny auction" business.

12

48.   The sale of compounding / sample / VIP bids in ZeekRewards dwarfed the sale of "retail" bids. According to the ZeekRewards database, ZeekRewards sold approximately $820 million in compounding / sample / VIP bids, but only about $10 million in retail bids were sold.

49.   While over $400 million dollars was paid out to ZeekRewards Affiliates over the course of the scheme, the money used to fund ZeekRewards' distributions to Affiliates came almost entirely from new participants rather than income from the Zeekler penny auctions. Only about $10 million dollars in retail bids were sold (of which $3.6 million reflected purchases by net losing Affiliates). So, the "profit" from the penny auction business, if there was any at all, was too small to support even 3% of the total payments made to participants.

50.   Burks and the other Insiders were aware that the payouts to Affiliates would be funded by new participants rather than retail profits from the penny auctions. Dawn Wright-Olivares excitedly told Burks early in the scheme, "I think we can blow this OUT together- we've already attracted a great many big fishes."

ZeekRewards Compensation Plan

51.   ZeekRewards succeeded because it promoted a lucrative "compensation plan," offering large amounts of passive income to entice individuals to participate in the scheme.

52.   The participants in the ZeekRewards scheme invested money in the scheme by buying so-called "bids/points," "memberships," "subscriptions," customer names, and other items related to the scheme.

13

53.   ZeekRewards was a common enterprise in that the participants relied on Burks and RVG to run the "penny auction" business, which was claimed to be the source of profits for the company. The participants in ZeekRewards expected that they would receive profits from the Zeekler penny auction or other Zeek efforts.

54.   The compensation plan consisted primarily of two components: (1) the "Compounder," also known as the "Retail Profit Pool" or "RPP," which supposedly allowed participants to collectively share up to 50% of Zeek's net retail profits and receive a 125% return on investment; and (2) the "Matrix," which was a multi-level marketing commission program.

55.   Initially, ZeekRewards promised a 125% return on a passive investment, describing the program as follows: "What if you found a very simple and quick way to earn 125% profit on the dollars you spend with us without ever having to sell a thing or recruit a soul?"

56.   In a pitch entitled "Latest Zeek Compounder News" on January 10, 2011, RVG wrote: "ZeekRewards is a new kind of loyalty program that gives a limited number of early adopters the opportunity to compound up to 125% of each bid purchased," and went on to say that there is "no recruiting, . . . your money [is] compounding for you daily." Other recruiting emails claimed, "the minimal requirement is to simply place one free ad *somewhere* each day" and "if you do then the company will rebate you up to 125% of each bid purchased." (emphasis in original email).

57.   Another pitch touted the income participants would receive: "I found something I believe is absolutely out of this world . . . it's called the 'Compounder' and

14

"grows income for you by compounding it daily;" . . . "the new system [lets] you earn every 24 hours and can generate for you 4 or 5 figures or more per month . . . ." "[I]f you've ever wanted to earn 5 figures or more monthly, passively, then this is your chance." Similarly, de Brantes boasted that by participating in ZeekRewards: "Many are currently receiving $2,000 to $3,000 per month PASSIVELY." (emphasis in original).

58.   Early ZeekRewards participants were told to expect profit shares of .5% to 4% *daily*. The first day the Compounder share percentage was allocated to participants was January 20, 2011, and the share percentage was 3.24%.

59.   As the scheme progressed, participants continued to be told to expect large, consistent daily returns. On May 14, 2011, Paul Burks told Michael VanLeeuwen ("Coach Van") that "our goal has always been 1% Mon-Thurs and 1/2% weekends, Fri-Sun. We have always maintained those averages and exceeded them often."

60.   And, even after counsel advised against publicly promoting a 125% return, RVG continued to tell Affiliates and prospects to expect large returns. For example, de Brantes told an affiliate in July 2011:

> [O]ur average has been between 1.6–1.8% which would actually be
> a great deal more than 125%. The attorneys our [sic] advising us on
> what we can and can't say and now it's our job to figure out how
> much we need to pay daily to get everyone exactly what we intend to
> give (it makes it a little tricky but it is our intention to maintain a
> system that pays 125% without saying it anywhere on the site). It's
> my understanding that to reach 125% we'll need to pay 1.38% per
> day. Our programmers and strategists are working around the clock
> to land on the right method, percentages, and presentation for all of
> this. Right now we're still working on the 125% cap system. We
> just aren't saying 125%.

15

61.   Therefore, Affiliates paid and invested money into ZeekRewards with the expectation that they would profit from their payments based on the success of the company's operations.

62.   All the income received by ZeekRewards and Zeekler, regardless of source, was pooled and comingled in a cast of financial institutions that changed as the scheme evolved or as financial companies refused to work with RVG.

63.   Although the specifics and the terminology of the ZeekRewards "Compensation Plan" changed from time to time as Burks and the other Insiders tried to prolong and prop up the scheme, the two pillars of the plan for most Affiliates were always: (1) "profit" sharing (first called the Compounder then later the Retail Profit Pool (or "RPP")) and (2) the multi-level marketing pyramid that paid Affiliates a "commission" on the membership fees paid by recruited "downline" Affiliates (known as the Matrix).

The Compounder a/k/a Retail Profit Pool

64.   ZeekRewards' Affiliates' primary money making tool was the "Compounder." To participate in the Compounder, Affiliates purchased "compounding" bids, which earned Affiliates one point for each "compounding" bid that they purchased from the company.

65.   To become an Affiliate "qualified" to receive points required little or no effort, despite the bogus claim that Affiliates "earned" points. As discussed in more detail below, Affiliates were required to place daily one free digital ad (prepared by the company) for Zeekler.com. Later, Affiliates were told they needed to "give away" the

16

bids in order to obtain points, although in practice this so-called "requirement" was easily met: Affiliates could simply pay extra to have the company "give away" the bids for them. This, in turn, was yet another revenue source for the company.

66.   As the inducement to purchase these "compounding" bids, ZeekRewards told Affiliates that the company would give a portion of the company's daily earnings or profits (often claimed to be 50%) to point-holding Affiliates. The size of the daily "profit sharing" payment each affiliate received through the Compounder was based upon the number of points the affiliate held in his or her account.

67.   The size of each Affiliate's daily award depended only on the Affiliate's point total and was not based on the amount of services provided to ZeekRewards. Thus, regardless of the Affiliates' efforts, buying more points resulted in a larger profit share, just like having more shares of stock results in a larger dividend for a stockholder.

68.   ZeekRewards described the "Compounder" process as follows: "At the end of each business day (7days a week) the company determines its daily overall profitability and rebates a percentage back to its Active Advertising Affiliates based on each individual Premium Members Compounder Bid Balance."

69.   Each day, affiliates had a choice to be paid all or a portion of the so-called "profit" award in cash or to use the "cash" award to buy more bids/points, which then added to the bid / points balance and "compounded" as the daily percentage awards were made.

70.   Burks and the other insiders understood that the compensation plan would be unsustainable in both the short run and the long run because there would not be

17

enough new participants to support full daily cash payments to a growing number of existing Affiliates.

71.   Prior to the shutdown of ZeekRewards, there were over 3 billion VIP bid points in the ZeekRewards system. Based on the actual average daily "profit" percentage of 1.43% used during the scheme, the daily "profit" award to Affiliates would be over $40,000,000 on 3 billion points. The amount of money paid in to ZeekRewards daily was far less than $40 million. Therefore, if RVG had been required to pay the daily awards supposedly available to Affiliates in cash, ZeekRewards would have quickly collapsed.

72.   Specifically, during the last month ZeekRewards operated (July 16, 2012 to August 15, 2012) the daily average RPP award was $38,237,036, but the daily receipts (from all sources, not just retail auctions) were much smaller, averaging approximately $8,850,000. Thus, not only were the ZeekRewards payouts made from the money put in by other participants, but the so-called "profit" awards greatly exceeded total receipts, which, of course, was unsustainable.

73.   So, to maintain the program for as long as possible and generate the most income, ZeekRewards actively discouraged Affiliates from requesting actual payment of all their profit awards in cash. Instead, Affiliates were encouraged to let their balances "compound" and only take 20% or less of their "earnings."

74.   Dawn Wright-Olivares explained and promoted the plan in a Skype chat as follows:

> Here's a scenario here where you could be receiving $3,000 per month RESIDUALLY. Let's use a 1% daily cash-back figure in this example (Please note: This is only an example and the actual amount

18

will vary day to day). When you reach 50,000 points in your account, then you could start doing an 80/20 cash-out plan. Pay close attention? When you hit 50,000 points in your account, if the daily cash-back percentage is 1%, ZeekRewards will be awarding you with $500.00 each day. First of all, did you catch that? ... you're making $500 per day ... it's your money! Ok, the 80/20 plan works like this, take 80% of that $500 (or $400) and purchase more VIP bids to give away to new customers as samples to continue growing your points balance. Then, keep doing what you've been doing every day, which primarily consists of giving free bids away as samples and placing one free ad per day for Zeekler.com's penny auctions and submitting into your ZeekRewards back office. Then, pull out 20% of the $500 (or $100) and request a check weekly. That's $700 per week, or about $3,000 per month in residual income! And keep in mind, these amounts can continue to grow day after day and month after month.

75. ZeekRewards eventually changed the name of the Compounder to the "Retail Profit Pool," or "RPP." In addition, they changed the name of compounding bids to "VIP bids" or "sample bids." However, while the names changed, the essential nature of the "profit" sharing scheme remained the same.

76. In one email, when referring to compounding bids being renamed VIP bids, Wright-Olivares wrote, "wherever you see a (compounding) next to VIP – you will know that these terms are interchangeable," and she later wrote that "no change has been made in how they operate, qualify or earn."

77. Indeed, Wright-Olivares admitted that she thought the name changes were a joke. In a June 15, 2011 email to O.H. Brown, an RVG advisor whose company created marketing videos for ZeekRewards, about a company webinar script, she said: "you'll see where I started to say Retail Profit Pool (lol) instead of Compounder…. We're going to call compounding bids – VIP bids."

19

78.   However, whether it was called the Compounder or the Retail Profit Pool, the program was a fraud because the payments had no relation to actual "retail" profits nor were they calculated from real receipts or expenses.

79.   Instead, the alleged "profit percentage" was nothing more than a number made up by Burks or one of the other Insiders. Most days, Burks made up the number. As Danny Olivares explained to RVG's internet provider, "Paul [Burks] goes in nightly and opens up adm_displayCompunder3.asp and enters a decimal percentage." Sometimes, the number was made up by Dawn Wright-Olivares or Danny Olivares.

80.   Rather than reflecting the typical variances that might be expected in a company's profits, the alleged profits paid in ZeekRewards were remarkably consistent, falling nearly always between 1% and 2% on Monday through Thursday and between .5% and 1% on the weekends, Friday through Sunday. The goal of this fake consistency was to project the appearance of a stable source of income to entice new participants and to encourage existing Affiliates to allow their bid balances to compound rather than request payment of their daily award in cash.

81.   With RVG's knowledge, Affiliates regularly touted the consistent payments in their recruiting of new participants. For example, "Coach Van's" email footer said: "It has been going like clockwork for over 220 days, 7 days per week.".... "EVERYONE...GETS...PAID...FIRST...DAY!" . . . This works every time with just one minute per day! If you're not getting paid every single day for 1 minute of work, . . . [sic] why not?" . . . "100 percent of our active members are paid daily 100 percent of the time within their first 24 hours without any referrals."

20

82. The payouts were so consistent that when a mistake was made (such as when an extra decimal place was added to the "profit" percentage or the lower "weekend" percentage was used on a "weekday") Affiliates would immediately complain. For example, on August 3, 2012, de Brantes sent Danny Olivares a Skype message saying, the "Thursday [RPP] commission's % are running like a weekend commission % and everyone is going crazy." Olivares replies that, he is "working on it."

83. And, the Insiders realized that not paying Affiliates, even once, was not an option if they wanted to keep the scheme going. On May 20, 2012, there were problems with payments to affiliates. Dawn Wright-Olivares texted Danny Olivares and instructed him to post an update letting affiliates know their payments would eventually be processed and commissions would be paid, telling him, "[t]he fastest way to get charge [sic] as a Ponzi scheme is for distributors to claim they are not getting paid."

84. Burks deliberately evaded affiliate questions asking how the RPP was calculated. In a Skype chat with an affiliate, he said: "[a] proprietary system is used to determine the amount of profit sharing that is done each day. We do not divulge the details of how those numbers are determined. Our stated target of minimum of 1% weekdays (Mon-Thur) and .5% weekends (Fri-Sun) has always been met and exceeded. It is clearly not directly tied to the number of auctions in a particular day. It is the overall average that counts."

85. Behind the scenes, the insiders were not even subtle about the fake earnings numbers. Often, the company simply used the previous week's daily RPP percentages. For example, on one occasion, Danny Olivares sent a text message to multiple insiders

21

stating, "Need a % for rpp when you can." Dawn Wright-Olivares responded, "Do whatever was last Monday." Or, from Paul Burks: "Hey Dan. Sorry about last night. What percent did you use?" Danny Olivares: "Same as last Friday. 0.009."

86. On another occasion, Burks wrote in a Skype message to Olivares that the RPP would be ".0089 unless you have already grabbed last week[']s :)."

87. Sometimes, Burks even told Danny Olivares *in advance* what a day's profit number would be, such as on September 14, 2011, when in the early morning Burks told him "to start the RPP run shortly after 7p.m. using .00179 as the percentage" because Burks was not going to be able to run it himself.

88. Even if the Insiders had intended to calculate actual profits (which they plainly did not), RVG did not maintain financial records sufficient to allow Burks or anyone else to calculate a daily retail profit for the company.

ZeekRewards' "Advertising" Requirement

89. In an unsuccessful effort to avoid the obvious legal infirmity of Affiliates simply buying points in return for the expectation of a share of the profits (like a stock purchase), ZeekRewards told Affiliates that in order to supposedly "earn" their points, they were required to place a short, free digital ad each day on one of the many free classified websites available on the internet.

90. Affiliates were told to merely copy and paste free ads created by ZeekRewards into a free digital classified ad website. Affiliates then submitted the ad's internet link to ZeekRewards to verify that they had placed the ad. Placing more ads or better ads did not change an Affiliate's share of the profits in any way.

22

91.   And, the ad "requirement" was not imposed on all Affiliates. Burks even wrote a computer program that allowed a number of Affiliates who managed multiple accounts to avoid placing the ads altogether. As Burks wrote in an email to Danny Olivares on January 23, 2011, "This allows us to defer to some of our major people like Agnita Solomon who manage dozens of accounts so that they don'e [sic] have to place so many ads every day."

92.   The ad process was intended to be very simple and was widely advertised as taking only 3-5 minutes each day. For example, Burks routinely told Affiliates: "Placing an ad takes three to five minutes a day and can be done from anywhere there is an Internet connection."

93.   Indeed, because of how minimal the task was, Burks was irritated by Affiliates who complained when they were not paid: "I am afraid I don't have a lot of patience anymore for people who are making hundreds of dollars a day for placing an ad and they get mad when their card declines and they miss a day. Tough luck."

94.   The company did not believe that these digital ads made any material difference in the success of the Zeekler auctions and did no research to determine if the ads were successful.

95.   In reality, the ads were just an attempt to manufacture a cover for what was nothing more than the investment of money by Affiliates with the expectation of receiving daily "profit" distributions.

23

ZeekRewards' Bid "Give Away" Requirement

96.   In a further effort to justify the Affiliates' investments of money, beginning in August 2011, ZeekRewards purportedly required Affiliates to "give away" their purchased VIP bids to earn points. The claimed intent of this "requirement" was to promote use of the auctions by new retail customers who received these free bids.

97.   However, Burks and the insiders knew that in practice the bid "give away" program (like the free ads) had no material impact on the success of the penny auctions.

98.   First, the company made little or no attempt to determine if bids had in fact been given to legitimate prospective retail customers. Many Affiliates simply listed fake email addresses, addresses of other existing Affiliates or those planning to be affiliates, family members, and other non-productive locations for where the bids had been given away. In some cases, the company just agreed not to require the affiliate to give away their bids to earn points.

99.   Also, both as a way to minimize any real effort by Affiliates and a way to make more money, Affiliates were given the opportunity to pay to have the company (supposedly) give the bids away on behalf of the affiliate. Points were earned when the bids were given to the company (supposedly) to be given away.

100.   In fact, the company did not find prospective retail customers to whom it could give away all the bids, so millions of bids remained in the company unused. But, ZeekRewards did make an additional $2.00 - $2.50 per customer "sold" to Affiliates. And, because there were alleged limits on the number of bids that could be given away to any one person based on the Affiliate's membership level, tying the "give away" of bids

24

to the accrual of points drove "upgrades" in membership levels which increased revenues even more.

101. Danny Olivares explained the process of how VIP bids were automatically given away to accrue points for Affiliates as follows: After a VIP bid is purchased, the "Company pool automates the process of giving bids away as samples. Giving the bids away as samples is what generates VIP points. Which the rpp uses to calculate your award. So we come full circle."

102. Burks told Affiliates that the company-wide Bid Pool would "take ALL of the sting out of the whole bid-give requirement! . . . [Y]ou will be able to automatically give your bids each day" and "you will automatically receive the VIP points as soon as you receive your daily RPP award each day. . . . All you'll have to do is select the "Give my bids to the Zeek bid pool" option and the system will automatically give your bids to your customers and every customer that registers @ Zeekler.com that wants free bids! If you do not have any customers then you simply purchase them as you need them from the customer co-op, and that will be automated as well!"

103. Later, Affiliates were not allowed to simply pay the company to "give away" the bids for them, but they were allowed to pay third parties to do so. ZeekRewards made no effort to determine if these bids were in fact given to legitimate potential retail customers.

The Matrix

104. The second broad component of the ZeekRewards compensation plan was paying Affiliates to recruit other Affiliates in a pyramid-style payment system. ZeekRewards referred to this system as the "Matrix."

105. The Matrix pyramid was initially a "2x21" matrix in which Affiliates made multi-level marketing commissions for 21 levels down in their "organization." Later, ZeekRewards used a "2x5 forced-fill matrix," which is a pyramid with 63 positions that paid a bonus to Affiliates for every "downline" investor within each affiliate's personal matrix, plus a "matching bonus" for every 5th level where certain qualifiers were met, so in effect the commissions could be earned indefinitely.

106. To get bonuses through the Matrix, Affiliates just had to (1) enroll in a monthly subscription plan requiring payments of $10, $50, or $99 per month; and (2) recruit at least two other "Preferred Customers" (i.e., investors who also enrolled in a monthly subscription plan).

107. Once qualified, affiliates earned bonuses and commissions for every paid subscription within their "downline" pyramid, whether or not they personally recruited everyone within the matrix. Simply put, Affiliates were rewarded merely for recruiting new investors without regard to any efforts by the Affiliates to sell bids or products or otherwise materially support the Zeekler retail business.

108. The funds raised through the Matrix were commingled with the money raised through the Compounder / Retail Profit Pool (and what little money came in from

26

the retail auction business), so nearly all the money used to pay the pyramid commissions came from other investors in the scheme.

109. While some commissions were available to Affiliates on customers' purchases of retail bids for use in the Zeekler auctions, Affiliates did not need to sell retail bids to customers in order to receive commissions through the Matrix. Furthermore, overall commissions from the sale of retail bids to end-user customers were miniscule. These retail commissions, referred to by RVG as "Zap Commissions," were merely incidental to the overall commissions earned through the Matrix for downline subscription payments and through the Compounder/RPP.

110. As with the Compounder, the Insiders changed the terminology for the Matrix, but they never changed the real essence of the scheme. Dawn Wright-Olivares explained the cosmetic changes to the Matrix this way: "you [will] in effect be paid on levels 5-10".... "but we can't SAY that. Deep matrices get shut down. So instead...we say that you are getting a matching bonus on all of the 2x5's on your 5th level. It's semantics, but semantics mean a great deal with regulators." ... "[I] don't really understand how they can say they have levels 10, 15, etc. when it's a 2x5, but if we can get away with it this way - then it's my vote to leave it alone."

111. Similarly, Keith Laggos, a ZeekRewards advisor, emailed Dawn Wright-Olivares (copying Burks) in July 2011: "when talking about matching bonuses, you are showing being paid on 1 to 10, 1 to 15 and 1 to 20 levels. This defeats what we did by going to a 2x5 matrix. You should say a 100% matching on all your 5th, 15th and 20th

level affiliates' 2 x 5 matrixes. I know you want to show they get paid on 20 levels in a 2 by 20 matrix, but that is when you can get a pyramid investigation or charge."

The "Sweet 16"

112. In addition to the Compounder/RPP and the Matrix, a select group of individuals were allowed an additional revenue source, referred to as the "Sweet 16."

113. The Sweet 16 was another means by which RVG made payments on a passive investment. It did not involve the sale of a product, nor did it require a member to recruit other participants into the program.

114. As RVG advertised in late 2010 or early 2011, the Sweet 16 was a program where participants received "a 1/16 share at the diamond level" on paid subscriptions in the then-2x21 matrix "across the entire width of the matrix."

115. Participation in the Sweet 16 cost a one-time fee of $999.

116. Each month, RVG totaled commissions from all subscription renewals for the entire Matrix and divided a portion of those commissions among the Sweet 16 members.

117. On information and belief, Sweet 16 payments to investors totaled more than $4.7 million over the life of the scheme.

The "Row of 16"

118. In addition to the Sweet 16, two insiders were allowed payments through a revenue source referred to as the "Row of 16."

119. Dawn Wright-Olivares and Danny Olivares were the only two members of the Row of 16.

28

120.   These Row of 16 payments were generally calculated as sixteen times the highest Sweet 16 payment amount.

121.   The Row of 16 was nothing more than a gift or bonus to these two individuals.

122.   As with the other "compensation" payments made to Affiliates, these payments were made with money received from Affiliates purchasing VIP bids or subscription renewals, not from a legitimate retail activity.

123.   Dawn Wright-Olivares and Daniel Olivares received more than $5.8 million in Row of 16 payments over the life of the scheme.

The Insiders' Efforts to Avoid Discovery of
the ZeekRewards Ponzi and Pyramid Scheme

124.   RVG's insiders often worried about being caught and sought to make the unlawful scheme seem legitimate in many ways.

125.   As described above, the changing of terminology or the rules of the game, but not the substance of the scheme, was a common practice. Throughout 2011 and 2012, Burks and the Insiders regularly changed the names of the program elements or demanded that Affiliates stop using certain words, which accurately described the scheme but highlighted its illegality.

126.   For example, on July 26, 2011, de Brantes emailed an Affiliate with a list of things the Affiliate can and cannot say, including: "compounder, compound, compounded, compounding, 125%, Members, Interest, Investment, Mature." On the list of sanitized things the Affiliate could say: "You make a purchase and re-purchase; You

earn bids; The bids retire on a 90 day timeline averaging 1.5% a day; You get cash rewards; Retail Profit Pool; Everyone is an Affiliate and they own business center subscriptions; Your Bid balance can increase as oppose to mature."

127. Also, RVG employees openly discussed the words that could and could not be said, even adding a bit of black humor as the scheme headed towards its inevitable demise. On June 8, 2012, de Brantes and others discussed "training" Affiliates on "the top 10 or 12 words that every Affiliate should erase from their vocabulary". The list included "investment, put money in, roi [return on investment], fund, passive income, passive returns, returns and points are not dollars." In response to this list, Ken Kilby (a supposed "compliance officer") suggested adding: "BBB, Attorney General, FBI, FTC, Report, turn you in."

128. Beyond the shifting terminology, Burks and the Insiders tried to bolster the perception of the legitimacy of the scheme by running "Compliance" courses for Affiliates. As with the advertising or bid give-away "requirements," the "compliance" courses were just an effort to obscure the fraud and wrap it in a cloak of propriety, while making even more money in the process.

RVG's False 1099 Tax Filings

129. For the year 2011, ZeekRewards issued many Affiliates IRS Form 1099s, the form given to independent contractors. Of those 2011 1099s issued to Affiliates, nearly 10,000 were filed with the IRS.

130. First, Affiliates were not "independent contractors." RVG, not the Affiliates, was totally responsible for the company's websites, handled all payments,

30

managed the bank accounts and payment service providers, managed affiliate and customer accounts, created all advertisements, sponsored recruiting videos and calls, sponsored training videos and calls, and tracked and determined all Matrix bonus payments. And, further, the Affiliates did no real work to obtain the supposed "income" they received from the Compounder/RPP and the vast majority of the Matrix payments.

131. More importantly, in an effort to further the appearance that the scheme was a legitimate business enterprise, ZeekRewards reported affiliate income on the 1099s that had not been paid out to Affiliates.

132. Instead, much of the reported "income" was based on the Affiliates' reinvesting their daily awards into the scheme through "bid repurchases" and subscription payments as if this money was actual income earned by the Affiliates, when in fact the income was fictitious and never paid to Affiliates.

133. In total, ZeekRewards reported affiliate income of over $87 million for the year 2011 on the 1099s issued, while ZeekRewards actually paid out less than $12 million in cash to Affiliates during that year.

134. Therefore, Affiliates were forced to pay taxes on phantom income that they never actually received, and ZeekRewards was able to use the false tax notices to perpetuate the scheme.

Insiders' Use of Affiliates' Investments for Personal Enrichment

135. The Insiders not only paid the early investors with the money that flowed into the scheme. They also paid themselves and their families and friends.

31

136. Over the course of the scheme, Burks received payments of more than $10 million from RVG. On information and belief, Burks used investor money to provide cash gifts of more than $250,000 to his son, and more than $30,000 to his daughter.

137. Wright-Olivares misappropriated over $7.8 million through the scheme. With these investor funds, she repaid personal loans, renovated her home, purchased an RV, bought multiple vehicles, and engaged in several other suspicious transactions.

138. In addition, Wright-Olivares looted RVG of significant funds after it had become apparent that the scheme would soon end. In August 2012, she received over $1.7 million from RVG, with most of this sum being paid directly to an account held by her shell corporation, Wandering Phoenix LLC. Wright-Olivares then redistributed more than $1.2 million of these funds to her personal account and de Brantes' personal account, as well as to others involved with RVG, including OH Brown, Robert Mecham, Peter Mingils, Aaron Baker, and Barbara Ghent. These payments were sometimes accompanied by invented one-year "consulting agreements" for the respective individuals' purported services.

139. Further, Wright-Olivares paid out $150,000 to Jonathan Wright, Suzanne Wright, and Ben Powell Construction on August 17, 2012, the day ZeekRewards was shut down and the freeze order took effect. Moreover, even a week after the freeze order was in place, Wright-Olivares was still redistributing the illicit funds, paying over $90,000 to Aaron Baker, John Wright, and her own accounts on August 24, 2012.

140. Burks and Wright-Olivares, along with the other orchestrators of the scheme, engaged in self-dealing with no regard for the fact that in a matter of months or

32

weeks, ZeekRewards would be unable to pay back those individuals who unwittingly bought into the lie.

FIRST CLAIM FOR RELIEF
Fraudulent Transfer of RVG Funds in Violation of the North Carolina Uniform Fraudulent Transfer Act
(Against all Defendants)

141. The Receiver realleges and incorporates by reference the foregoing paragraphs.

142. In the course of operating the ZeekRewards scheme, Burks and others – through RVG – made numerous "profit payments," "commission" payments, bonuses and other payments to each of the Insiders as described above in excess of the amount of money paid to RVG. These excess payments are collectively referred to as the "Transfers."

143. The Transfers were made within four years before the date of this action.

144. Each of the Transfers constitutes a "transfer" of an asset or an interest in an asset within the meaning of N.C. Gen. Stat. §39-23.1(12).

145. All of the Transfers occurred during the course of a Ponzi and/or pyramid scheme, when participant money was commingled and the Receivership Entities were effectively insolvent.

146. Each of the Transfers was to, or for the benefit of, one or more of the Defendants.

33

147. Each of the Transfers was made with money misappropriated from one or more of the Receivership Entities. At all times relevant herein, the Receivership Entities had a claim to the funds used for the Transfers.

148. Each of the Transfers was made without receipt of reasonably equivalent value from the Defendants.

149. Each of the Transfers was made by Burks and others to further the Ponzi and/or pyramid scheme and was made with the actual intent to hinder, delay or defraud some or all of the Receivership Entities' then existing creditors.

150. In the alternative, at the time of each of the Transfers, the Receivership Entities were insolvent or became insolvent as a result of the Transfer, were engaged in a business or transaction, or were about to engage in a business or transaction, for which the remaining assets of the Receivership Entities were unreasonably small in relation to the business or transaction or intended to incur, or believed that they would incur, debts that would be beyond their ability to pay as such debts became due.

151. The Transfers constitute fraudulent transfers avoidable by the Receiver pursuant to N.C. Gen. Stat. §39-23.4(a)(1), N.C. Gen. Stat. §39-23.4(a)(2) or N.C. Gen. Stat. §39-23.5 and recoverable from the Defendants pursuant to N.C. Gen. Stat. §39-23.7 and N.C. Gen. Stat. §39-23.8.

152. Pursuant to N.C. Gen. Stat. §39-23.4(a)(1), N.C. Gen. Stat. §39-23.7, N.C. Gen. Stat. §39-23.8 and 28 U.S.C. §2201, the Receiver is entitled to a Judgment: (1) avoiding the Transfers; and (2) recovering the Transfers, or the value thereof, from the Defendants for the benefit of the Receivership Estate.

34

SECOND CLAIM FOR RELIEF
Common Law Fraudulent Transfer
(Against all Defendants)

153.   The Receiver realleges and incorporates by reference the foregoing paragraphs.

154.   The Transfers were made within three years before the date of this action.

155.   Each of the Transfers constitutes a transfer of an asset or an interest in an asset of the Receivership Entities.

156.   All of the Transfers occurred during the course of a Ponzi and/or pyramid scheme, when participant money was commingled and the Receivership Entities were insolvent.

157.   Each of the Transfers was to, or for the benefit of, one or more of the Defendants.

158.   Each of the Transfers was made with money misappropriated from one or more of the Receivership Entities. At all times relevant herein, the Receivership Entities had a claim to the funds used for the Transfers.

159.   Each of the Transfers was made without receipt of reasonably equivalent value from the Defendants.

160.   At the time of each of the Transfers, the Receivership Entities were insolvent, or became insolvent, as a result of the Transfer.

161.   The Transfers constitute fraudulent transfers avoidable by the Receiver and recoverable from the Defendants.

35

162.   Accordingly, pursuant to 28 U.S.C. §2201, the Receiver is entitled to a Judgment: (1) avoiding the Transfers; and (2) recovering the Transfers, or the value thereof, from the Defendants for the benefit of the Receivership Estate.

THIRD CLAIM FOR RELIEF
Breach of Fiduciary Duty
(Against all Defendants)

163.   The Receiver realleges and incorporates by reference the foregoing paragraphs.

164.   RVG reposed trust and confidence in the Defendants. By virtue of this trust and their positions and responsibilities at RVG, each of the Defendants owed a fiduciary duty to RVG to act honestly and in RVG's best interests and not for their own interests or the interests of those other than RVG.

165.   By their unlawful and improper conduct described above, the Defendants breached their fiduciary duties to RVG.

166.   The Defendants' breaches of their fiduciary duties have directly and proximately caused substantial harm to RVG, including, but not limited to, the financial claims of the victims of the Zeek Ponzi and/or pyramid scheme against RVG.

167.   RVG is entitled to recover from the Defendants the amount of damages proximately caused by their conduct in an amount to be proven at trial.

168.   The Defendants' breach of their fiduciary duties was willful, wanton, and outrageous, and RVG is entitled to an award on punitive damages against the Defendants to deter such conduct in the future.

36

FOURTH CLAIM FOR RELIEF

Conversion

(Against all Defendants)

169.   The Receiver realleges and incorporates by reference the foregoing paragraphs.

170.   The Defendants received money from RVG in the form of bonuses and other payments of money to which they were not entitled and/or directed the payments of money from RVG to others who were not entitled to receive that money within the three years prior to the filing of this action.

171.   The Defendants had no right to receive or direct the payment of those funds from RVG.

172.   By their wrongful use of that property as described above and their failure to return that property to RVG, the Defendants have unlawfully converted that property for their own use and unjust benefit without justification or permission from RVG.

173.   As a direct and approximate cause of this conversion of property, RVG has suffered damages, including irreparable harm and loss, and is entitled to recover those damages from the Defendants.

174.   The Defendants' conversion of RVG's property was and is wanton and willful and in malicious disregard of RVG's rights, which warrants an award of punitive damages to RVG to deter such conduct in the future.

37

FIFTH CLAIM FOR RELIEF
Unjust Enrichment
(Against all Defendants)

175.   The Receiver realleges and incorporates by reference the foregoing paragraphs.

176.   The Defendants each benefited from the receipt of money from the Receivership Entities in the form of bonuses, compensation, and other payments which were the property of the Receivership Entities and for which the Defendants did not adequately compensate RVG or provide value.

177.   The Defendants have unjustly failed to repay RVG for the excessive benefits they received.

178.   The enrichment was at the expense of the Receivership Entities and ultimately at the expense of RVG's creditors / victims.

179.   Equity and good conscience require full restitution of the monies received by the Defendants for distribution to RVG's creditors / victims.

180.   Accordingly, the Receiver, on behalf of RVG, is entitled to an award of full restitution from the Defendants in an amount to be determined at trial.

SIXTH CLAIM FOR RELIEF
Constructive Trust
(Against all Defendants)

181.   The Receiver realleges and incorporates by reference the foregoing paragraphs.

38

182. As alleged above, the assets of the Receivership Entities have been wrongfully diverted as a result of fraudulent transfers, unjust enrichment, conversion, breaches of fiduciary duty and other wrongful conduct for the Defendants' individual interests and enrichment.

183. The Receiver has no adequate remedy at law.

184. Because of the past unjust enrichment and the fraudulent transfers, the Receiver is entitled to the imposition of a constructive trust with respect to any transfer of funds, assets, or property from the Receivership Entities, as well as any assets received by Defendants in the past or on a going forward basis as a result of those transfers from the Receivership Entities.

185. The Receiver is entitled to and demands title, possession, use and enjoyment of the foregoing property for the benefit of the Receivership Estate.

PRAYER FOR RELIEF

WHEREFORE, the Receiver respectfully requests that the Court:

1. Award compensatory and punitive damages against Defendants Paul Burks, Dawn Wright-Olivares, Danny Olivares, Darryle Douglas, and Roger Plyler in an amount to be determined at trial on the Receiver's Claims for Breach of Fiduciary Duty, Conversion, Unjust Enrichment, and Constructive Trust.

2. Enter an injunction against the Defendants prohibiting each of them from dissipating their assets pending satisfaction of the Judgment against them.

3. Enter a declaratory Judgment against the Defendants determining that the payments they received from RVG and/or ZeekRewards were fraudulent transfers from

39

RVG, ordering that the payments and/or net winnings of each of the Defendants is Receivership Property and subject to a constructive trust for the benefit of the Receivership Estate and ordering the repayment of those payments and/or net winnings back to RVG.

4.   Award prejudgment and post-judgment interest, costs and such other and further relief against all Defendants and the Net Winner Class as the Receiver is entitled to recover.

Dated: February 28, 2013   Respectfully submitted,

/s/ Irving M. Brenner
Kenneth D. Bell, Esq., Receiver
Irving M. Brenner (NC Bar No. 15483)
Jennifer L. King (NC Bar No. 34158)
Susan Rodriguez (NC Bar No. 40035)
Matthew E. Orso (NC Bar No. 42409)
McGuireWoods LLP
201 North Tryon Street, Suite 3000
Charlotte, North Carolina 28202
(704) 373-4620
(704) 373-8836 (fax)
kbell@mcguirewoods.com
ibrenner@mcguirewoods.com
jlking@mcguirewoods.com
srodriguez@mcguirewoods.com
morso@mcguirewoods.com

Exhibit 8

UNITED STATES DISTRICT COURT
WESTERN DISTRICT OF NORTH CAROLINA
CHARLOTTE DIVISION

SECURITIES AND EXCHANGE COMMISSION,

Plaintiff,

v.

REX VENTURE GROUP LLC
d/b/a ZEEKREWARDS.COM, and
PAUL R. BURKS,

Defendant.

3:12cv 519

C.A. No. ___-___ (   )

CONSENT OF DEFENDANT PAUL R. BURKS

1.   Defendant Paul R. Burks ("Defendant") waives service of a summons and the complaint in this action, enters a general appearance, and admits the Court's jurisdiction over Defendant and over the subject matter of this action.

2.   Without admitting or denying the allegations of the Complaint (except as to personal and subject matter jurisdiction, which Defendant admits), Defendant hereby consents to the entry of judgment in the form attached hereto (the "Agreed Judgment as to Burks") and incorporated by reference herein, which, among other things, permanently restrains and enjoins Defendant from violation of Sections 5(a), 5(c) and 17(a) of the Securities Act of 1933 ("Securities Act") [15 U.S.C. §§ 77e(a), 77e(c) and 77q(a)], and Section 10(b) of the Securities Exchange Act of 1934 ("Exchange Act") [15 U.S.C. § 78j(b)], and Rule 10b-5 thereunder [17 C.F.R. § 240.10b-5], and from directly or indirectly participating in, or facilitating, the solicitation of any investment in any security or in the offering of any security.

1

3. Defendant agrees to disclaim and relinquish, and agrees that the Court shall order Defendant to disclaim and relinquish, all legal and equitable right, title, claim, or interest in Rex Venture Group LLC, including: all subsidiaries, whether incorporated or unincorporated; all businesses or business names under which it does business and; and all assets in Rex Venture Group LLC's possession, custody or control, including assets held in accounts in any financial institution.

4. Defendant hereby consents to the entry of Agreed Order Appointing Temporary Receiver and Freezing Assets of Defendant Rex Venture Group LLC filed in connection with this action (the "Agreed Order Appointing Receiver and Freezing Assets") and incorporated by reference herein. Defendant neither admits nor denies the factual statements contained in the Agreed Order Appoint Receiver and Freezing Assets. Defendant agrees to cooperate with the appointed receiver and the Commission in all aspects as set forth in the Agreed Order Appointing Receiver and Freezing Assets, including, but not limited to: preserving, marshaling, accessing and repatriating all assets of Rex Venture and accessing any other information concerning Rex Venture, including access to its books, records and accounts. The preceding sentence should not be construed to inhibit, however, Burks ability to assert any and all applicable privileges in proceedings in which Burks is adverse to the Receiver, nor shall it require production of attorney work product created by Burks' counsel representing him in his personal capacity.

5. Defendant hereby consents to the entry of the Agreed Judgment as to Burks in the form attached hereto and incorporated by reference herein, which, among other things, orders Defendant to pay a civil penalty in the amount of $4,000,000.00 (four million dollars) under

2

234

Section 20(d) of the Securities Act [15 U.S.C. § 77t(d)] and Section 21(d)(3) of the Exchange Act [15 U.S.C. § 78u(d)(3)].

6.   Defendant acknowledges that the civil penalty paid pursuant to the Agreed Judgment as to Burks may be distributed pursuant to the Fair Fund provisions of Section 308(a) of the Sarbanes-Oxley Act of 2002. Regardless of whether any such Fair Fund distribution is made, the civil penalty shall be treated as a penalty paid to the government for all purposes, including all tax purposes. To preserve the deterrent effect of the civil penalty, Defendant agrees that he shall not, after offset or reduction of any award of compensatory damages in any Related Investor Action based on Defendant's payment of disgorgement in this action, argue that he is entitled to, nor shall he further benefit by, offset or reduction of such compensatory damages award by the amount of any part of Defendant's payment of a civil penalty in this action ("Penalty Offset"). If the court in any Related Investor Action grants such a Penalty Offset, Defendant agrees that he shall, within 30 days after entry of a final order granting the Penalty Offset, notify the Commission's counsel in this action and pay the amount of the Penalty Offset to the United States Treasury or to a Fair Fund, as the Commission directs. Such a payment shall not be deemed an additional civil penalty and shall not be deemed to change the amount of the civil penalty imposed in this action. For purposes of this paragraph, a "Related Investor Action" means a private damages action brought against Defendant by or on behalf of one or more investors based on substantially the same facts as alleged in the Complaint in this action.

7.   Defendant agrees that he shall not seek or accept, directly or indirectly, reimbursement or indemnification from any source, including but not limited to payment made pursuant to any insurance policy, with regard to any civil penalty amounts that Defendant pays pursuant to the Agreed Judgment as to Burks, regardless of whether such penalty amounts or any

3

part thereof are added to a distribution fund or otherwise used for the benefit of investors. Defendant further agrees that he shall not claim, assert, or apply for a tax deduction or tax credit with regard to any federal, state, or local tax for any penalty amounts that Defendant pays pursuant to the Agreed Judgment as to Burks, regardless of whether such penalty amounts or any part thereof are added to a distribution fund or otherwise used for the benefit of investors.

8.   Defendant acknowledges that this Consent and the Agreed Judgment as to Burks are based in part upon Defendant's sworn representations in Defendant's Statement of Financial Condition dated [_____] and other documents and information submitted to the Commission. Defendant further consents that if at any time following the entry of the Agreed Judgment as to Burks the Commission obtains information indicating that Defendant's representations to the Commission concerning Defendant's assets, income, liabilities, or net worth were fraudulent, misleading, inaccurate, or incomplete in any material respect as of the time such representations were made, the Commission may, at its sole discretion and without prior notice to Defendant, petition the Court for an order requiring Defendant to pay disgorgement, pre-judgment and post-judgment interest thereon, and the maximum civil penalty allowable under the law. In connection with any such petition, the only issue shall be whether the financial information provided by Defendant was fraudulent, misleading, inaccurate, or incomplete in any material respect as of the time such representations were made. In any such petition, the Commission may move the Court to consider all available remedies, including but not limited to ordering Defendant to pay funds or assets, directing the forfeiture of any assets, or sanctions for contempt of the Court's Agreed Judgment as to Burks. The Commission may also request additional discovery. Defendant may not, by way of defense to such petition: (1) challenge the validity of this Consent or the Agreed Judgment as to Burks; (2) contest the allegations in the Complaint;

4

(3) assert that payment of disgorgement, pre-judgment or post-judgment interest, or a civil penalty should not be ordered; (4) contest the amount of disgorgement or pre-judgment or post-judgment interest; (5) contest the imposition of the maximum civil penalty allowable under the law; or (6) assert any defense to liability or remedy, including but not limited to any statute of limitations defense.

9.　Defendant waives the entry of findings of fact and conclusions of law pursuant to Rule 52 of the Federal Rules of Civil Procedure.

10.　Defendant waives the right, if any, to a jury trial and to appeal from the entry of the Agreed Judgment as to Burks.

11.　Defendant enters into this Consent voluntarily and represents that no threats, offers, promises, or inducements of any kind have been made by the Commission or any member, officer, employee, agent, or representative of the Commission to induce Defendant to enter into this Consent.

12.　Defendant agrees that this Consent shall be incorporated into the Agreed Judgment as to Burks with the same force and effect as if fully set forth therein.

13.　Defendant will not oppose the enforcement of the Agreed Judgment as to Burks on the ground, if any exists, that it fails to comply with Rule 65(d) of the Federal Rules of Civil Procedure, and hereby waives any objection based thereon.

14.　Defendant waives service of the Agreed Judgment as to Burks and agrees that entry of the Agreed Judgment as to Burks by the Court and filing with the Clerk of the Court will constitute notice to Defendant of its terms and conditions. Defendant further agrees to provide counsel for the Commission, within thirty days after the Agreed Judgment as to Burks is filed

5

with the Clerk of the Court, with an affidavit or declaration stating that Defendant has received and read a copy of the Agreed Judgment as to Burks.

15.   Consistent with 17 C.F.R. 202.5(f), this Consent resolves only the claims asserted against Defendant in this civil proceeding. Defendant acknowledges that no promise or representation has been made by the Commission or any member, officer, employee, agent, or representative of the Commission with regard to any criminal liability that may have arisen or may arise from the facts underlying this action or immunity from any such criminal liability. Defendant waives any claim of Double Jeopardy based upon the settlement of this proceeding, including the imposition of any remedy or civil penalty herein. Defendant further acknowledges that the Court's entry of a permanent injunction may have collateral consequences under federal or state law and the rules and regulations of self-regulatory organizations, licensing boards, and other regulatory organizations. Such collateral consequences include, but are not limited to, a statutory disqualification with respect to membership or participation in, or association with a member of, a self-regulatory organization. This statutory disqualification has consequences that are separate from any sanction imposed in an administrative proceeding. In addition, in any disciplinary proceeding before the Commission based on the entry of the injunction in this action, Defendant understands that he shall not be permitted to contest the factual allegations of the Complaint in this action.

16.   Defendant understands and agrees to comply with the Commission's policy "not to permit a defendant or respondent to consent to a judgment or order that imposes a sanction while denying the allegations in the complaint or order for proceedings." 17 C.F.R. § 202.5. In compliance with this policy, Defendant agrees: (i) not to take any action or to make or permit to be made any public statement denying, directly or indirectly, any allegation in the complaint or

6

creating the impression that the complaint is without factual basis; and (ii) that upon the filing of this Consent, Defendant hereby withdraws any papers filed in this action to the extent that they deny any allegation in the complaint. If Defendant breaches this agreement, the Commission may petition the Court to vacate the Agreed Judgment as to Burks and restore this action to its active docket. Nothing in this paragraph affects Defendant's: (i) testimonial obligations; or (ii) right to take legal or factual positions in litigation or other legal proceedings in which the Commission is not a party.

17.   Defendant hereby waives any rights under the Equal Access to Justice Act, the Small Business Regulatory Enforcement Fairness Act of 1996, or any other provision of law to seek from the United States, or any agency, or any official of the United States acting in his or her official capacity, directly or indirectly, reimbursement of attorney's fees or other fees, expenses, or costs expended by Defendant to defend against this action. For these purposes, Defendant agrees that Defendant is not the prevailing party in this action since the parties have reached a good faith settlement.

18.   Defendant acknowledges and agrees that, by bringing this action against Defendant and Rex Ventures LLC involving securities offered through ZeekRewards.com and ZeekRewardsNews.com, the Commission has not taken any position on the legality of Zeekler.com or any other subsidiary of Rex Ventures, whether incorporated or unincorporated, or any businesses or business names under which Rex Venture does business.

19.   Defendant agrees that the Commission may present the Agreed Judgment as to Burks to the Court for signature and entry without further notice.

20.   Defendant agrees that this Court shall retain jurisdiction over this matter for the purpose of enforcing the terms of the Agreed Judgment as to Burks.

Dated: 8/17/12   _Paul R Burks_
                                  PAUL R. BURKS

On _8-17_____, 201_2_ _Paul R. Burks_____, a person known to me,
personally appeared before me and acknowledged executing the foregoing Consent.

                                  _Marie G Seguin_____
                                  Notary Public
                                  Commission expires: 07-24-15

Approved as to form:

signature
Attorney for Defendant

Exhibit 9

IN THE UNITED STATES DISTRICT COURT FOR THE
WESTERN DISTRICT OF NORTH CAROLINA
CHARLOTTE DIVISION

SECURITIES AND EXCHANGE)
COMMISSION,)
)
        Plaintiff,)
)
vs.   )   Civil Action No. 3:12 cv 519
)
REX VENTURES GROUP, LLC)
d/b/a ZEEKREWARDS.COM, and)
PAUL BURKS,)
)
        Defendants.)
)

DEFENDANT PAUL BURKS' RESPONSE TO RECEIVER'S MOTION SEEKING AMENDMENT OF AGREED ORDER APPOINTING TEMPORARY RECEIVER AND FREEZING ASSETS OF DEFENDANT

NOW COMES defendant Paul Burks, and responds in opposition to the motion filed by

Kenneth D. Bell ("Receiver") seeking amendment of the Agreed Order Appointing Temporary

Receiver and Freezing Assets of Defendant Rex Ventures Group, LLC (Doc. No. 4) ("Agreed

Order"). Mr. Burks opposes the Receiver's request to expand the definition of "Recoverable

Assets," as it specifically pertains to Paul Burks, beyond the scope of the consent order entered

by this Court on August 17, 2012.[1] In support of this motion, the defendant shows the following:

     1.   The instant action stems from an investigation by the Securities & Exchange

Commission ("SEC") into Rex Ventures Group, LLC and its sole shareholder Paul Burks. Prior

to entering into a consent agreement with the SEC, Rex Ventures Group, LLC operated

---

[1] Because it clearly fits within the text and spirit of the Agreed Order, Mr. Burks does not oppose modifying the Agreed Order to enable the Receiver to more clearly define—and better receive—funds identified as "cashier's checks, certified checks, money orders, and other forms of payment that are being held by the Receivership Defendant that have not been deposited with a bank." (Doc. 14 ¶ 6)

1

Zeekler.com, a penny auction website, and ZeekRewards.com, an internet-based affiliate program used to promote the Zeekler.com website.

2.   On August 17, 2012, following a period of cooperation between Mr. Burks and Rex Ventures Group, LLC, and the SEC—cooperation that included the production of hundreds of thousands of documents, including financial records, e-mails, and all manner of electronic files—the defendants entered into a consent agreement with the SEC. Immediately after these filings took place, the Court, *inter alia*, entered the Agreed Order.

3.   The language of the Agreed Order is clear. This Court appointed the Receiver to marshal the assets of the Receivership Defendant, Rex Ventures Group, LLC, and its order defined the scope of his authority consistent with that mandate. Rex Ventures Group, LLC is the sole Receivership Defendant, and "Receivership Assets" are defined as assets of the business, namely, "those assets: (a) held or possessed by Receivership Defendant; (b) held in constructive trust for the Receivership Defendant; and (c) fraudulently transferred by the Receivership Defendant." (Doc. 4 at 2)

4.   Without sufficient justification or cause, the Receiver now seeks to expand his powers and previously defined scope of authority in order to include Mr. Burks' personal accounts.

5.   While asserting that the Agreed Order "does not specifically address the freezing of assets" in Mr. Burks' possession, (Doc. 14 ¶ 5) the Receiver ignores the fact that the Agreed Order clearly designates the specific assets that are to go into receivership. Pursuant to the Agreed Order, the Court appointed a temporary receiver "for the purpose of marshaling and preserving all assets of the Receivership Defendant," and accordingly froze certain assets of Rex Ventures Group.

2

6.   The Receiver's argument in support of expanding his reach into Mr. Burks' personal assets is unsupported. Indeed, there is no factual basis for the Receiver's motion other than references to the SEC's Complaint, assertions which Mr. Burks neither admits nor denies. The Receiver has not referenced any facts, affidavits, or other evidence in support of his assertion that freezing Mr. Burks' personal assets is necessary. Thus, there is no record to support the Receiver's motion.

7.   Relying solely on the SEC's assertions in its Complaint, the Receiver's motion accuses Mr. Burks of having "misappropriated and secreted approximately $11 million." Continuing to quote from the SEC's Complaint, the Receiver asserts that "approximately $4 million [of the $11 million] ... remain[ed] in the possession, custody or control of Burks as of August 17, 2012." (Doc. 14 ¶ 3)

8.   As the SEC and federal government are well aware, more than half of this approximately $11 million was paid to the Internal Revenue Service for 2011 and 2012 estimated taxes. Moreover, as the filings in this matter make clear, Mr. Burks was also assessed a $4 million fine by the government.[2]

9.   Lacking a factual basis to support his motion, the Receiver lacks a legal basis, as well. Ordinarily, a party seeking an asset freeze must demonstrate that the party is "likely to succeed on the merits." *Securities and Exchange Commission v. Cavanagh*, 155 F.3d 129, 132 (2nd Cir. 1998). Here, however, Mr. Burks has settled the SEC's claim against him. There is, therefore, nothing upon which to base a determination of likelihood of success on the merits. The Receiver has not met his burden.

---

[2] Mr. Burks wired $3,615,254.27 to the government today and made arrangements for the balance-- $384,745.73-- to be wired tomorrow morning.

3

10. Not only has the Receiver failed to assert a factual basis for his motion to expand his reach, no such factual basis exists. Rex Ventures Group, LLC generated revenue from three sources: (1) retail bid sales; (2) Zeekler.com penny auction sales; and (3) membership in the ZeekRewards.com affiliate program. Upon information and belief, revenues from retail bids alone were substantially greater than moneys retained by Mr. Burks. These sales were made absent any connection to the allegedly improper business conduct that resulted in the Agreed Order. Indeed, the only revenue stream that is traceable to any allegedly improper conduct is revenue earned from the ZeekRewards.com affiliate program.

11. There is no basis and no need to freeze Mr. Burks' personal funds. Mr. Burks has never expatriated the assets of Rex Ventures Group, LLC or his personal money. He has fully cooperated in the SEC investigation, which included examination of relevant financial records. He is 65 years old, married, a two time cancer survivor, and has lived in Lexington, North Carolina for 23 years. He has never been a defendant in any action, civil or criminal, until this matter. Mr. Burks is aware of the importance of this proceeding and will abide by any orders this Court imposes.

WHEREFORE, the Defendant requests that the Court deny the Receiver's motion.

4

244

This the 30th day of August, 2012

Respectfully submitted,

s/ Noell P. Tin

Noell P. Tin
Tin Fulton Walker & Owen, PLLC
301 East Park Ave.
Charlotte, NC 28203
Phone: (704) 338-1220
Fax: (704) 338-1312
ntin@tinfulton.com
COUNSEL FOR MR. BURKS

CERTIFICATE OF SERVICE

I certify that I have served the foregoing DEFENDANT PAUL BURKS' RESPONSE TO RECEIVER'S MOTION SEEKING AMENDMENT OF AGREED ORDER APPOINTING TEMPORARY RECEIVER AND FREEZING ASSETS OF DEFENDANT on opposing counsel by submitting a copy thereof through Electronic Case Filing, to be sent to:

John J. Bowers
Securities & Exchange Commission
100 F Street, NE
Washington, DC 20815
Email: bowersj@sec.gov

Kenneth D. Bell
McGuireWoods LLP
201 North Tryon Street
P.O. Box 31247
Charlotte, NC 28231
Email: kbell@mcguirewoods.com

This the 30th day of August, 2012.

s/Noell Tin
Noell P. Tin

246

Exhibit 10

IN THE UNITED STATES DISTRCT COURT FOR THE WESTERN DISTRICT OF
NORTH CAROLINA CHARLOTTE DIVISION
SECURITIES AND
EXCHANGE COMMISSION,

Plaintiff,

v.

Civil Action No. 3:12-cv-519

REX VENTURES GROUP,
LLC
d/b/a
ZEEKREWARDS.COM, and
PAUL BURKS,

Defendants.

**BRIEF IN SUPPORT OF EMERGENCY MOTION FOR AN ORDER
REQUIRING RELEASE OF THIRD-PARTY ASSETS FROZEN IN RESPONSE
TO THIS COURT'S AUGUST 17, 2012 ORDER**

David Sorrells, David Kettner, and Mary Kettner (collectively "Movants") file this brief

as follows:

I. SUMMARY

On August 17, 2012, the Court entered an Agreed Order Appointing Temporary Receiver

and Freezing Assets, which order was amended on August 30, 2012. ("Agreed Order" [Doc. 4].)

Sometime between August 17, 2012 and August 20, 2012, the Receiver and/or the SEC delivered

copies of the Agreed Order to several e-wallet companies, including NxSystems, Inc. ("NxPay"),

SolidTrustPay, and Payza/Alert Pay (the "E-wallet Companies") for the purpose of recovering

Recoverable Assets (as defined in the Agreed Order), including assets belonging to Paul Burks

and Rex Venture Group. Movants are each former affiliates of ZeekRewards.com ("Affiliates")

and each an owner of an e-wallet account at one of the E-wallet Companies which has been frozen even though their accounts do not contain any Recoverable Assets. The Receiver is aware that the E-wallet Companies have frozen thousands of such accounts and originally took the position with Movants' counsel that he did not request the E-wallet Companies to freeze those accounts and that he never intended that result. Indeed, the Receiver initially acknowledged on November 19, 2012 that: "Nothing in the preliminary liquidation plan suggests that I claim that individual accounts (other than for Burks or Rex Venture Group) are presently part of the Receivership assets" In reliance on the Receiver's representations, Movants' counsel delayed filing a motion seeking an evidentiary hearing to determine the true status of the funds in the e- wallet accounts and asking the Court to order those funds released to Affiliates. Instead, Movants' counsel made contact with NxPay's general counsel and later with its president, each of whom offered assurances that NxPay was merely trying to reconcile its accounts and would, when that reconciliation was complete, release funds in accounts not in the name of Paul Burks or Rex Venture Group to the Affiliates. On December 5, 2012, Movants' counsel learned that several Affiliate NxPay accounts had been zeroed out and that NxPay customer service was telling Affiliates that NxPay had turned their money over to the Receiver or the SEC. When questioned about that on December 6, 2012, the Receiver responded: "I was informed yesterday by counsel for NXPay that they interpret the Court's Orders to freeze Receivership assets to include identifiable transfers from RVG/Zeek to individuals' accounts. I agree with their interpretation of the Orders, and have informed them of my position."

Because the Agreed Order does not give the Receiver the authority to claw-back assets not belonging to Paul Burks or his family members or Rex Venture Group or its related entities, Movants request the Court to enter an order requiring NxPay and the other E-wallet Companies to release assets which they froze because of the Agreed Order but which are in accounts not

2

containing Recoverable Assets. Further, to the extent NxPay and other E-wallet Companies have turned over Affiliate funds to the Receiver or to the SEC, Movants' request that the Court entered an order requiring that those funds be returned and that the accounts from which those funds were converted be released to the account owner.

II. STATEMENT OF FACTS[1]

Rex Ventures Group, LLC operated a penny auction website called Zeekler.com and a related promotional program called ZeekRewards.com. Individuals signed up as "Affiliates" of the ZeekRewards program on a monthly basis. For that month, each Affiliate agreed to purchase sample bids for Zeekler.com, distribute them to new bidders, and place a free Zeekler.com advertisement on the Internet every day. In return, Affiliates earned Profits Points that made them eligible to receive daily rewards. The daily reward was a *pro rata* payment totaling up to 50% of the company's daily net profits relating to the penny auction, which the Affiliates could choose to convert into additional Profit Points or to receive as a cash payment in their own personal deposit accounts at NxPay, SolidTrustPay, and Payza/Alert Pay. (Exhs. A, B and C, ¶ 2.)

Amounts maintained by NxPay, SolidTrustPay and Payza/Alert Pay are known as "e-wallet" accounts. They are virtually identical to normal bank accounts one would have at a local bank. The account holder completes paperwork to open the account and the account is owned exclusively by the person who opens the account. Only the account holder can withdraw funds from the account. The account is held in the name of the account holder. In short, the account holder is the sole owner of the account and all funds contained in it. (Exhs. A, B and C, ¶ 3.)

---

[1] This motion is supported by the following declarations: (i) the Declaration of David Sorrells is being separately filed in accordance with LR 7.1(C)(3) as **Exhibit A**; (ii) the Declaration of Mary Kettner is being separately filed as **Exhibit B**; and (iii) the Declaration of David Kettner is being separately filed as **Exhibit C**.

3

Movants were each Affiliates in the ZeekRewards program who maintained personal accounts at NxPay. The Movants' accounts were in their own name and the funds in the accounts were owned by the Movants and are not, in any respect whatsoever, held for or owned by the Receivership Defendant. The Receivership Defendant does not own, possess or have a beneficial interest, direct or indirect, in the accounts or the funds in them. The Receivership Defendant had no right to access the funds in the accounts by charge-back or otherwise. (Exhs. A, B and C, ¶ 4.)

Movants each earned the money in their e-wallet accounts by participating in the ZeekRewards program. Stated very simply, Affiliates of Zeek Rewards, including Movants, had to work hard to be part of the group that earned a percentage of the daily profits generated from bids sold to play the penny auctions. This work included: (i) making efforts to drive new customers to the penny auction site (Zeekler.com); and (ii) marketing the Zeekler.com penny auction site by placing advertisements in one or many of hundreds of online locations to bring exposure and Internet traffic to Zeekler.com. (Exhs. A, B and C, ¶ 5.)

The most successful Affiliates worked the hardest, placed numerous ads, and explained the Zeekler.com penny auction to groups of people several times a month. Some of the Movants, for example, traveled extensively to maintain contact with their network of peers and to educate them, among other things, on how to be successful in the program. These Movants' successes were a direct result of the amount of time and effort they poured into the effort to promote the penny auction. (Exhs. A, B and C, ¶ 6.)

Some of the Movants have already paid taxes on the revenue they generated from their participation in ZeekRewards. Each of the Movants was counting on receiving the money frozen in their e-wallet accounts for purposes of paying their quarterly taxes in September 2012.

4

Further, each of the Movants, like many of the thousands of other individuals who had the money in their e-wallet accounts frozen, made their hard work and participation in the ZeekRewards program their primary livelihood and primary source of income. Therefore, the loss of that income and the loss of the funds in the e-wallet accounts has caused them a significant amount of hardship, not the least of which is potentially unpaid tax liabilities and the loss of the means of their livelihood. (Exhs. A, B and C, ¶ 7.)

On August 17, 2012, the Court entered an Agreed Order Appointing Temporary Receiver and Freezing Assets. ("Agreed Order" [Doc. 4].) The Agreed Order appointed Kenneth D. Bell as temporary receiver ("Receiver") for and over the estate of the Receivership Defendant (defined as Rex Venture Group, LLC d/b/a ZeekRewards.com any of its subsidiaries, whether incorporated or unincorporated, and any businesses or business names under which it does business). (Agreed Order [Doc. 4], ¶¶1 and 2.)

The Agreed Order contained, at paragraph 3, an asset freeze provision which states, in pertinent part ". . . all Receivership Assets and Recoverable Assets are frozen until further order of this Court. . . . This freeze shall include, but not be limited to, Receivership Assets and/or Recoverable Assets that are on deposit with financial institutions such as banks, brokerage firms, and on-line interest-based payment processors." The term "Receivership Assets" is defined in the second recital paragraph of the Agreed Order as "all assets of the Receivership Defendant."

However, the term "Recoverable Assets" is not defined anywhere in the Agreed Order.[2]

---

[2] On August 24, 2012, the Receiver filed a Motion Seeking Amendment of the Agreed Order [Doc. 14] in which he recognized

that the Agreed Order did not define the term "Recoverable Assets" [Motion ¶7]. As a basis for the amendment request the Receiver referenced two specific things: (1) "misappropriated assets" (alleged fraudulent transfers to the individual Defendant's family members) and (2) funds in the nature of checks and money orders mailed by customers to the corporate Defendant prior to the Receivership. On August 30, 2012, the Court issued an Order Granting in Part and Denying in Part the Receiver's Motion ("Amended Order" [Doc. 21]) which, inter alia, defined "Recoverable Assets" as those having been fraudulently transferred by the Defendant.

5

Between August 17 and August 20, 2012, upon information and belief, the Receiver and/or the SEC sent the Agreed Order to each of the E-wallet Companies. By email letter dated August 20, 2012, NxPay notified each of the Movants, and thousands of other account holders, that each of their accounts had been frozen. (Exhs. A, B and C, ¶ 8.) A true and correct copy of this letter is attached to the Declarations of each of the Movants as Exhibit 1. Specifically, and apparently as a direct result of the Receiver and/or the SEC sending the Agreed Order to NxPay, the following accounts owned exclusively by each of the Movants were frozen and the Movants have had no access to the funds since that time:

Account Holder	Institution	Amount Frozen
David Sorrells	NxPay	$373,375.66
David Kettner	NxPay	$33,626.80
Mary Kettner	NxPay	$25,319.67

(Exhs. A, B and C, ¶ 9.)

On November 19, 2012, the undersigned informed the Receiver that many accounts at the E-wallet Companies belonging to Affiliates ("Affiliate Accounts") had been frozen and that Movants intended to file a motion for an order releasing the accounts because they were wrongfully seized by the Receiver. In a conversation between the undersigned and the Receiver relating to that proposed motion, the Receiver represented that he had not seized those accounts, and in a subsequent e-mail exchange relating to the frozen e-wallet accounts, the Receiver wrote:

The US Secret Service obtained and executed seizure warrants for several accounts belonging to Burks or Rex Venture Group. I served on several institutions a copy of the Court's Order and requested compliance with its directives. Neither the USSS nor I ever asked or directed any institution to freeze assets belonging to any other person or entity. NxPay, and other institutions, have informed the USSS and me that all assets in the name of Burks or Rex Venture Group have been surrendered, and that only funds belonging to Burks or Rex Venture Group were surrendered. Nothing in the preliminary liquidation

6

plan suggests that I claim that individual accounts (other than for Burks or Rex Venture Group) are presently part of the Receivership assets.

(November 19, 2012 e-mail from the Receiver to Michael Quilling and Rodney Alexander (**Exhibit D**)).

Because it appeared that, as a result of their receipt of the Agreed Order, the E-wallet Companies had frozen thousands of accounts of innocent people who do not have possession of Recoverable Assets, and because it appeared that the Receiver never intended that result, counsel for the Movants suggested to the Receiver that it would be reasonable for the Receiver to take some action to notify the E-wallet Companies that the Agreed Order was not intended to cause the seizure or freezing of the Affiliate Accounts. In another e-mail dated November 19, 2012, the undersigned wrote to the Receiver:

Ken

Obviously, there is a result that you did not intend. If you did not intend it, and you had no authority to cause it, then you should be willing to take reasonable measures to correct it.
(E-mail dated November 19, 2012 (**Exhibit E**).)

On the morning of November 20, 2012, Movants' counsel delivered to the Receiver a proposed agreed order which recited the following:
The Receiver has been advised by counsel for several individuals who (i) own e-wallet accounts at NxPay, SolidTrustPay and Payza/Alert Pay and (ii) are not in possession of any Recoverable Assets as defined in the Order, that NxPay, SolidTrustPay and Payza/Alert Pay have frozen their accounts to the extent there were any funds in their accounts relating to Rex Venture Group, Zeekler.com or ZeekRewards. The Receiver has been advised independently by several other individuals who (i) own e-wallet accounts at NxPay, SolidTrustPay and Payza/Alert Pay and (ii) are not in possession of any Recoverable Assets as defined in the Order that NxPay, SolidTrustPay and Payza/Alert Pay have similarly frozen their accounts.

The Receiver has been advised that NxPay, SolidTrustPay and Payza/Alert Pay have apparently interpreted the Order as requiring them to freeze accounts at their respective institutions owned by persons/entities who are not the subject of these

7

proceedings and who are not in possession of Recoverable Assets. The Receiver did not intend that result and did not instruct the institutions to freeze or hold the accounts of individuals not in possession of Recoverable Assets. Accordingly, the Receiver agrees to the entry of this order providing the relief below:

(A copy of the proposed Agreed Order is attached hereto as **Exhibit F**.) The proposed Agreed Order requested the following relief:

It is ORDERED that NxPay, SolidTrustPay and Payza/Alert Pay, with the sole exception of accounts in the name of any one or more of the defendants listed in the caption of this order, shall immediately release any freeze or hold any of them has placed on any accounts at their respective institutions to the extent that freeze or hold was put in place as a result of the Order. This mandate shall not apply to any account on which a hold or freeze was placed for any reason other than the Order.

(Exhibit F.)

Even though the Receiver has conceded that "all assets in the name of Burks or Rex Venture Group have been surrendered," after having the opportunity to review the proposed agreed order, the Receiver responded as follows:

I cannot consent to this Order. It is up to the e-wallets to determine how to comply with the Court's order. If, as you say, they have chosen to temporarily freeze and analyze accounts to determine whether the accounts include Receivership assets, I have no authority to tell them otherwise. I also think it is not appropriate to ask the Court to enter an order telling the e-wallets how to comply with the Order without providing them an opportunity to be heard.

(E-mail dated November 20, 2012 **(Exhibit G)**.)

Although disagreeing with the Receiver's position with respect to requirement of notice to the E-wallet Companies, on November 20, 2012, Movants' counsel sent a letter to an attorney in the legal department for NxPay notifying him that, based on communications with the Receiver, the Receiver did not intend for NxPay to freeze the accounts of thousands of Affiliates who had no Recoverable Assets in their NxPay accounts. Thereafter, counsel for the Movants had a number of telephone conversations with counsel for NxPay in which he informed counsel for the Movants that only funds in the name of and belonging to one or both of the Defendants

8   Case 3:12-cv-00519-GCM   Document 81   Filed 12/11/12   Page 8 of 18

had been turned over to the Secret Service, and that the funds in the accounts of and belonging to Affiliates had not been turned over, were safe and were still frozen because of issues relating to their ACH processor, LST Financial in San Antonio, Texas. He asked that the Affiliates remain patient while the "reconciliation" process continued and he stated that progress was being made in that regard and the accounts would be released to the Affiliates shortly.

Thereafter, counsel for the Movants discussed the situation with counsel for Four Oaks Bank in North Carolina where the NxPay funds were actually on deposit and was told that, indeed, the funds were on deposit and that headway was being made in the "reconciliation" process. Within a couple of days, many of the Affiliates who checked their NxPay accounts online were able to see that the funds in their account were shown as "available" but still not subject to being transferred. (Exhs. A, B and C, ¶ 11.)

Thereafter, on December 3, 2012, counsel for the Movants had a lengthy discussion with representatives of the SEC regarding a number of issues including the frozen accounts. In that conversation, the SEC represented that it had served the Agreed Order on the E-wallet Companies and that the Secret Service had obtained the funds held at those institutions belonging to the Receivership Defendant. They professed to have no knowledge of the frozen accounts of the Affiliates.

Based on the foregoing, the undersigned recommended to the Movants and the thousands of other Affiliates on whose behalf they were acting to remain patient and let the "reconciliation" process continue. However, within only a couple of days, the Affiliates (including the Movants) who checked their NxPay accounts online learned that their account balances were now zero and that NxPay had issued a notice to them that their funds had been transferred to the SEC/Receiver. (Exhs. A, B and C, ¶ 11). It is difficult to arrive at any conclusion other than that, under the

9

pretense for the need to remain patient, NxPay has outright lied to counsel for the Movants while they secretly worked on a separate agenda—to turn Affiliate funds over to the Receiver or the SEC.

On December 6, 2012, counsel for the Movants attempted to discuss the situation with counsel for NxPay but he refused to respond. Counsel for the Movants also sent an email to the Receiver and an attorney for the SEC, which among other things, advised each of them that, contrary to prior representations, Movants' and other Affiliate accounts had been zeroed out, inquired as to whether the Receiver or the SEC was responsible for that result, and inquired as to whether either the Receiver or the SEC would oppose a motion in which Movants sought release of funds in the e-wallet accounts to Affiliates. An accurate copy of the December 6, 2012 email is attached as **Exhibit H**. The Receiver responded as follows:

> I was informed yesterday by counsel for NXPay that they interpret the Court's Orders to freeze Receivership assets to include identifiable transfers from RVG/Zeek to individuals' accounts. I agree with their interpretation of the Orders, and have informed them of my position. I have not provided legal advice to nor directed NXPay or any other institution on how to comply with the Court's Orders.

Exhibit H (December 6, 2012 5:53 PM email from the Receiver to Rodney Alexander.) The SEC responded and suggested further delay and further review of the issues, including efforts to determine the source of the funds in the e-wallet accounts. (*See* **Exhibit I**, attached hereto.) Because NxPay's general counsel had originally told Movants' counsel that NxPay's ACH provider was working diligently to reconcile Affiliate accounts so that those accounts could be released to Affiliates, and because the version of the facts Movants' counsel was receiving from Movants (who advised their counsel that NxPay customer service was telling them that their funds were being seized by the Receiver or the SEC) and the Receiver was at odds with what NxPay's counsel had previously represented, on the morning of December 7,

10

2012, Movants' counsel forwarded a copy of the email exchange between Movants' counsel, the Receiver and the SEC's counsel to NxPay's general counsel, Ken Phillips. The purpose of that email was to see if NxPay would confirm or deny whether it has transferred funds to either the SEC or the Receiver. Specifically, the email to NxPay's general counsel read as follows:

You and I have not had the pleasure of speaking. I am acting as local counsel for Michael Quilling in connection with the Rex Venture matter. I want to make sure that you are fully aware of the communications between counsel for some of the Affiliates, the Receiver and the SEC. It seems that the Receiver is providing us with information that is directly contrary to information you provided to Michael Quilling only days ago. While we have tried very hard to cooperate and be patient, it seems inescapable at this point that court intervention will be required. In that regard, please see below [referring to email exchanges quoted above].

To be clear, we do not believe that the orders entered in this case give the Receiver or any other party authority to seize assets, including the value of accounts at NxPay, not in the name of Paul Burks or his family members or Rex Venture Group or its subsidiaries or related companies. We have been told that NxPay is zeroing out Affiliate accounts and advising Affiliates that the SEC has seized those funds. If NxPay is zeroing out affiliate accounts and/or turning funds over to either the Receiver or the SEC, please provide me with any information or documentation available to you which you believes justifies such conduct.

An accurate copy of the December 7, 2012 email to Ken Phillips is attached as **Exhibit J**. Mr. Phillips has failed to respond.

Also on December 7, the SEC's attorney advised Movants' counsel as follows:

Before the SEC takes a position (and before you represent the SEC's position on your planned motion), we would like to understand what assets are at issue, and where they came from. Without this information, it is virtually impossible to understand whether particular assets fall within the Freeze Order

An accurate copy of the SEC's attorney's email is attached hereto as **Exhibit K**.

Finally, in regard to the exchanges relating to the apparent seizure by the Receiver of funds in the e-wallet accounts, Movants' counsel responded to the SEC's counsel on the morning of December 7, 2012 as follows:

I am perplexed by your email. I thought it was fairly clear that assets that are at issue are the assets in the names of former Affiliates which assets are or were

11

distributed to various e-wallet companies and then placed into subaccounts in the names of Affiliates. With respect to the specific email exchange below and our separate email exchange from earlier this morning, we are discussing very specifically funds in the names of Affiliates who had e-wallet accounts at NxPay.

With respect to your statement that "we [presumptively the SEC] would like to understand what assets are at issue, and where they came from," I believe that you and the Receiver are in a much better position to understand where those assets came from. At what I presume is over $1 million in Receivership fees at this point, I cannot imagine that the Receiver does not have some idea where the funds in the accounts at issue originated. If the Receiver is unaware of where the funds in the accounts at issue originated, then it seems untenable for the Receiver to claim that they are subject to the Orders at issue. Please let me know if I am missing something here.

(An accurate copy of this December 7, 2012 email is attached as **Exhibit L**)

Based on the information available to the undersigned, the Movants BELIEVE the funds are still under NxPay's control and on actual deposit with Four Oaks Bank in North Carolina despite NxPay's written representations to the Affiliates that they have been transferred to the Receiver. The Movants request that this Court order that all funds in all Affiliate accounts be released immediately.

III.
ARGUMENT AND AUTHORITIES

The Receiver acknowledged on November 19, 2012 that he never intended for the E-wallet Companies to freeze any assets other than those defined as Recoverable Assets in the Agreed Order. (*See* **Exhibit D**.) The Receiver further acknowledged on November 19, 2012 that he already had recovered from the E-wallet Companies all of the funds he believed he was entitled to recover under the authority of the Agreed Order. (*Id.*) The Receiver is also now on notice that the E-wallet Companies, apparently based on their receipt of the Agreed Order, have frozen thousands of accounts of innocent people and started wiping out the funds in those accounts and apparently, at least according to NxPay customer service, begun the process of turning those funds over to the Receiver or the SEC. Notwithstanding the Receiver's original

12

position that he had recovered from the E-wallet Companies all of the funds he believed he was entitled to under the Agreed Order, the Receiver now professes to believe, apparently after having been convinced by NxPay's general counsel, that the Agreed Order is broader than the Receiver initially construed it, and that it is broad enough to reach assets in Affiliate e-wallet accounts. (*See* **Exhibit H.**) However, according to the SEC's attorney, the SEC does not even have sufficient information to determine where the funds in those accounts came from. (*See* **Exhibit K.**) Consequently, neither the Receiver nor the SEC can legitimately take the position that the funds in the e-wallet accounts are subject to seizure or freezing under the Agreed Order.

Notwithstanding the Receiver's knowledge that E-wallet Companies have frozen thousands of accounts which the Receiver never intended to impact, and notwithstanding the almost certainty that their conduct is based upon their receipt of the Agreed Order, and notwithstanding that neither the Receiver nor the SEC apparently knows the origin of the funds in the e-wallet accounts, the Receiver is unwilling to take any action to stop the E-wallet Companies from zeroing out Affiliate accounts and from apparently delivering Affiliate monies to the Receiver or the SEC. The Receiver's conduct in knowingly allowing the E-wallet Companies continue to freeze assets the Receiver did not intend to impact after having been put on notice of those facts is tantamount to a taking without due process of law.

"Procedural due process" constrains the government from depriving individuals of liberty or property interests under the Due Process Clause of the Fifth Amendment. *Mathews v. Eldridge*, 424 U.S. 319, 332 (1976). At a minimum, individuals are entitled to notice and an opportunity to be heard. *Schroeder v. N.Y.*, 371 U.S. 208, 212 (1962); *Mullane v. Cent. Hanover Bank & Trust Co.*, 339 U.S. 306, 314 (1950). Due process is not a "technical conception with a fixed content unrelated to time, place and circumstances." *Cafeteria Workers v. McElroy*, 367

13

U.S. 886, 895 (1961). It is "flexible and calls for such procedural protections as the particular situation demands." *Morrissey v. Brewer*, 408 U.S. 471, 481 (1972). In this case, the Court must analyze the governmental and private interests affected by the Receiver's decision to unilaterally seize Movants' accounts. *Arnett v. Kennedy*, 416 U.S. 134, 167-168 (1974;

      Goldberg v. Kelly, 397 U.S. 254, 263-266 (1970); *Cafeteria Workers*, 367 U.S. at 895.

The Receiver has, inadvertently or not, caused thousands of accounts held by Affiliates to be frozen. The funds in the e-wallet accounts had been distributed on a final basis to Movants and others similarly situated. Once distributed, the Receivership Defendant no longer had any interest whatsoever in those funds. Therefore, those funds were and are the property of Movants and other owners of e-wallet accounts whose funds were seized. The Receiver's conduct in refusing to take any action to provide the E-wallet Companies with clarification of the intent of the Agreed Order, and allowing those accounts to remain frozen as a result of the E-wallet Companies receipt of the Agreed Order amounts to a wrongful taking without due process and violates the due process principles set forth above.

The Receiver's active refusal to take any action to cause the E-wallet Companies to release the assets they have wrongfully frozen, in conjunction with the active conduct of the E-wallet Companies in wrongfully freezing the assets of thousands of Affiliates, effectively results in thousands of pre-judgment attachments in violation of Rule 64. Rule 64 expressly incorporates state procedures for pre-judgment attachments. FED. R. CIV. P. 64(a). In North Carolina, attachment is ancillary to a pending principal action and is intended to bring property of a defendant within the legal custody of the court so that it may later be applied to the satisfaction of a money judgment against the defendant in the principal action. N.C. GEN. STAT. § 1-440.1(a). It is available in the following proceedings:

14

Attachment may be had in any action the purpose of which, in whole or in part, or in the alternative, is to secure a judgment for money, or in any action for alimony or for maintenance and support, or an action for the support of a minor child, but not in any other action.

N.C. GEN. STAT. § 1-440.2; see also § 1-440.11(a). For an attachment proceeding to be lawful, the attached property must belong to the defendant debtor. N.C. GEN. STAT. § 1-440.4; see also *Rose, Rand, Ray, Winfrey & Gregory, P.A. v. Salter*, No. 88-2608, 1989 WL 64134, *2 (4th Cir. Jun. 5, 1989). The property sought to be attached must also be located within the State of North Carolina (N.C. GEN. STAT. § 1-440.4). Because pre-judgment attachment is a "narrow and exceptional" remedy, its procedures are strictly enforced by the Federal Courts. *Allstate Ins. Co. v. Weir*, 531 F.Supp.2d 674, 677-78 (E.D.N.C. 2008).

In this instance it is clear that the Receiver is not entitled to a Rule 64 pre-judgment attachment. None of the account owners is a defendant in any lawsuit. Not only has the Receiver not made an application for a Rule 64 attachment, he has not even filed a lawsuit against the Movants or anyone else. Instead, during the last six weeks the Receiver has begun sending overly broad and oppressive subpoenas to about 1,200 Affiliates which contain a demand to pay to him their alleged profits (a copy of the subpoena and the cover letter containing the demand for payment to each of the Movants is attached to the Declaration of each

of the Movants as Exhibit 2).[3] Significantly, the Receiver's demands do not articulate a legal

theory to support those demands.

Request for Emergency Evidentiary Hearing

Movants respectfully request that the Court hold an emergency evidentiary hearing with respect to this Motion. The matters presented in this Motion are extremely important and impact

---

[3] These subpoenas also demand that each Affiliate produce documentation regarding every asset owned by the Affiliate as if the Receiver is somehow entitled to post-judgment discovery even though he has not yet filed a lawsuit.

the lives of potentially 2.2 million people according to the Receiver's estimates. The Receiver should be called upon to explain to the Court why, if the Agreed Order does not apply to the Affiliates' accounts, and if the Receiver has already recovered the assets he sought to recover from the E-wallet Companies, and why, if the Receiver is aware that thousands of Affiliate accounts have been frozen by the E-wallet Companies, he is unwilling to take any action to rectify the problem he caused, but claims he did not intend to cause.

Further, the evidence available to the undersigned and to Movants leads them to believe that Rex Ventures, ZeekRewards.com and Zeekler.com operated as a unique, if highly profitable, business model and not a Ponzi scheme. One is illegal, one is not. Among many other things, the Receiver should be required to establish that Rex Ventures, ZeekRewards.com and Zeekler.com actually operated as a Ponzi scheme or that there was some other securities law violation justifying the Receiver's pursuit of innocent Affiliates.

WHEREFORE, Movants respectfully ask the Court to order the immediate release of all accounts at NxPay, SolidTrustPay, or Payza/Alert Pay that are held in their name or in the name of the other Affiliates and for such other and further relief, general or special, at law or in equity, to which they may otherwise be entitled.

Respectfully submitted,

QUILLING, SELANDER, CUMMISKEY
& LOWNDS, P.C.

/s/ Michael J. Quilling
Texas Bar No. 16432300, *pro hac vice*

2001 Bryan Street, Suite 1800
Dallas, Texas 75201
Telephone: (214) 871-2100
Facsimile: (214) 871-2111
16

E-mail: mquilling@qslwm.com and

ALEXANDER RICKS PLLC

Rodney E. Alexander
N.C. Bar No. 23615

2901 Coltsgate Rd., Suite 202
Charlotte, NC 28211
Telephone: (704) 365-3656
Facsimile: (704) 365-3676
E-mail: rodney@alexanderricks.com

CERTIFICATE OF SERVICE

I hereby certify that on December 11, 2012, I electronically filed the foregoing document with the Clerk of Court using the CM/ECF system, which will electronically serve the referenced document on the parties' counsel who are registered CM/ECF users, including:

John J. Bowers
Stephen L. Cohen
J. Lee Buck, II
Brian M. Privor Alfred
C. Tierney
U.S. Securities and Exchange
Commission 100 F Street, N.E.
Washington, D.C. 20549

Noell P. Tin
C. Melissa Owen
Jacob H. Sussman Jeremy
D. Freeman Sarah E.
Bennett
Tin Fulton Walker & Owen
PLLC 301 East Park Avenue
Charlotte, NC 28203

Kenneth D. Bell
Irving M. Brenner
Jennifer L. King
McGuire Woods LLP
201 North Tryon Street
P. O. Box 31247
Charlotte, NC 28231

In addition, I hereby certify that on December 11, 2012, I sent a copy of this document to NxPay's general counsel via email at kphillips@nxsystemsinc.com and via Federal Express to:

Kenneth S. Mitchell-Phillips,
Sr. Corporate Counsel
12400 SE Freeman Way, Suite 100
Portland, OR 97222

/s/ Rodney E. Alexander _____ Rodney E. Al

4844-6060-9298, v. 1

18

BONUS SECTION
"HOW TO" START YOUR OWN MLM

If you're like most people, you have dreamed and wondered what it would be like to start your own Network Marketing Company or the three letter lighting rod identifier "MLM". Most people feel they have to locate a product that can be resold at 1,000 percent of its wholesale cost to the company.

The challenge is if this product is a replacement of what someone would purchase at the local Walmart, like a vitamin, meal replacement, lotion, or perfume; well that is a hard sale. Most people remember the early pioneers in this area; the stories were how they were more pure, special features made their product better but most just knew it was a "Box of Rocks". That was the term used to say, "This is my cost to do business", and knowing that they would never use the products purchased and would hope to convince others to buy the products, in hopes of earning massive commissions.

If you are dreaming of doing this, stand in line, as there is in most cases, one new MLM started each week. Most of them are touting lotions and pills. The competition is fierce and you are likely to fail if this is the direction you are looking to go.

What this section is going to cover is:

- How and why each plan works
- The unique differences in various plans

So let's jump in to the ways each plan works. First we will focus on the Unilevel, made famous by Amway, second the Stair Step Breakaway, third the Matrix forced and non-forced, the last the Binary and some combination of both. So on to the Unilevel, here is a quick graphic to explain. What you need to know is a Unilevel is simply the ability to sign up as many people as you want and they are considered on your front level. In fact, most Unilevels allow you to earn between 5 and 7 levels below the people you personally put in the business.

Unilevel

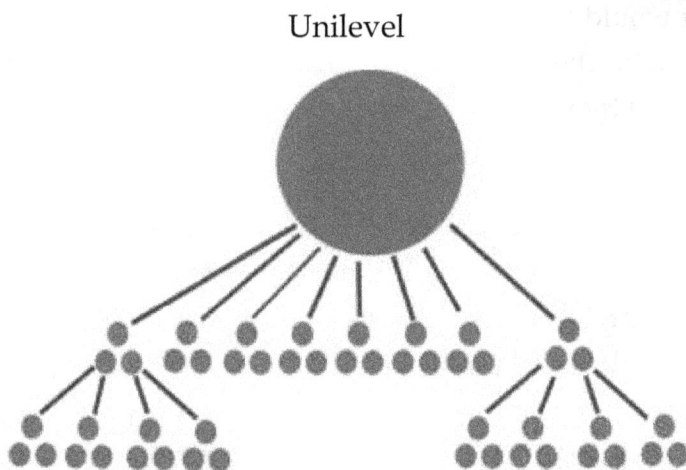

The Inilevel plan is, one level below the other

This plan shows that you can have many people on the front line, their success is not guaranteed and thus the image will not grow in a perfect diagram, but some will put more effort than others and this will lead to some wild looking diagrams.

This plan does not inspire people to work quickly and promote fast growth, but it is one that if worked long term has the best possibility of proving long-term residual income. But as with all the advancements made over the last 50 plus years, the company that made this famous now has reported gross sales of over $11 billion a year with over 13,000 employees and millions of distributors. [50]

Stair Step/Breakaway

[50] http://en.wikipedia.org/wiki/Amway

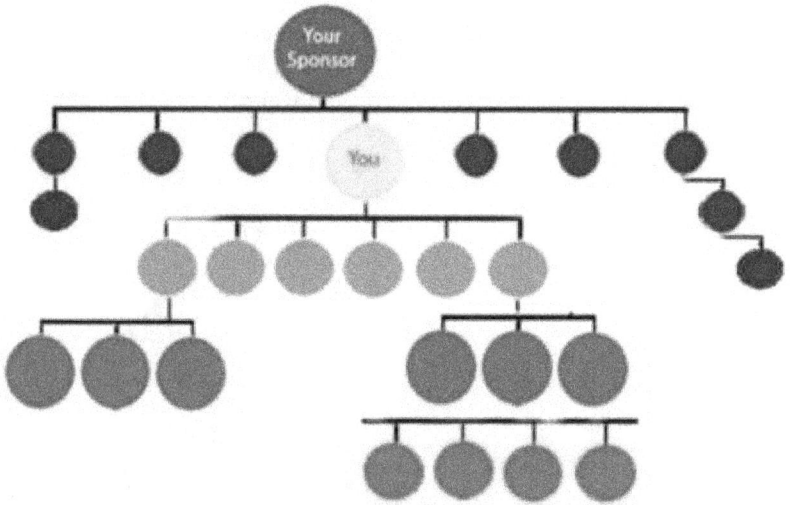

The Stair Step Breakaway is the next program that has been used. In fact this plan has been used in conjunction with Unilevel plans where the new distributor would enter at a new distributor level recruit their first 12 people only to have their sponsor get the benefit from this 12. Then they would break away and then be directly under someone one level higher. Now this sounds complicated and it may seem impossible to think anyone would go to work under this type of plan, but in fact it was quite successful for a little known company called Fortune High Tech Marketing or (FHTM). One thing to take from this is to understand the new distributor was made to go work to have the opportunity to work with the successful guys.

This system resulted in a high failure rate. If you reached the second level which was Regional, your personal sponsor would be giving you 12 people until they made Regional. If they fall out at 6, or 9 people, they have just helped you put more people on your front line. So great deal if you make Regional, this forced the sponsor to work hard to make the new person drop everything and put you in front of everyone you knew. Here is the rub, once you have 12 people, your entire warm market is gone and you have to find new people to get to their warm market, a vicious circle.

Matrix

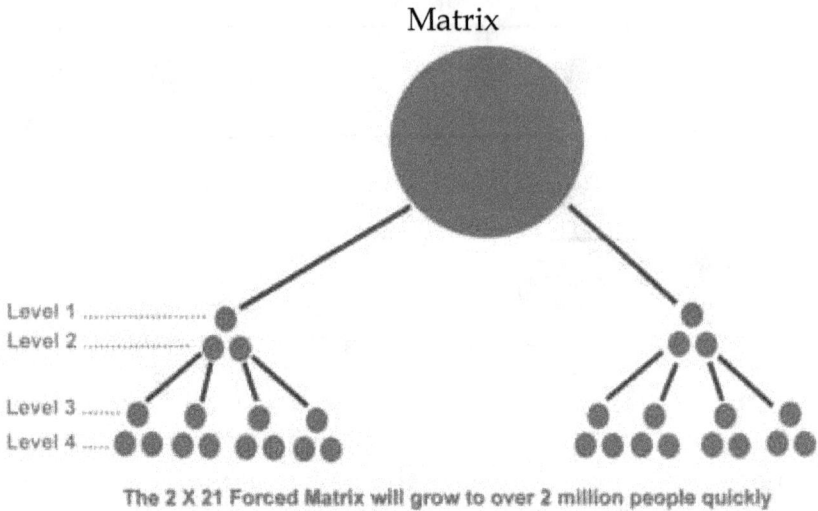

The 2 X 21 Forced Matrix will grow to over 2 million people quickly

The next one is Matrix, and I would like to spend a little more time on this program as this is the one that Zeek employed to make the millions of dollars in a short and rapid time. Now for anyone that understands a Matrix, it is like a Unilevel but has a limited width, and a limited depth, but in most cases allows you to make money on everyone in the new Matrix you have started. For example if you were in Zeek they had a 2 X 21 Forced Matrix. The forced part is if someone above you sponsored someone and in the Matrix you are in has all spots filled, but under you is an open spot, the person is placed directly in your open spot on your Matrix.

Wow, what a gift, but in fact the personal sponsorship benefit will go directly to the sponsor but the Matrix dollars you get to join in. So it is possible in a Matrix to sponsor the number required which could be from 3 to 20 people and have the ability to earn money from everyone below you on a monthly Matrix payout.

So let's look at Zeek for a moment. If you had people in 6 levels below you and you accomplished the needed requirements, and you were earning $3.50 from each person 6 levels down that would be 126 people paying you $441.00 dollars a month. Not bad if you just signup let's say 5 people. But the power is if you stay and keep doing what you need to do to stay active. If the levels you earn from fill up to the 9th level, the people in your Matrix jump to 1,022 and your monthly payment jumps to $3,577 dollars.

As you can see this type of growth is exciting to anyone that understands the power of the program. With every Santa Clause, there is a Grinch, and the government will want companies to limit the levels to a max of 5. That is not the end of the story, there is nothing to say bonuses based on sales performance could not be used to make up the difference of a larger Matrix and this is the direction most will take. It is possible to have a series of bonuses that equal the Matrix bonus level of 21 levels down, but the sales needed to reach this would be quite large, for example to reach a full matrix of a 2 X 21 would be well over 2 million people and to capture 2 million people, you will need a highly motivated group. I would have to say that this one plan is by far the most attractive of all plans, but that is just a personal opinion.

The next is the Binary, now to understand this in simple terms it is designed to look just like the Matrix. Here is the rub, you work hard to build both sides up but the company pays you on the smaller leg, now the logic is you will work to build up the smaller leg to make it larger and then you will earn more on what used to be the large leg and now the smaller leg, so did you catch that? It is kind of like the cat chasing its tail knowing it will never run fast enough to catch it. Wow what a concept, but believe me, people are signing up for this every day. People real good at spinning silk into gold will convince you of the benefits of this program.

As I said earlier, I could spend many hours and devote many pages to going into great detail, but you are reading this Bonus Section to understand the value, benefit and understanding of all programs. If I can shorten the process and have you come away with an understanding of what to look for in starting or joining a program that is using one of these programs to compensate you, this should be of value to you.

Now what makes a Network marketing company look like a Good Risk?

Well, this is a moving target, as startups will promise the world and take in some cases early losses to generate early distributor growth and in some circles they will call the members affiliates. The early members joining will have great joining bonuses expanded commission plans and some well-known leaders will strike side deals to come and help promote. If you are the company looking to attract this type of leader, remember the old saying, "give a person a cookie, they will want a gallon of milk", simply put, there will be a never ending set of demands that will be requested. Soon you are beholding to the high profile leader that will lead to their demands being met or the every looming threat to take the people somewhere else.

What can you do to prevent this from happening? That answer is simple, control the weekly conference calls that you are hosting, invite the leader on the call, keep the backend affiliate area restricted from having anyone up line from sending out mass emails to anyone below them without first going to a holding area and approve before all messages sent. Keep all emails on the affiliate site to an email you provide under a second domain you control. So the people in the system only know of the email provided by the company.

As we keep going you get the idea, and remember the old saying, keep your friends close and your enemies closer. Now not saying that the big famous MLM leader is not your friend, but do you really feel your company is his/her last stop, most likely not!

If you run across a company that wants you to put up money to take part in future earnings like a rev-share, this is evidence that they need the startup funds and this can be a slippery slope. The more you give them the more they need to stay open and it takes a well discipline person to not fall victim to this temptation. I have seen very good people that fall prey to the temptation. The money has to come from sales of products or services only, if you have to put up money, for anything other than product or service that is a red flag. Keep in mind, Zeek was selling bids, and the goal was to encourage people to use the bids and lead to new purchases of bids, thus helping company grow. Whether it worked out that way is still being debated and will be for some time to come.

Licensing in different states is really not a licensing issue but more of a notification issue, with the exception of North Carolina. North Carolina is one state that will require a bond of $50,000 if your entry exceeds $250 per month. If you offer a program that has a free entry, this part can be bypassed. For the other states, just keep your entry to free and a max $249.99 and you can stay under the radar. In fact, if you can get your people to quickly sponsor and reach a level where they are free of a monthly fee, provided the group sales are always growing, you will stay clear of the regulators, as they are truly acting like a well-oiled sales machine.

But to cover some of the requirements of let's say Georgia, their requirement is to list them on one simple form that you appoint the State of Georgia as your agent in terms of being served. Connecticut is really simple, provide proof that you have filed for a Federal Trademark and Shazam, you have met the requirements. Florida has abolished it requirements so they feel as do the other 45 states that if you step out of line the FTC and or SEC will place their heavy foot on your neck. That is really the simple explanation, but if you are looking for a more detailed understanding, just contact the DSA (Direct Sales Association) they can be a wealth of knowledge. They can also recommend good legal counsel that specializes in this area. By all means, don't get your recommendation from any attorney that has to spend all their waking time promoting themselves on YouTube, Google Hangout, and webpages they have published to tout their ability. By all means, don't fall victim to the old adage, of thinking you are going to get an attorney to write you an opinion letter. In network marketing, there are wide opinions to what is correct and is not. A well respected attorney and I will mention his name, Steven Korotash with the law firm of K&L Gates, said something that I will always remember. Steven said, Opinions are just that Opinions, everyone has one, and the regulator, which may agree with your opinion, may not reflect the opinion of the person that replaces them. If you want a good legal defense, have an attorney review your business model, and find out if they feel they can defend the model. That is your best course of action, and understand in the end, the opinion letter may not stop the war drums you hear in the distance from a regulator coming to make an example out of your new business venture.

Robert Craddock

Index

www.ingramcontent.com/pod-product-compliance
Lightning Source LLC
Chambersburg PA
CBHW070303200326
41518CB00010B/1873